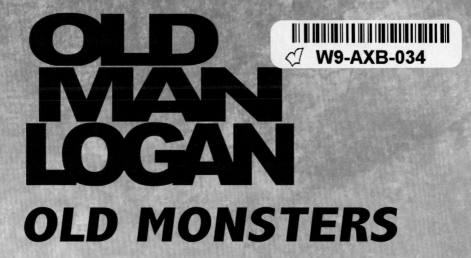

OLD MAN LOGAN

OLD MONSTERS

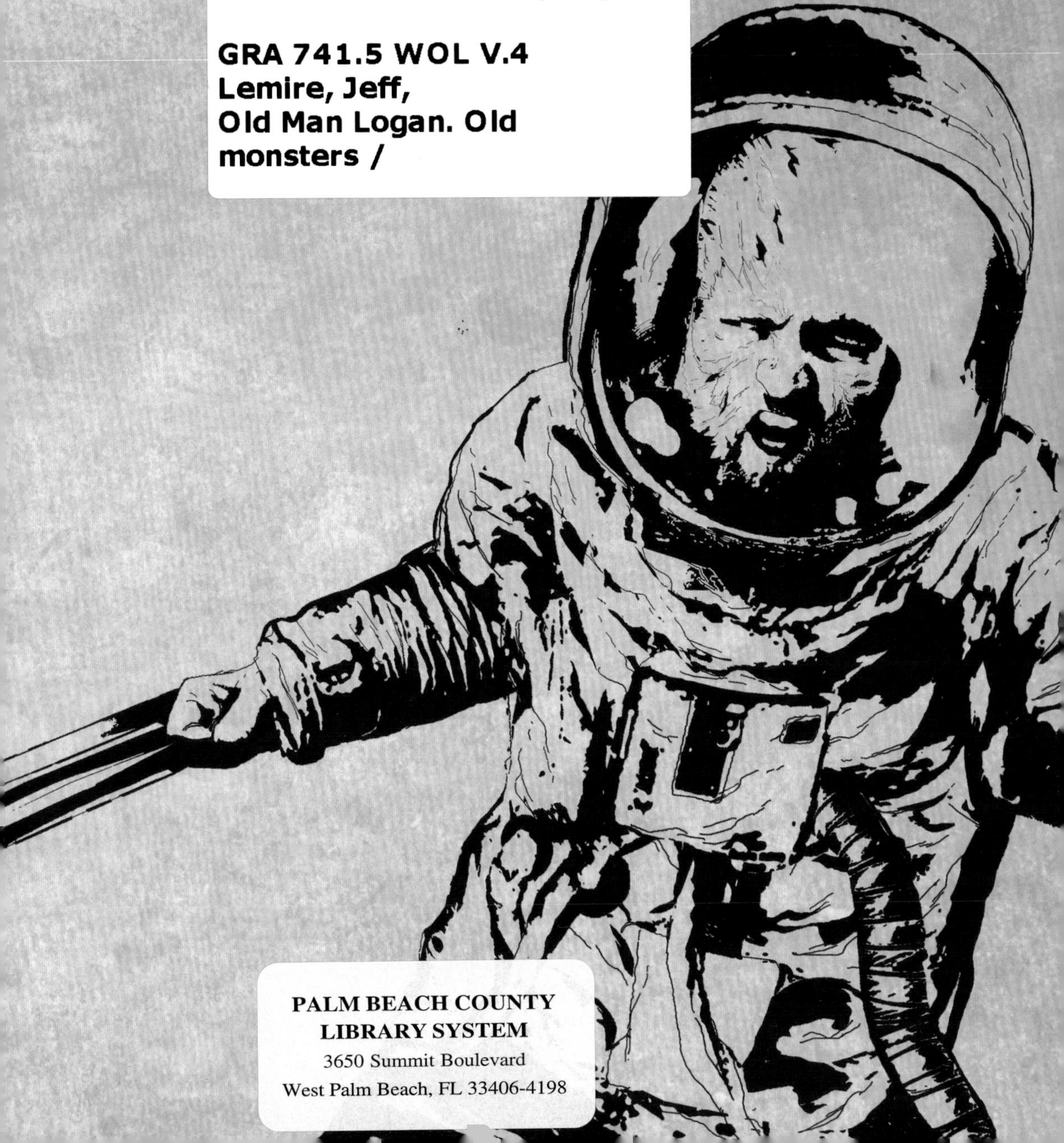

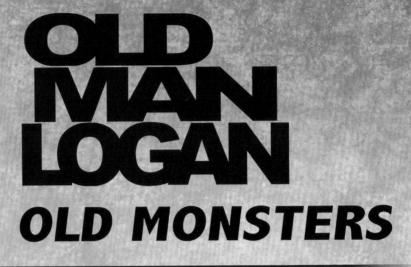

OLD MAN LOGAN

OLD MONSTERS

WRITER **JEFF LEMIRE**

"MONSTER WAR"

ARTIST **FILIPE ANDRADE**

COLORIST **JORDIE BELLAIRE**

"RETURN TO THE WASTELANDS"

ARTIST **ANDREA SORRENTINO**

COLORIST **MARCELO MAIOLO**

LETTERER **VC'S CORY PETIT**

COVER ARTISTS **ANDREA SORRENTINO &**
MARCELO MAIOLO

ASSISTANT EDITOR **CHRISTINA HARRINGTON**

EDITOR **MARK PANICCIA**

COLLECTION EDITOR **MARK D. BEAZLEY**
ASSISTANT EDITOR **CAITLIN O'CONNELL**
ASSOCIATE MANAGING EDITOR **KATERI WOODY**
ASSOCIATE MANAGER, DIGITAL ASSETS **JOE HOCHSTEIN**
SENIOR EDITOR, SPECIAL PROJECTS **JENNIFER GRÜNWALD**
VP PRODUCTION & SPECIAL PROJECTS **JEFF YOUNGQUIST**
SVP PRINT, SALES & MARKETING **DAVID GABRIEL**
BOOK DESIGNER **ADAM DEL RE**

EDITOR IN CHIEF **AXEL ALONSO**
CHIEF CREATIVE OFFICER **JOE QUESADA**
PRESIDENT **DAN BUCKLEY**
EXECUTIVE PRODUCER **ALAN FINE**

WOLVERINE: OLD MAN LOGAN VOL. 4 — OLD MONSTERS. Contains material originally published in magazine form as OLD MAN LOGAN #14-18. First printing 2017. ISBN# 978-1-302-90573-6. Published by MARVEL WORLDWIDE, INC., a subsidiary of MARVEL ENTERTAINMENT, LLC. OFFICE OF PUBLICATION: 135 West 50th Street, New York, NY 10020. Copyright © 2017 MARVEL No similarity between any of the names, characters, persons, and/or institutions in this magazine with those of any living or dead person or institution is intended, and any such similarity which may exist is purely coincidental. **Printed in Canada.** DAN BUCKLEY, President, Marvel Entertainment; JOE QUESADA, Chief Creative Officer; TOM BREVOORT, SVP of Publishing; DAVID BOGART, SVP of Business Affairs & Operations, Publishing & Partnership; C.B. CEBULSKI, VP of Brand Management & Development, Asia; DAVID GABRIEL, SVP of Sales & Marketing, Publishing; JEFF YOUNGQUIST, VP of Production & Special Projects; DAN CARR, Executive Director of Publishing Technology; ALEX MORALES, Director of Publishing Operations; SUSAN CRESPI, Production Manager; STAN LEE, Chairman Emeritus. For information regarding advertising in Marvel Comics or on Marvel.com, please contact Vit DeBellis, Integrated Sales Manager, at vdebellis@marvel.com. For Marvel subscription inquiries, please call 888-511-5480. **Manufactured between 4/7/2017 and 5/9/2017 by SOLISCO PRINTERS, SCOTT, QC, CANADA.**

10 9 8 7 6 5 4 3 2 1

After surviving a future known as the Wastelands where everything good in the world was destroyed, Old Man Logan awoke in the present, determined to prevent the death of his wife and children. Even after accepting that the past he remembers is not real, he is still haunted by his lost family.

Logan tries to be a lone agent, but isolating himself is not always possible.

In his past, Logan was a mentor to the young mutant Jubilee. In the Wastelands, he was responsible for Jubilee's death. In the present, though, Jubilee is thriving. She lives in Brooklyn, has a young son named Shogo and is currently a vampire.

OLD MAN LOGAN

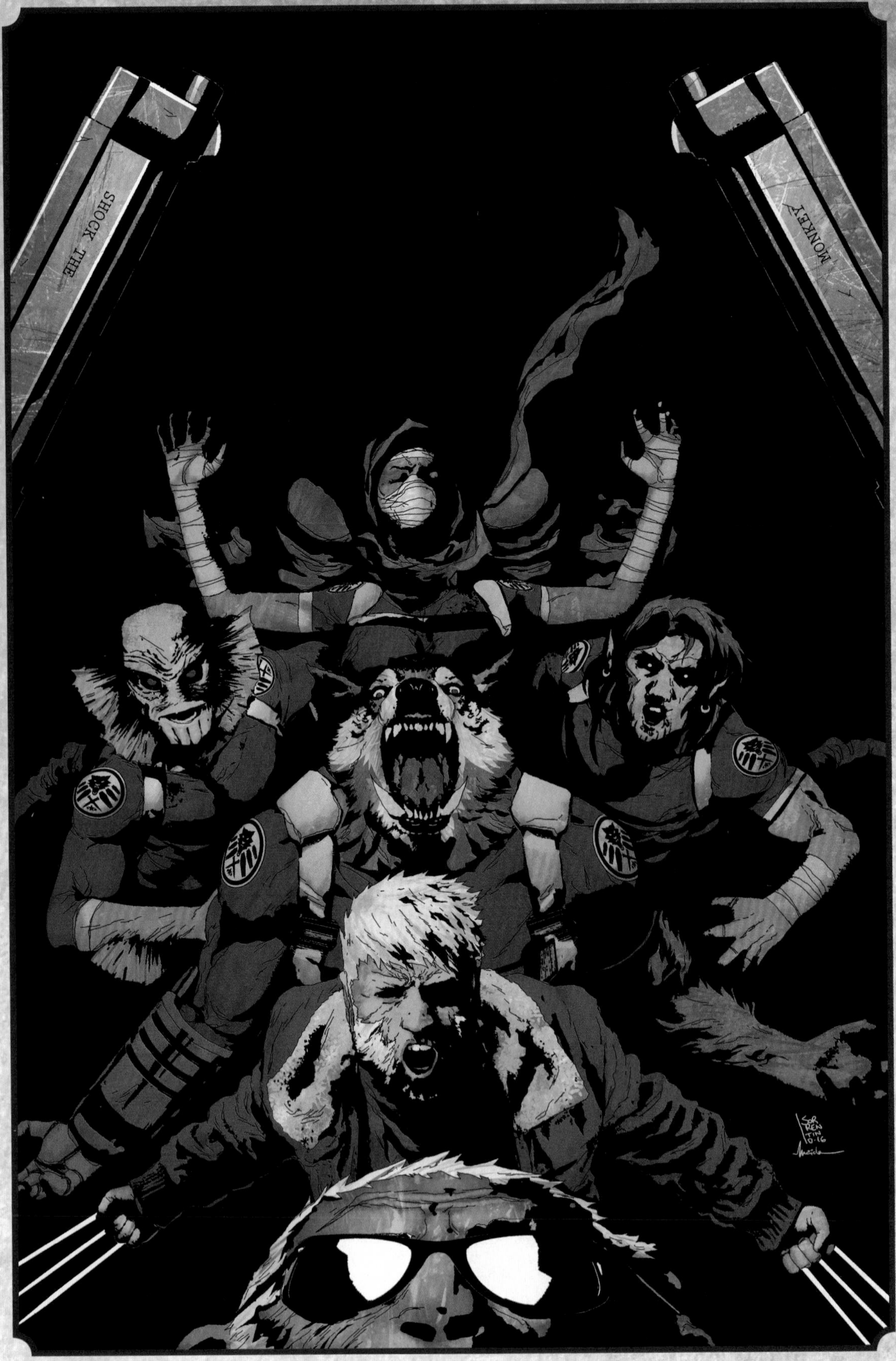
SHOCK THE
MONKEY

14

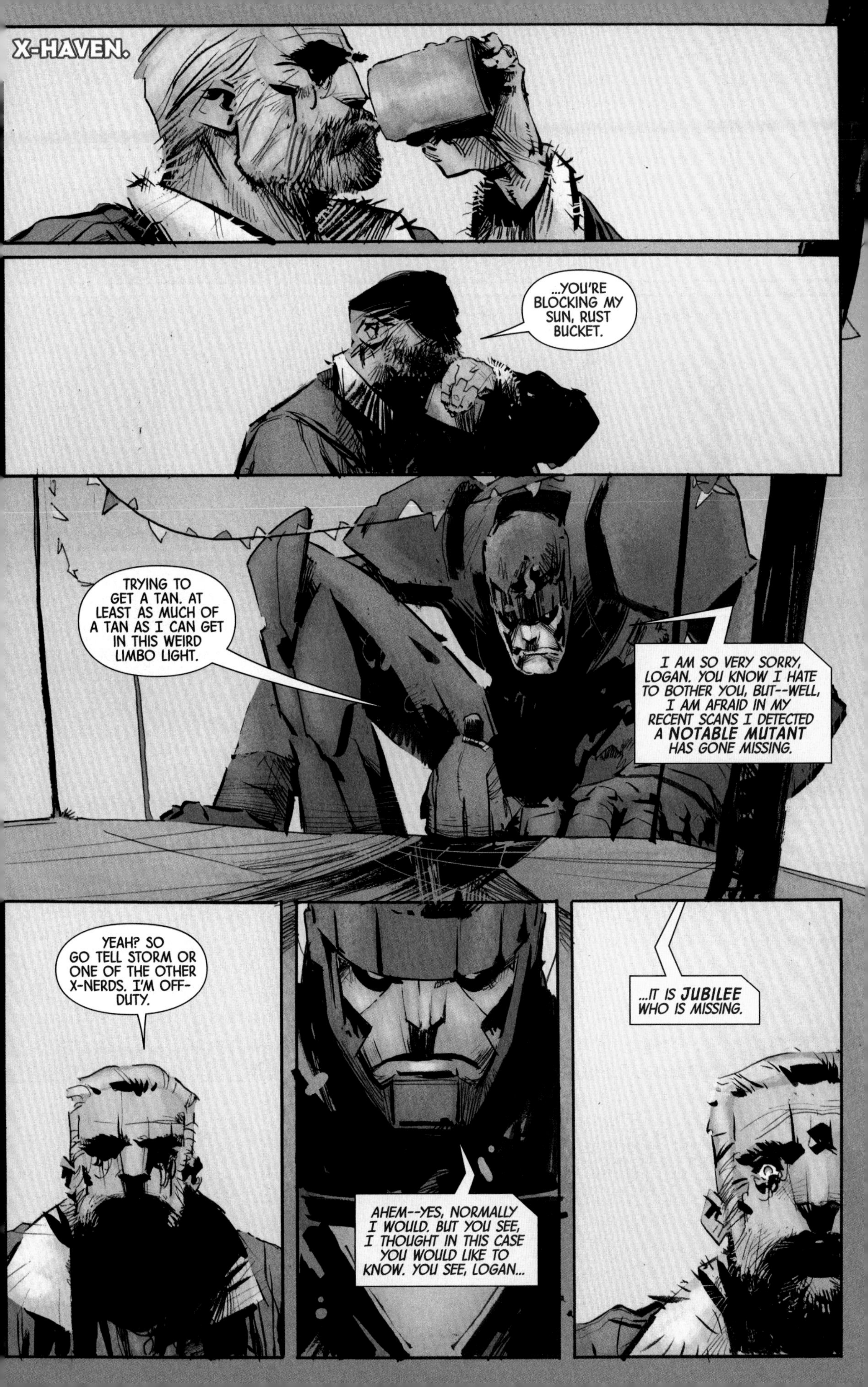
X-HAVEN.
...YOU'RE BLOCKING MY SUN, RUST BUCKET.
TRYING TO GET A TAN. AT LEAST AS MUCH OF A TAN AS I CAN GET IN THIS WEIRD LIMBO LIGHT.
I AM SO VERY SORRY, LOGAN. YOU KNOW I HATE TO BOTHER YOU, BUT--WELL, I AM AFRAID IN MY RECENT SCANS I DETECTED A NOTABLE MUTANT HAS GONE MISSING.
YEAH? SO GO TELL STORM OR ONE OF THE OTHER X-NERDS. I'M OFF-DUTY.
AHEM--YES, NORMALLY I WOULD. BUT YOU SEE, I THOUGHT IN THIS CASE YOU WOULD LIKE TO KNOW. YOU SEE, LOGAN...
...IT IS JUBILEE WHO IS MISSING.

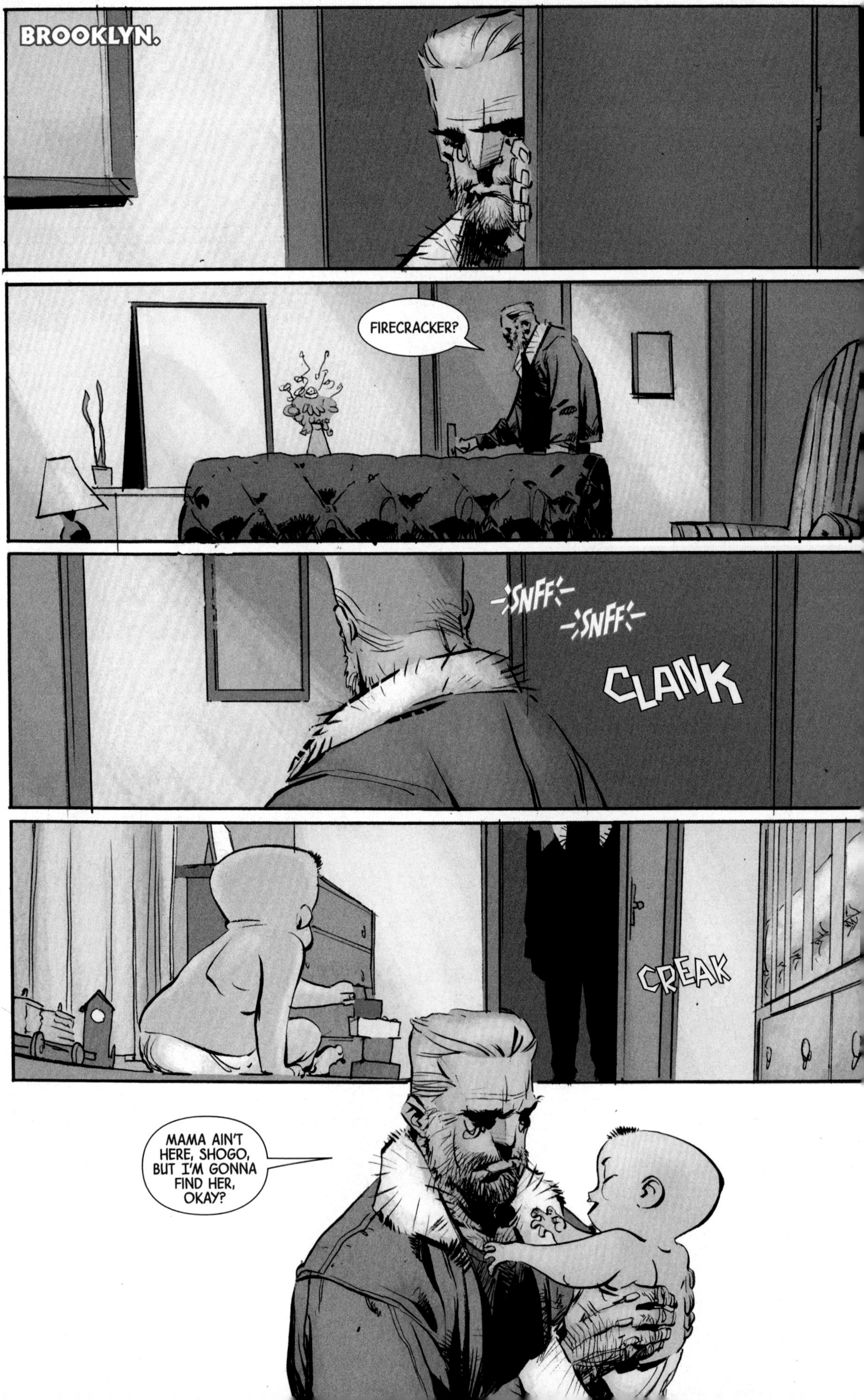
BROOKLYN.
FIRECRACKER?
SNFF
SNFF
CLANK
CREAK
MAMA AIN'T HERE, SHOGO, BUT I'M GONNA FIND HER, OKAY?

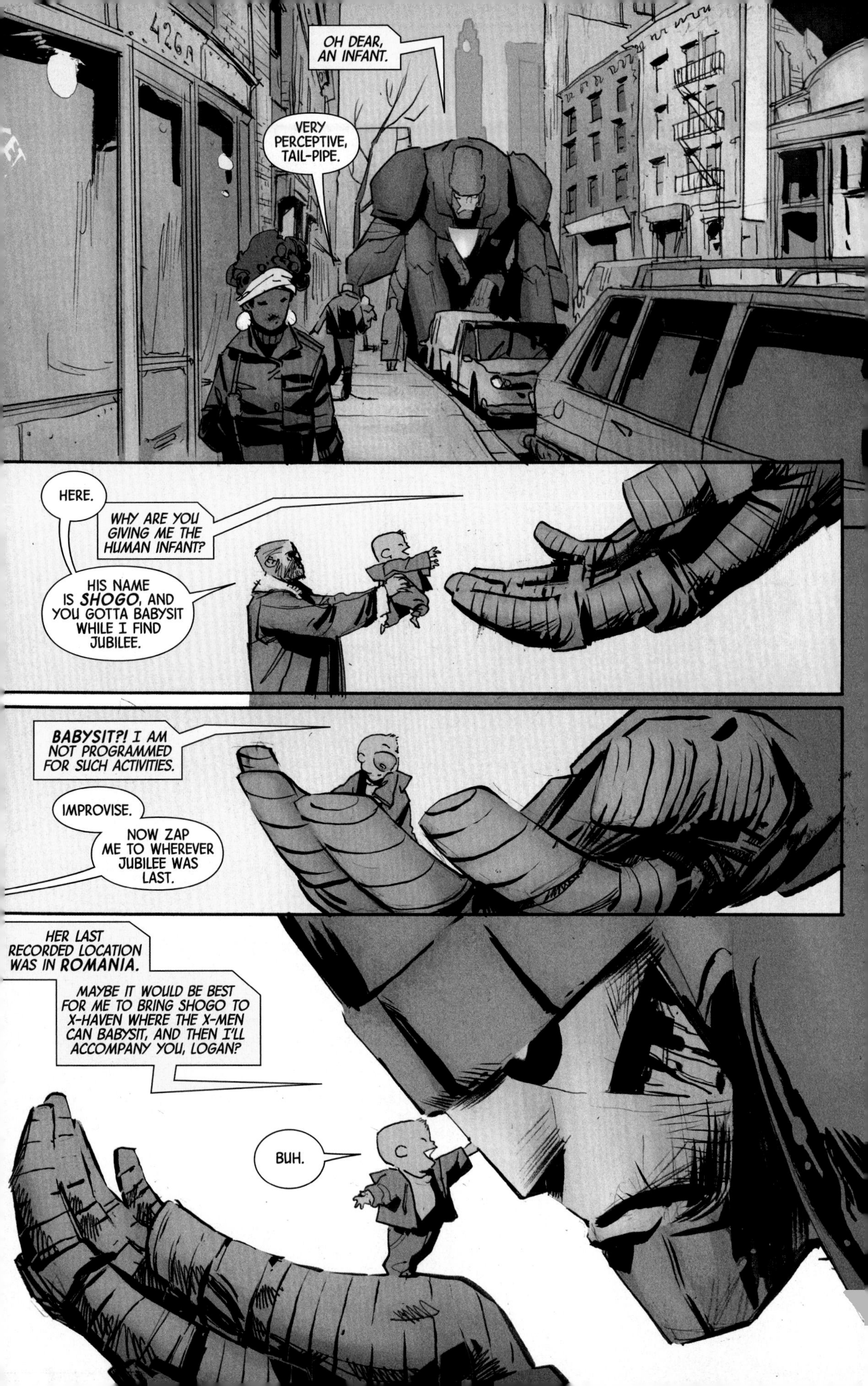
OH DEAR, AN INFANT.
VERY PERCEPTIVE, TAIL-PIPE.
HERE.
WHY ARE YOU GIVING ME THE HUMAN INFANT?
HIS NAME IS SHOGO, AND YOU GOTTA BABYSIT WHILE I FIND JUBILEE.
BABYSIT?! I AM NOT PROGRAMMED FOR SUCH ACTIVITIES.
IMPROVISE.
NOW ZAP ME TO WHEREVER JUBILEE WAS LAST.
HER LAST RECORDED LOCATION WAS IN ROMANIA.
MAYBE IT WOULD BE BEST FOR ME TO BRING SHOGO TO X-HAVEN WHERE THE X-MEN CAN BABYSIT, AND THEN I'LL ACCOMPANY YOU, LOGAN?
BUH.

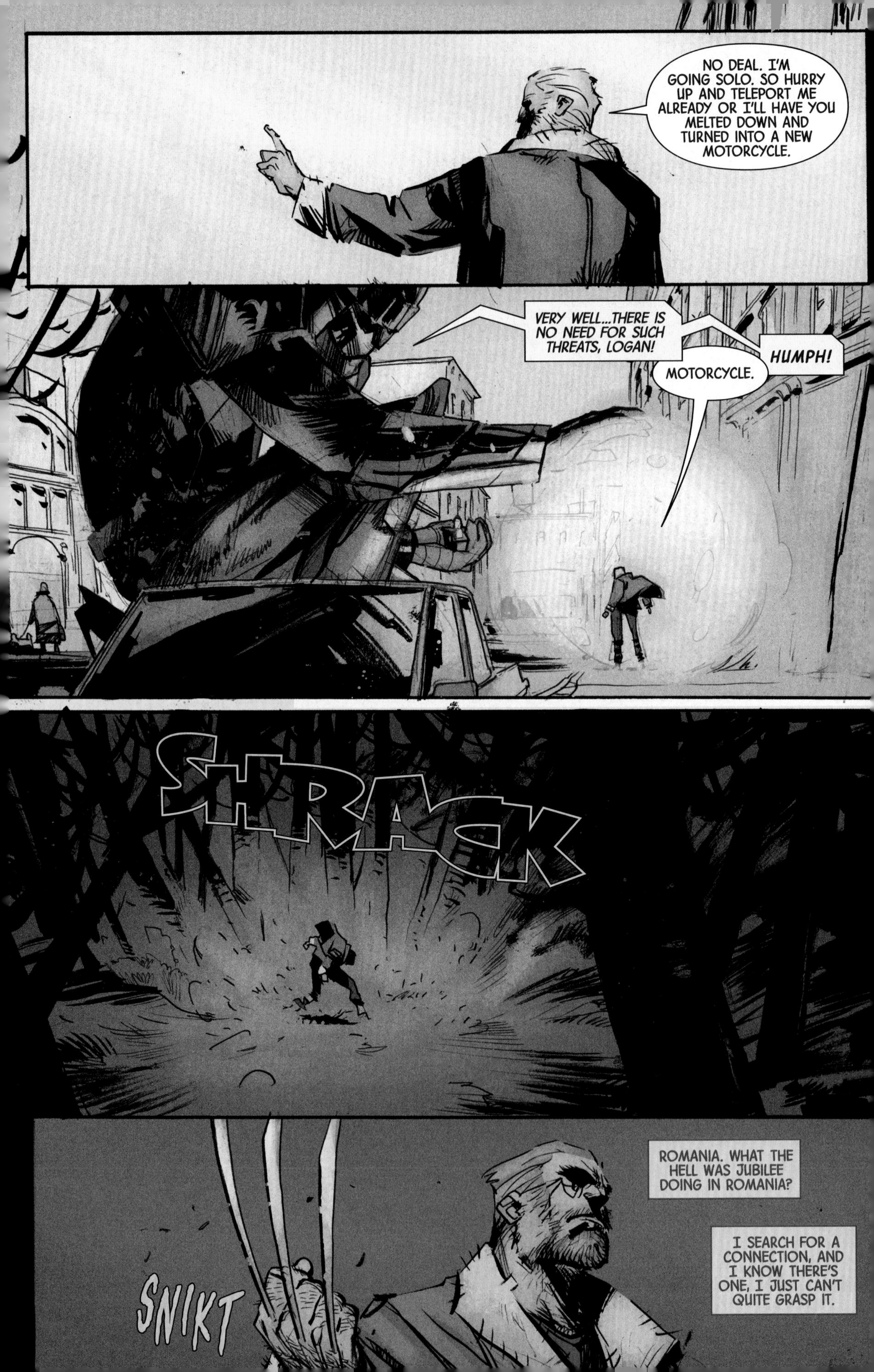
NO DEAL. I'M GOING SOLO. SO HURRY UP AND TELEPORT ME ALREADY OR I'LL HAVE YOU MELTED DOWN AND TURNED INTO A NEW MOTORCYCLE.
VERY WELL...THERE IS NO NEED FOR SUCH THREATS, LOGAN!
HUMPH!
MOTORCYCLE.
SHRACK
ROMANIA. WHAT THE HELL WAS JUBILEE DOING IN ROMANIA?
I SEARCH FOR A CONNECTION, AND I KNOW THERE'S ONE, I JUST CAN'T QUITE GRASP IT.
SNIKT

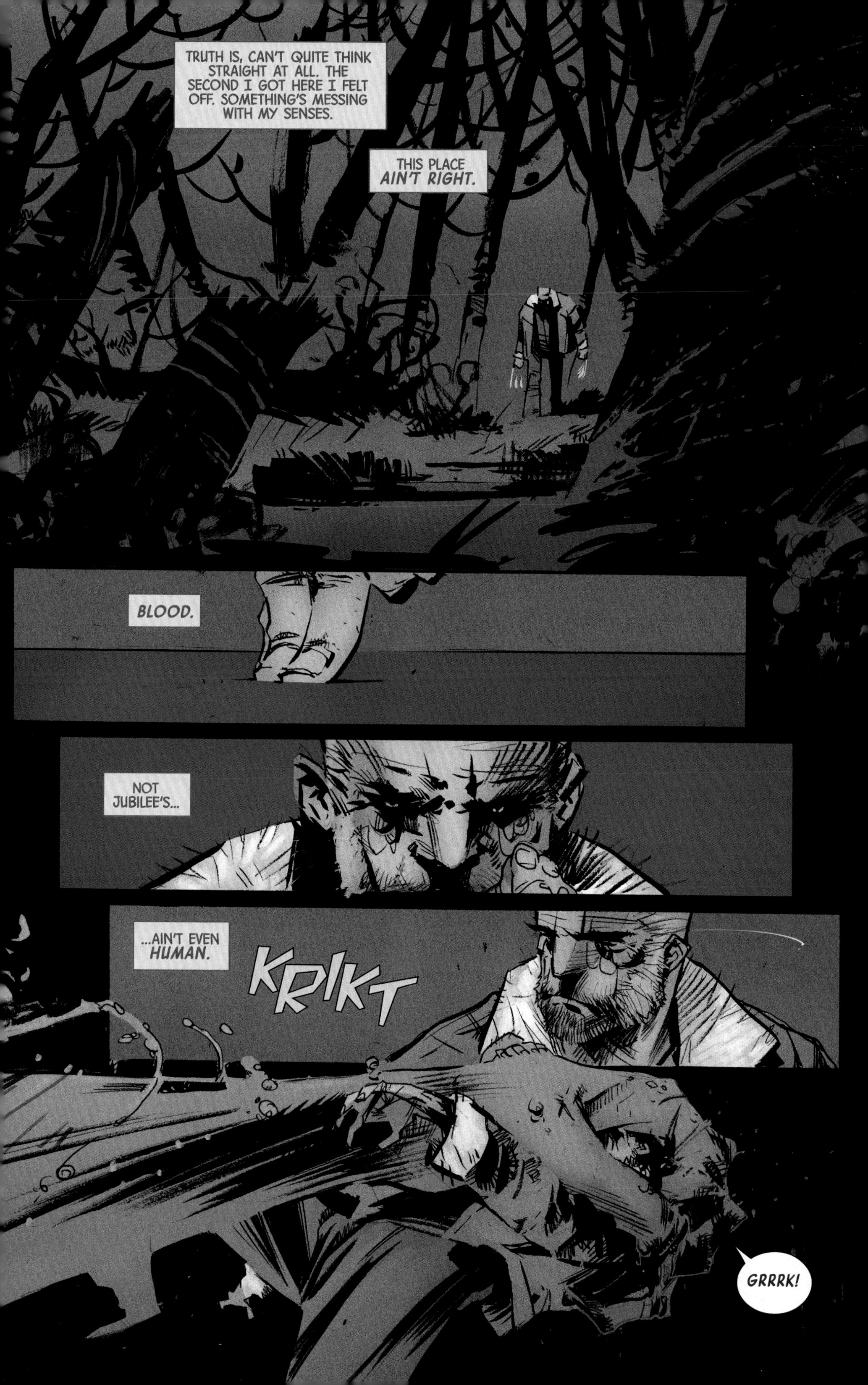
TRUTH IS, CAN'T QUITE THINK STRAIGHT AT ALL. THE SECOND I GOT HERE I FELT OFF. SOMETHING'S MESSING WITH MY SENSES.
THIS PLACE AIN'T RIGHT.
BLOOD.
NOT JUBILEE'S...
...AIN'T EVEN HUMAN.
KRIKT
GRRRK!

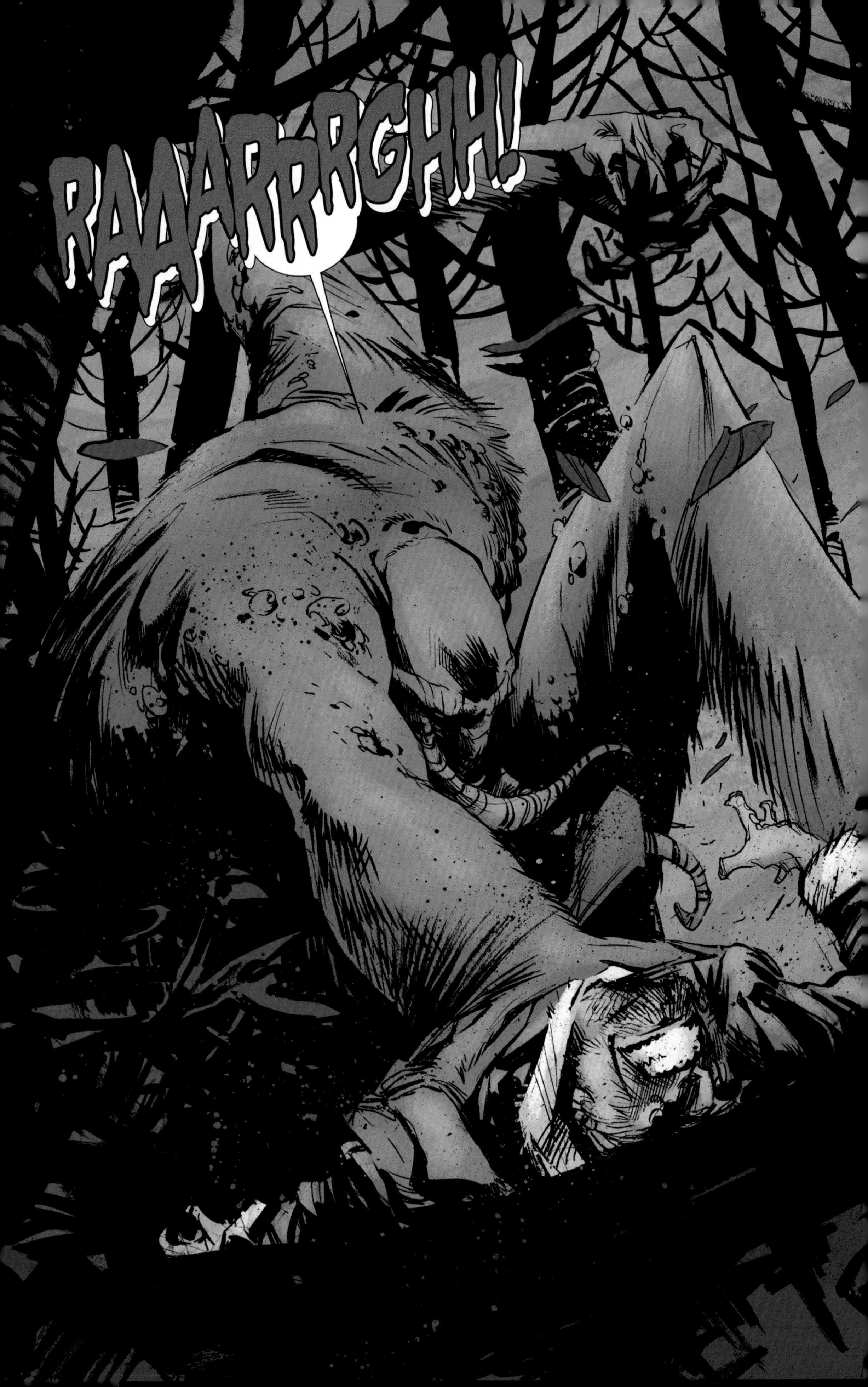
RAAARRRGHH!

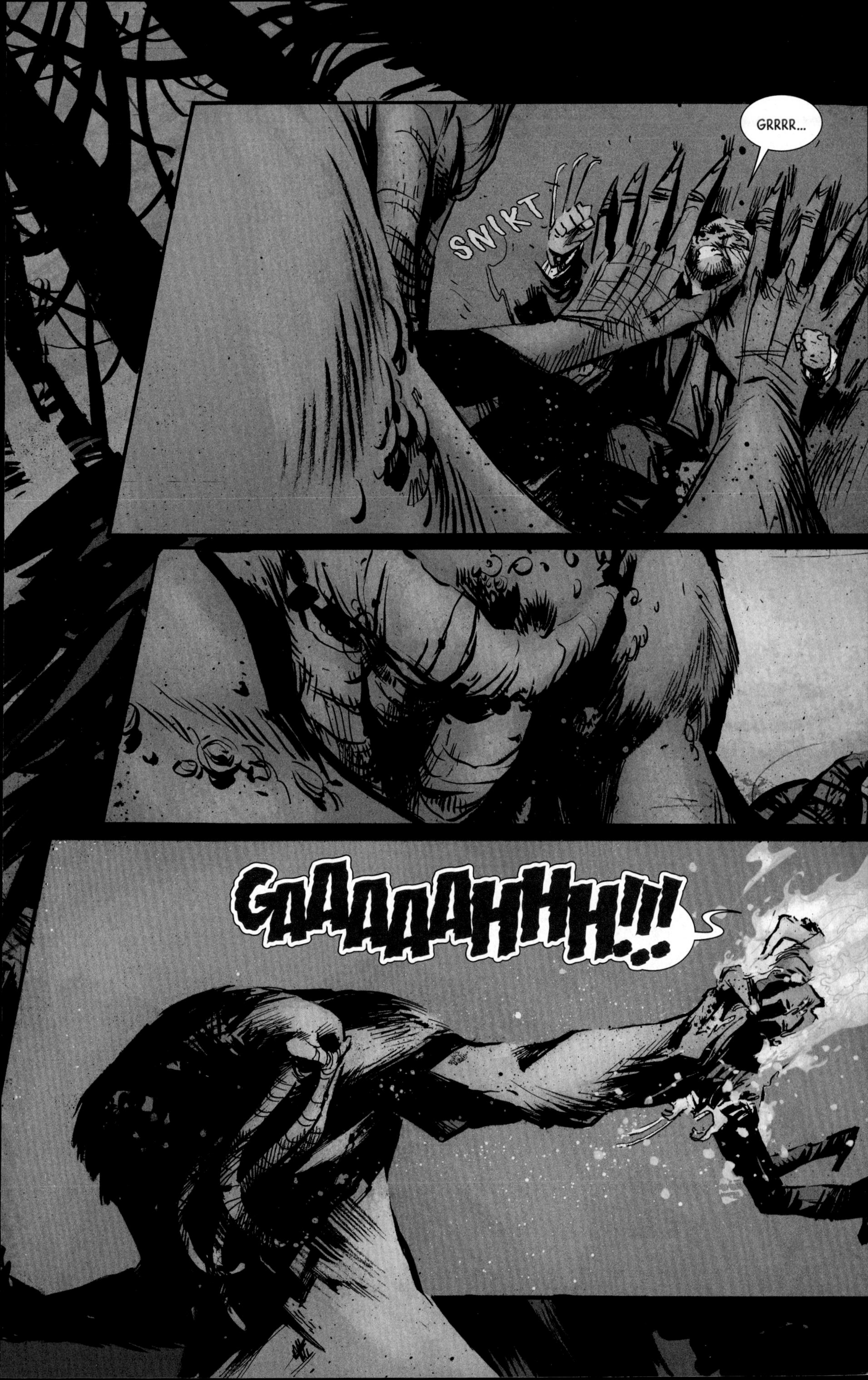
GRRRR...
SNIKT
GAAAAAHHHH!!!

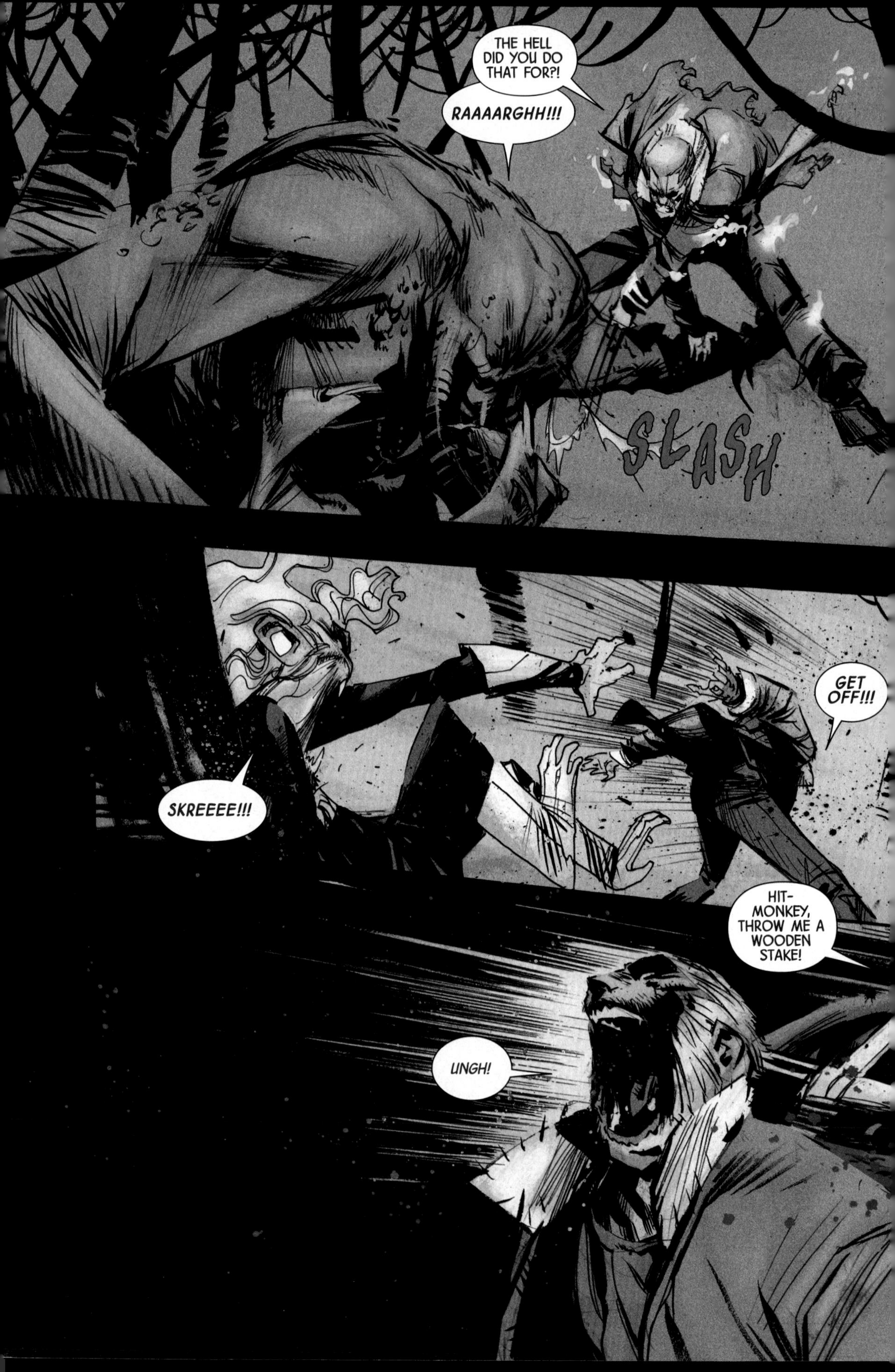
THE HELL DID YOU DO THAT FOR?!
RAAAARGHH!!!
SLASH
GET OFF!!!
SKREEEE!!!
HIT-MONKEY, THROW ME A WOODEN STAKE!
UNGH!

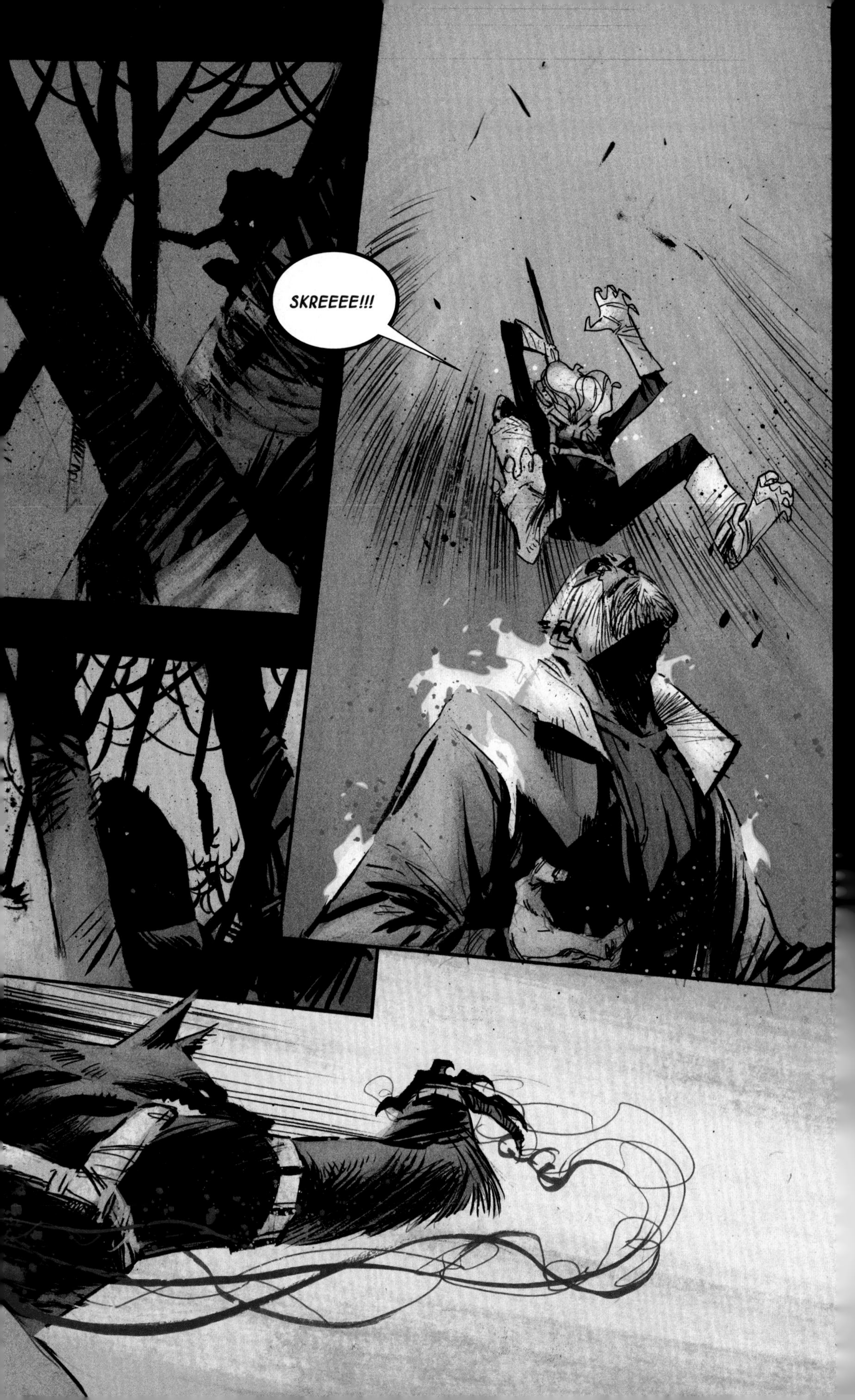
SKREEEE!!!

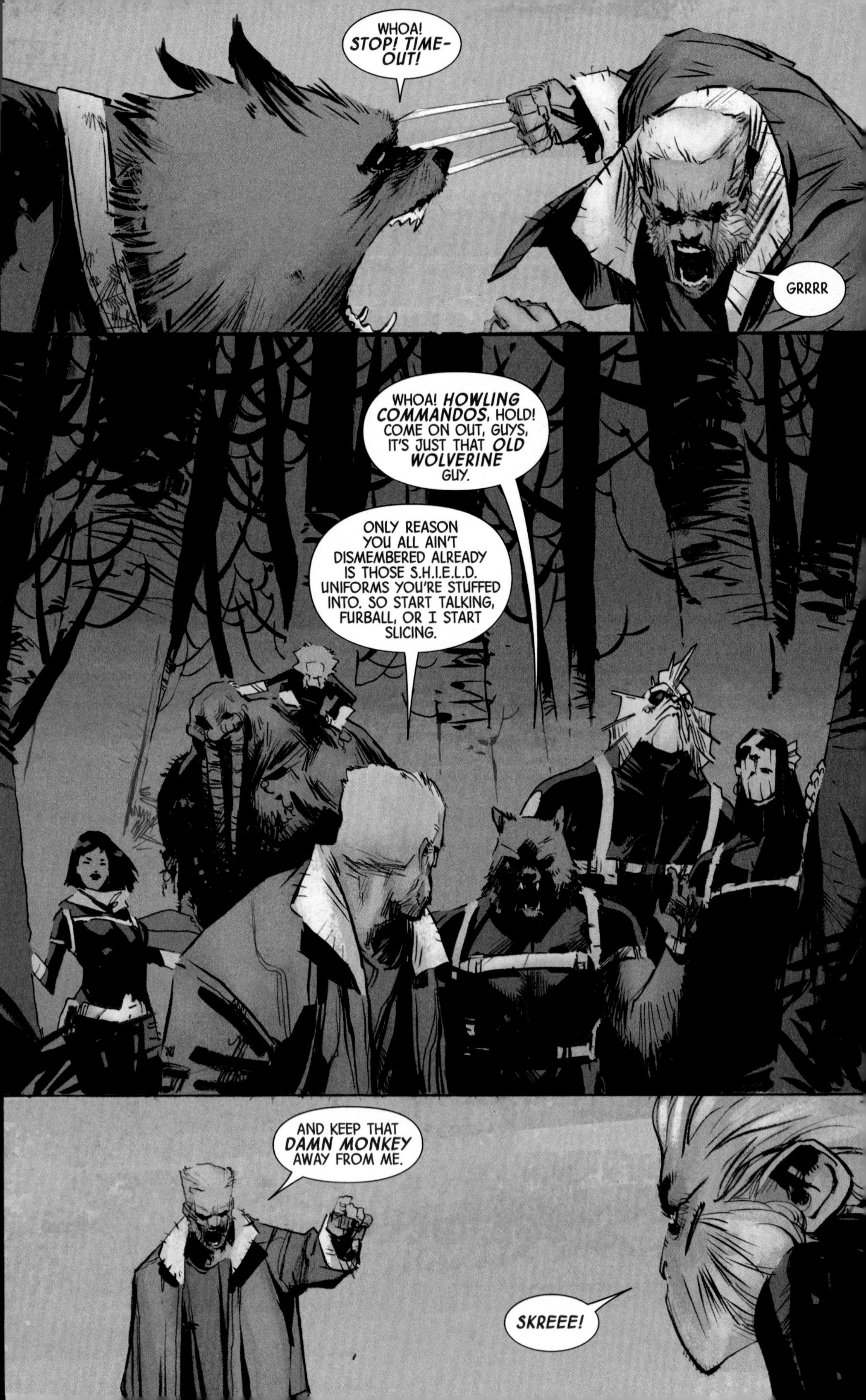
WHOA! STOP! TIME-OUT!
GRRRR
WHOA! HOWLING COMMANDOS, HOLD! COME ON OUT, GUYS, IT'S JUST THAT OLD WOLVERINE GUY.
ONLY REASON YOU ALL AIN'T DISMEMBERED ALREADY IS THOSE S.H.I.E.L.D. UNIFORMS YOU'RE STUFFED INTO. SO START TALKING, FURBALL, OR I START SLICING.
AND KEEP THAT DAMN MONKEY AWAY FROM ME.
SKREEE!

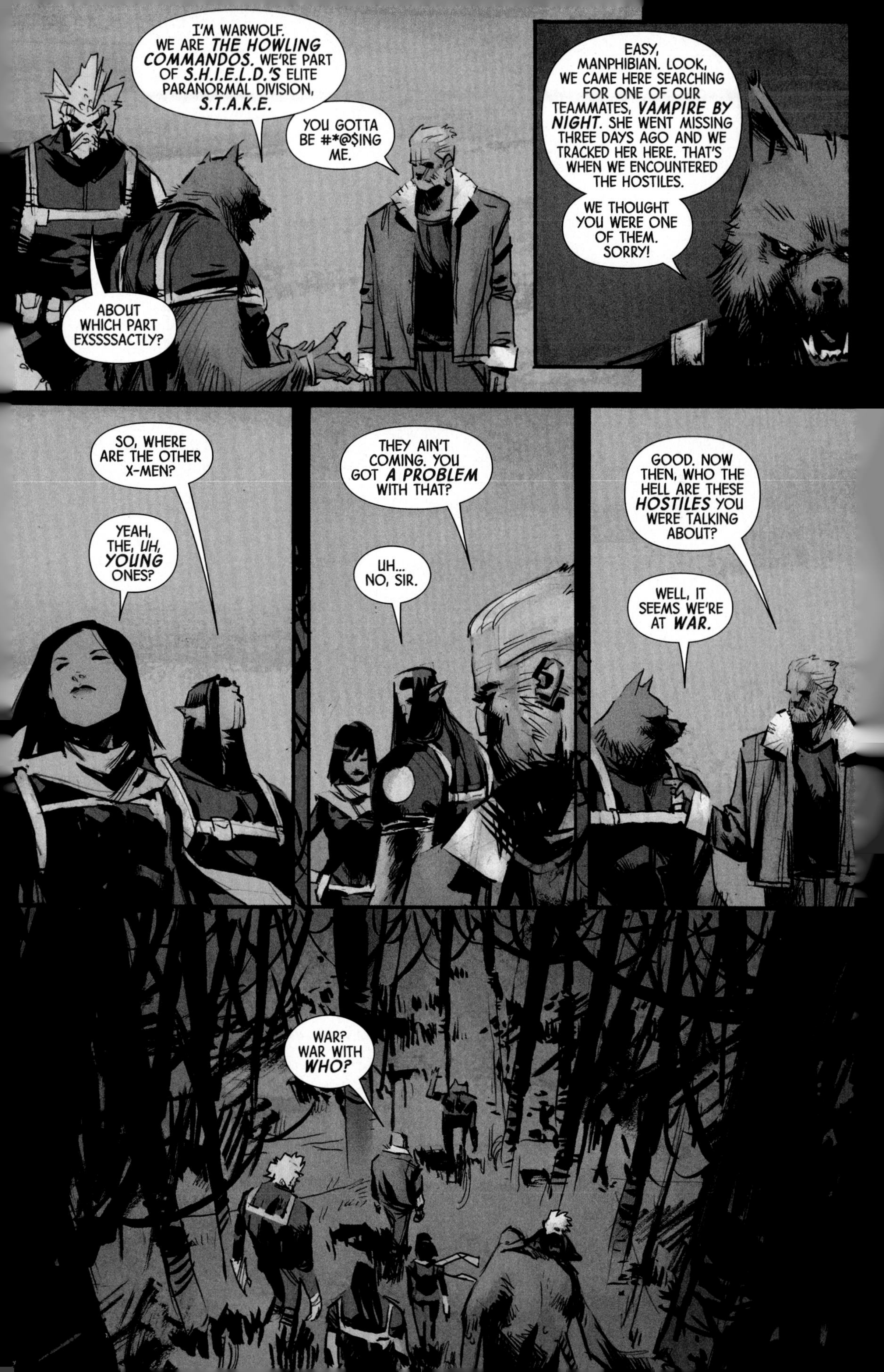
I'M WARWOLF. WE ARE THE HOWLING COMMANDOS. WE'RE PART OF S.H.I.E.L.D.'S ELITE PARANORMAL DIVISION, S.T.A.K.E.
YOU GOTTA BE #*@$ING ME.
ABOUT WHICH PART EXSSSSACTLY?
EASY, MANPHIBIAN. LOOK, WE CAME HERE SEARCHING FOR ONE OF OUR TEAMMATES, VAMPIRE BY NIGHT. SHE WENT MISSING THREE DAYS AGO AND WE TRACKED HER HERE. THAT'S WHEN WE ENCOUNTERED THE HOSTILES.
WE THOUGHT YOU WERE ONE OF THEM. SORRY!
SO, WHERE ARE THE OTHER X-MEN?
YEAH, THE, UH, YOUNG ONES?
THEY AIN'T COMING. YOU GOT A PROBLEM WITH THAT?
UH... NO, SIR.
GOOD. NOW THEN, WHO THE HELL ARE THESE HOSTILES YOU WERE TALKING ABOUT?
WELL, IT SEEMS WE'RE AT WAR.
WAR? WAR WITH WHO?

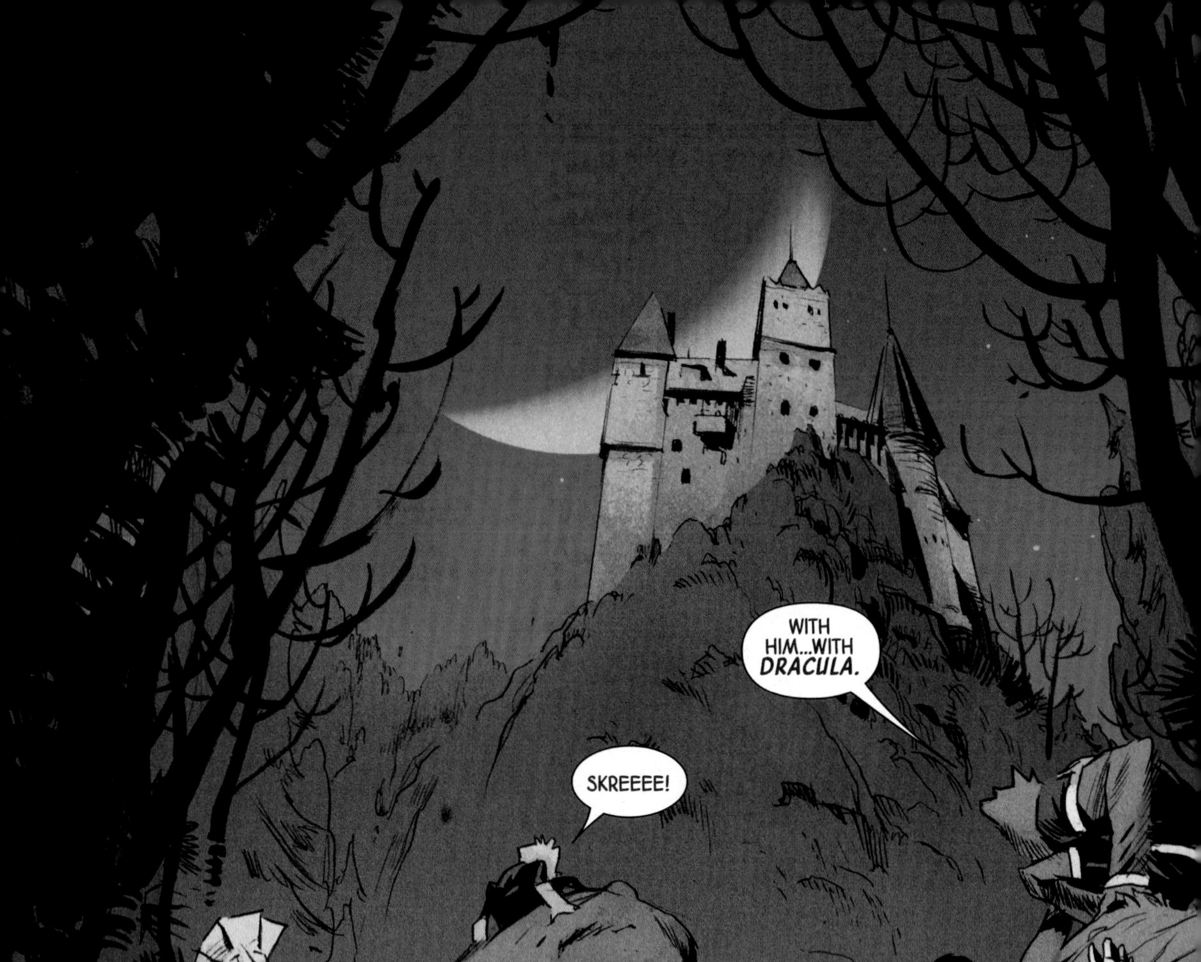
WITH HIM...WITH DRACULA.
SKREEEE!
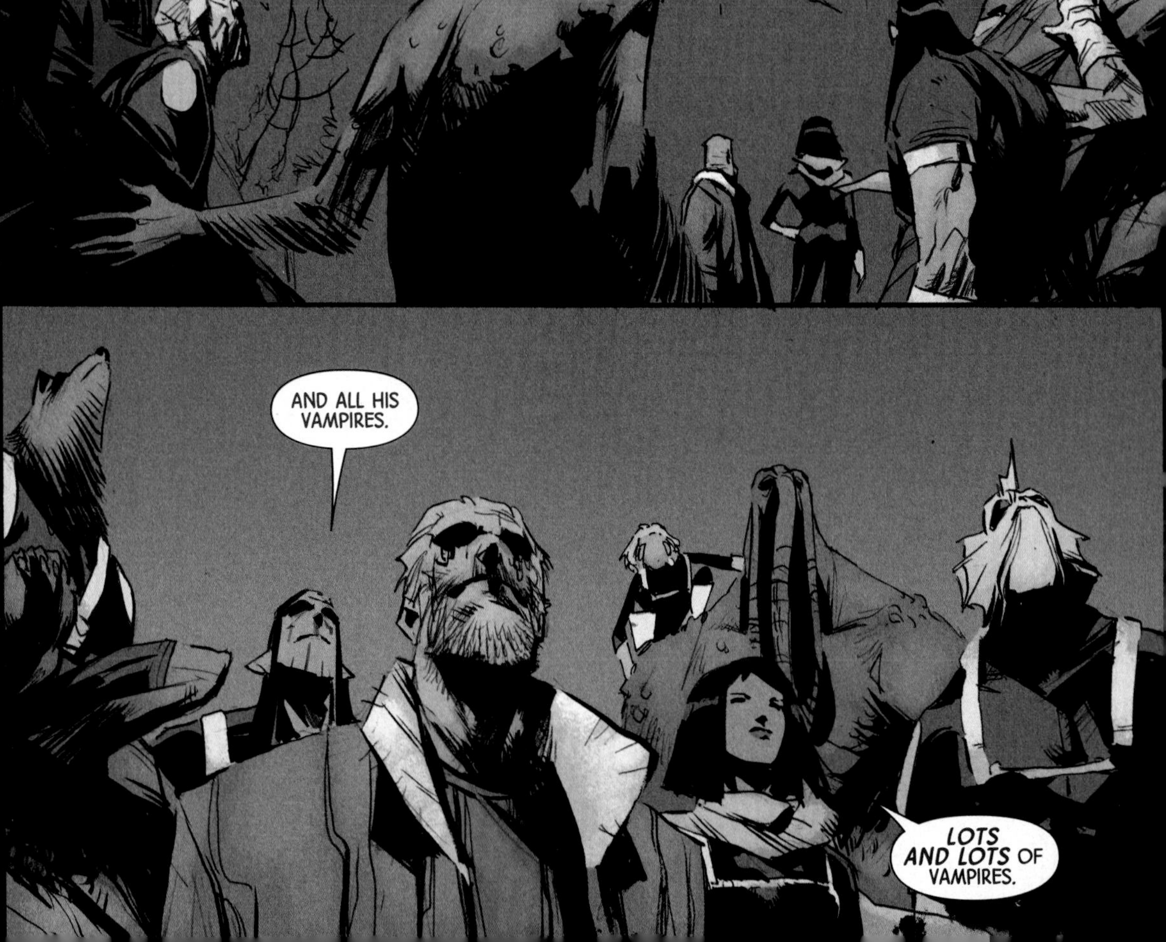
AND ALL HIS VAMPIRES.
LOTS AND LOTS OF VAMPIRES.

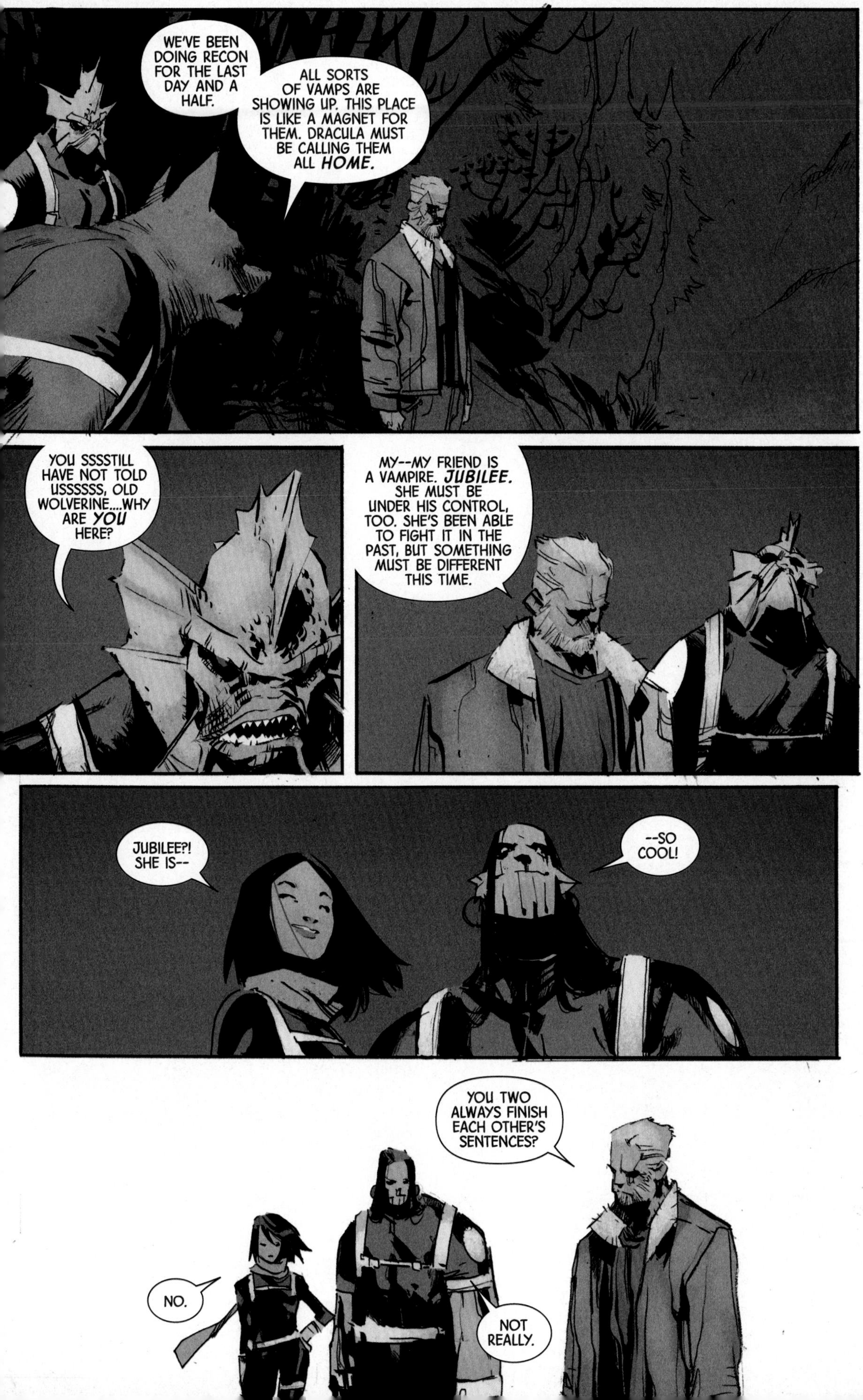
WE'VE BEEN DOING RECON FOR THE LAST DAY AND A HALF.
ALL SORTS OF VAMPS ARE SHOWING UP. THIS PLACE IS LIKE A MAGNET FOR THEM. DRACULA MUST BE CALLING THEM ALL HOME.
YOU SSSSTILL HAVE NOT TOLD USSSSSS, OLD WOLVERINE....WHY ARE YOU HERE?
MY--MY FRIEND IS A VAMPIRE. JUBILEE. SHE MUST BE UNDER HIS CONTROL, TOO. SHE'S BEEN ABLE TO FIGHT IT IN THE PAST, BUT SOMETHING MUST BE DIFFERENT THIS TIME.
JUBILEE?! SHE IS--
--SO COOL!
YOU TWO ALWAYS FINISH EACH OTHER'S SENTENCES?
NO.
NOT REALLY.

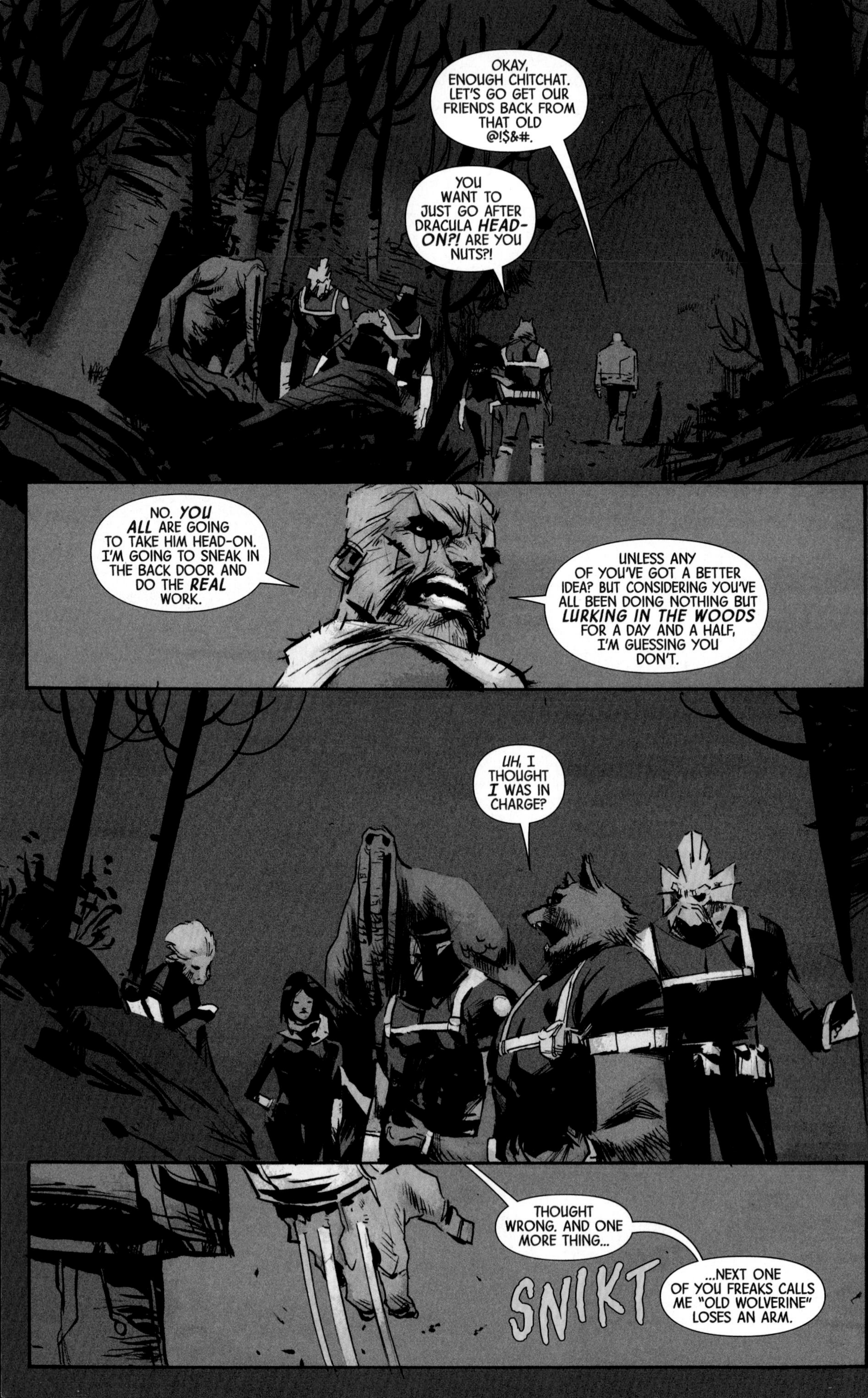
OKAY, ENOUGH CHITCHAT. LET'S GO GET OUR FRIENDS BACK FROM THAT OLD @!$&#.
YOU WANT TO JUST GO AFTER DRACULA HEAD-ON?! ARE YOU NUTS?!
NO. YOU ALL ARE GOING TO TAKE HIM HEAD-ON. I'M GOING TO SNEAK IN THE BACK DOOR AND DO THE REAL WORK.
UNLESS ANY OF YOU'VE GOT A BETTER IDEA? BUT CONSIDERING YOU'VE ALL BEEN DOING NOTHING BUT LURKING IN THE WOODS FOR A DAY AND A HALF, I'M GUESSING YOU DON'T.
UH, I THOUGHT I WAS IN CHARGE?
THOUGHT WRONG. AND ONE MORE THING...
SNIKT
...NEXT ONE OF YOU FREAKS CALLS ME "OLD WOLVERINE" LOSES AN ARM.

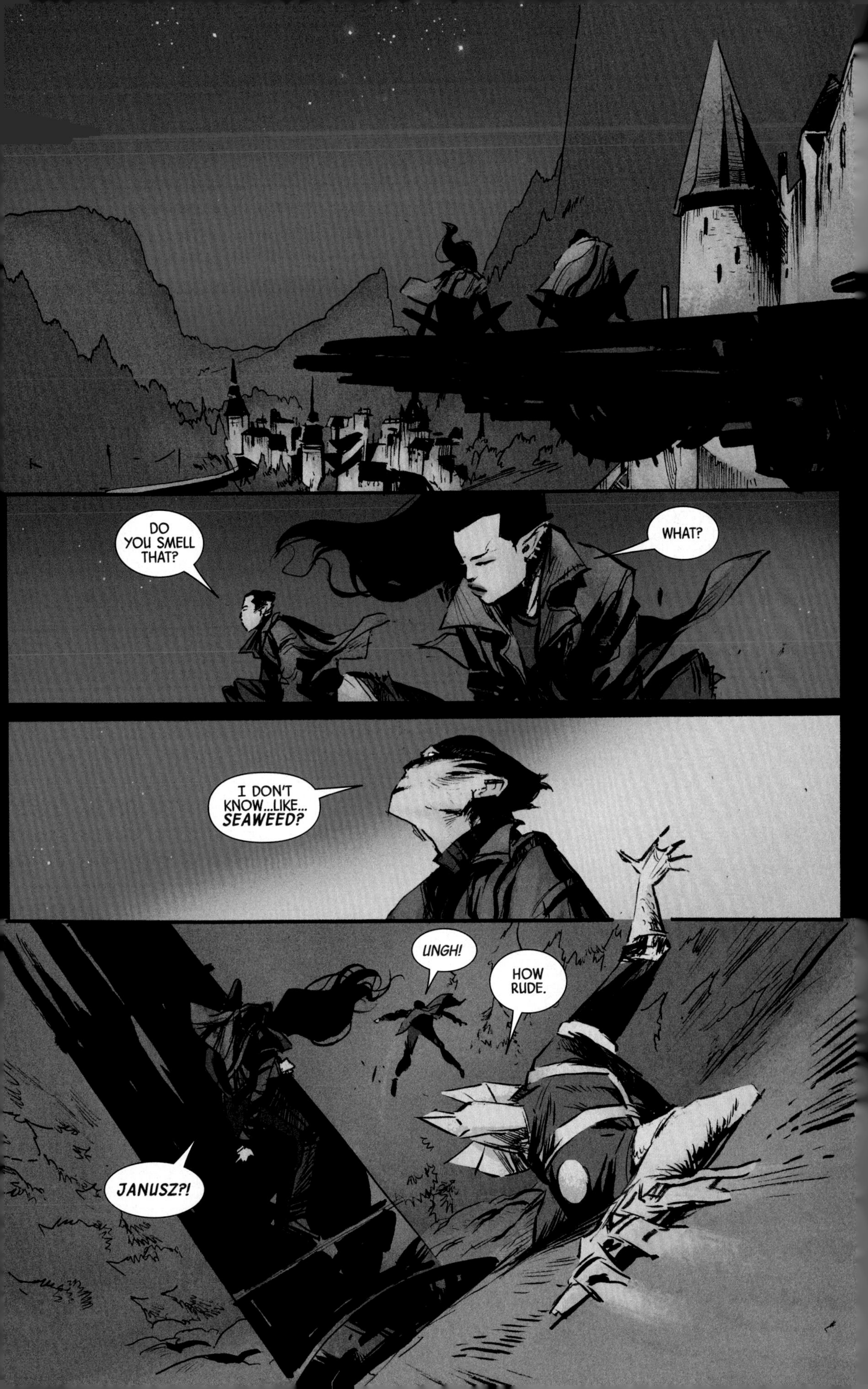
DO YOU SMELL THAT?
WHAT?
I DON'T KNOW...LIKE... SEAWEED?
UNGH!
HOW RUDE.
JANUSZ?!

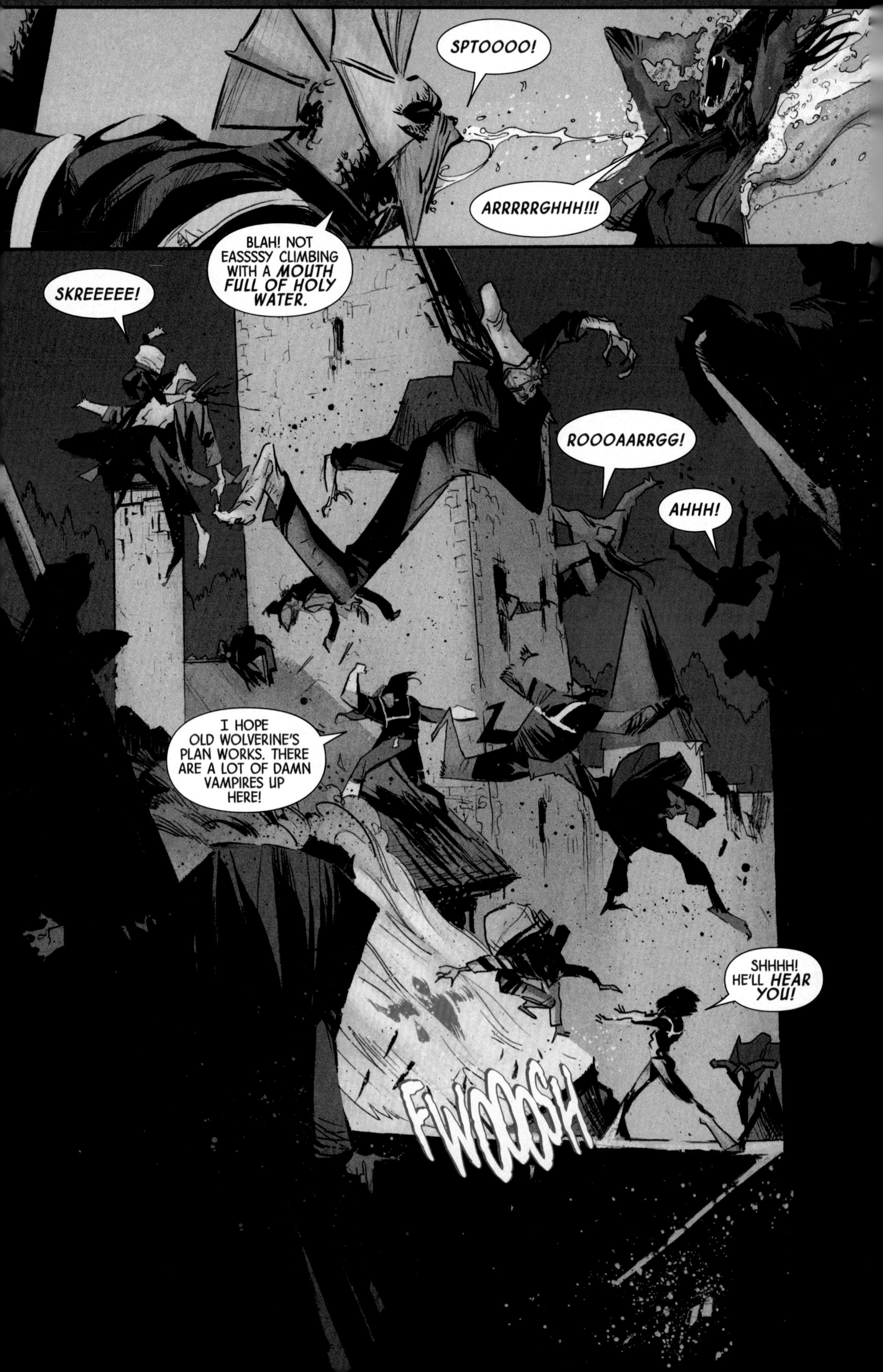
SPTOOOO!
ARRRRRGHHH!!!
BLAH! NOT EASSSSY CLIMBING WITH A MOUTH FULL OF HOLY WATER.
SKREEEEE!
ROOOAARRGG!
AHHH!
I HOPE OLD WOLVERINE'S PLAN WORKS. THERE ARE A LOT OF DAMN VAMPIRES UP HERE!
SHHHH! HE'LL HEAR YOU!
FWOOOSH

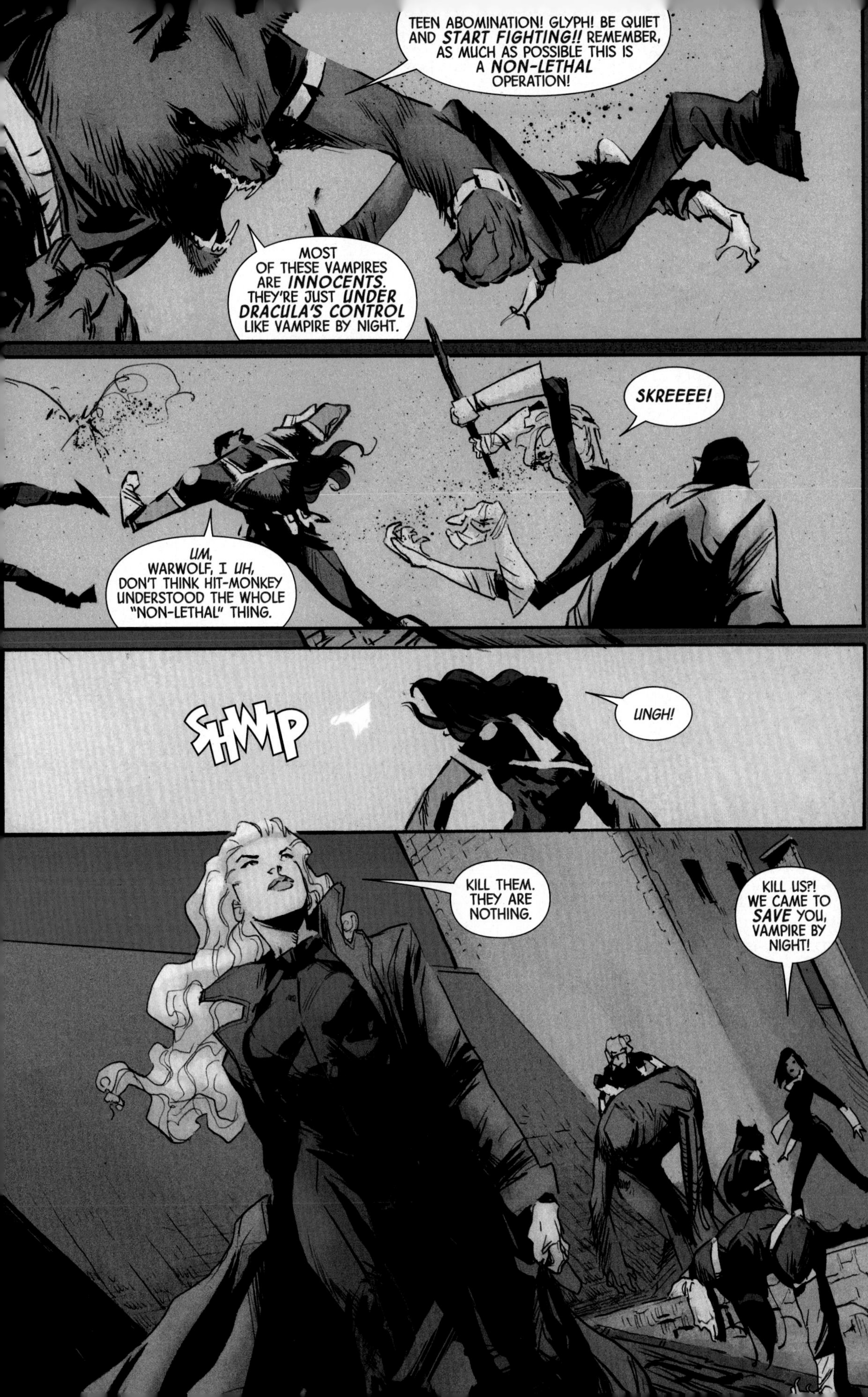
TEEN ABOMINATION! GLYPH! BE QUIET AND START FIGHTING!! REMEMBER, AS MUCH AS POSSIBLE THIS IS A NON-LETHAL OPERATION!
MOST OF THESE VAMPIRES ARE INNOCENTS. THEY'RE JUST UNDER DRACULA'S CONTROL LIKE VAMPIRE BY NIGHT.
SKREEEE!
UM, WARWOLF, I UH, DON'T THINK HIT-MONKEY UNDERSTOOD THE WHOLE "NON-LETHAL" THING.
SHWIP
UNGH!
KILL THEM. THEY ARE NOTHING.
KILL US?! WE CAME TO SAVE YOU, VAMPIRE BY NIGHT!

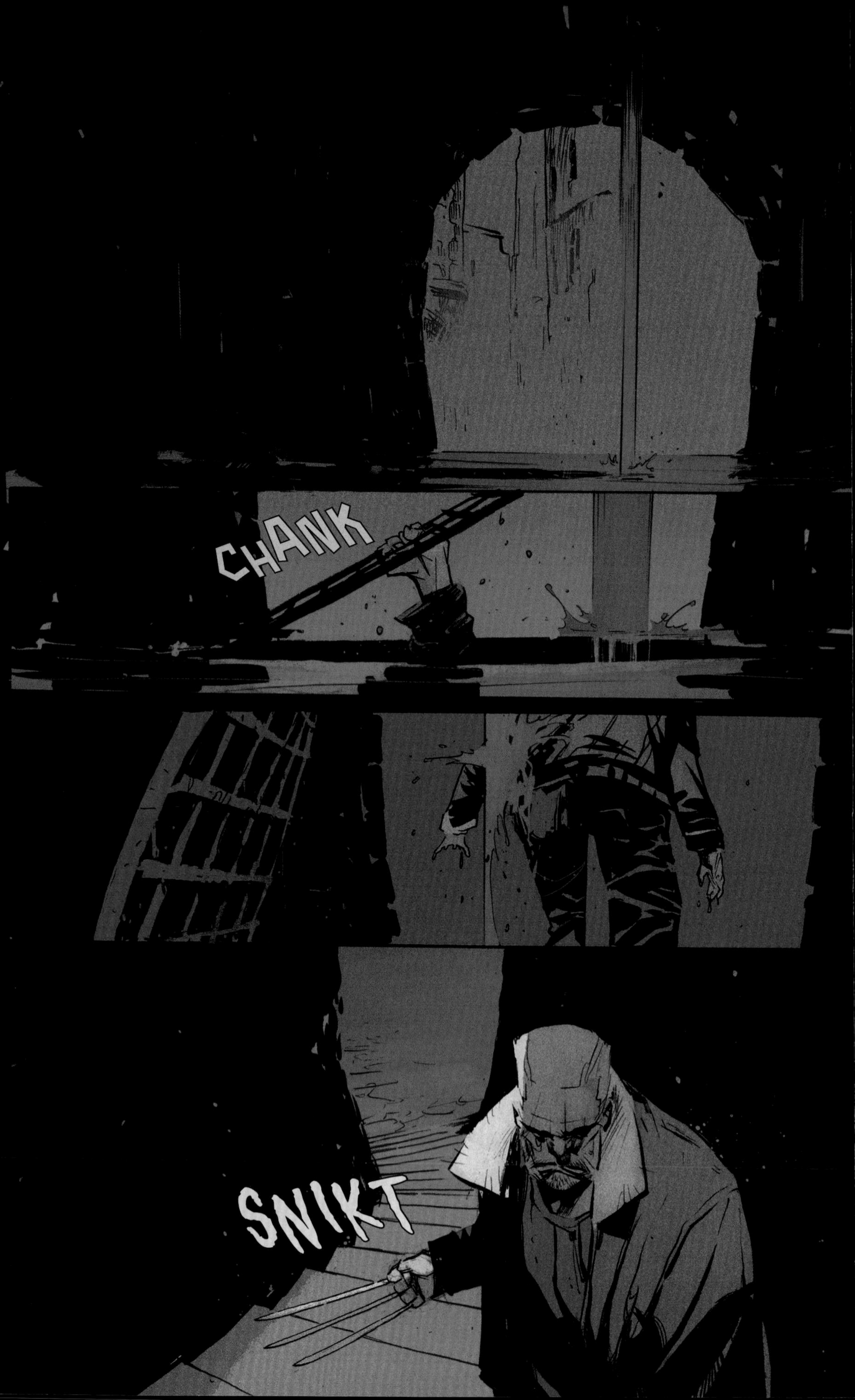
CHANK
SNIKT

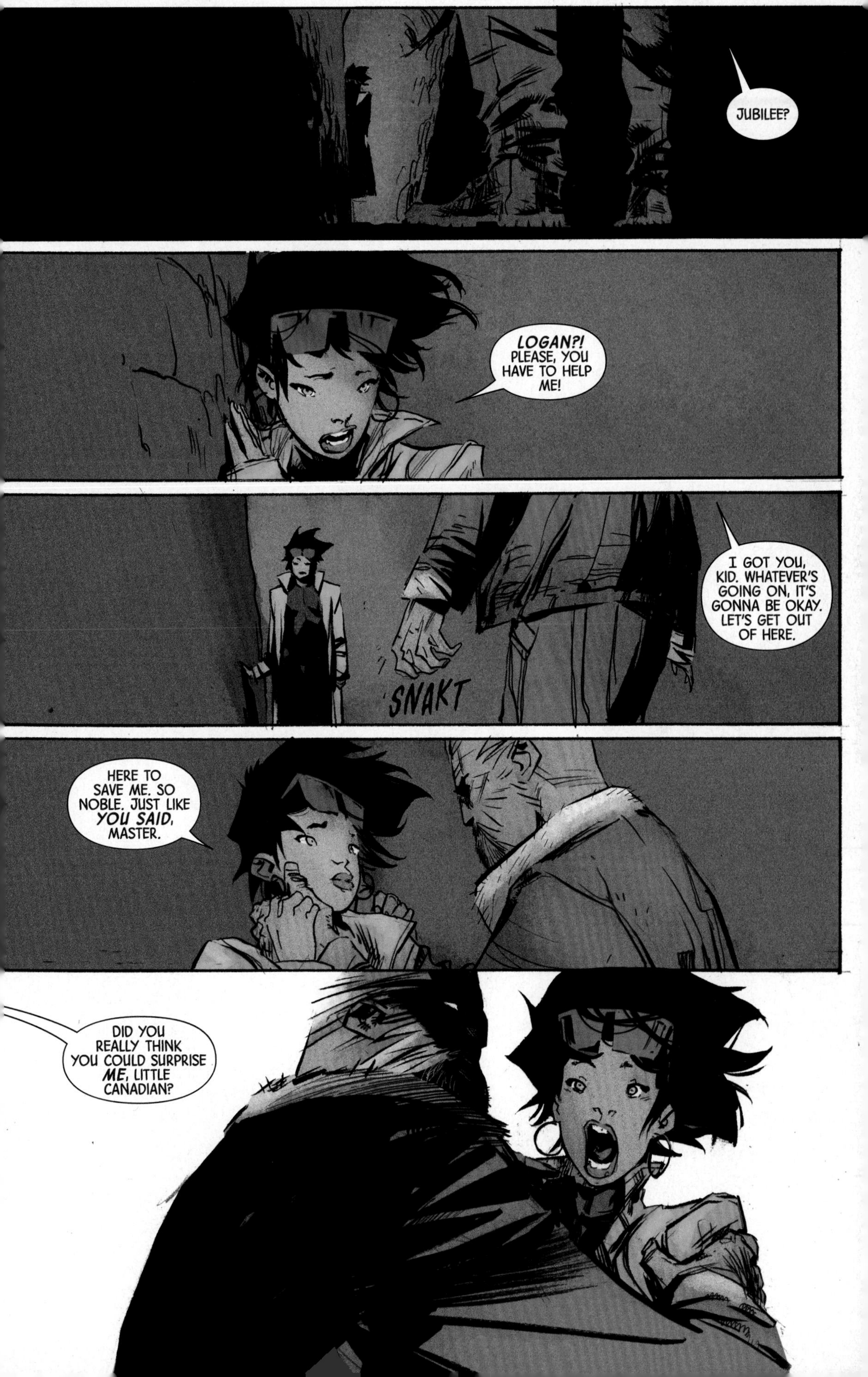
JUBILEE?
LOGAN?! PLEASE, YOU HAVE TO HELP ME!
I GOT YOU, KID. WHATEVER'S GOING ON, IT'S GONNA BE OKAY. LET'S GET OUT OF HERE.
SNAKT
HERE TO SAVE ME. SO NOBLE. JUST LIKE YOU SAID, MASTER.
DID YOU REALLY THINK YOU COULD SURPRISE ME, LITTLE CANADIAN?

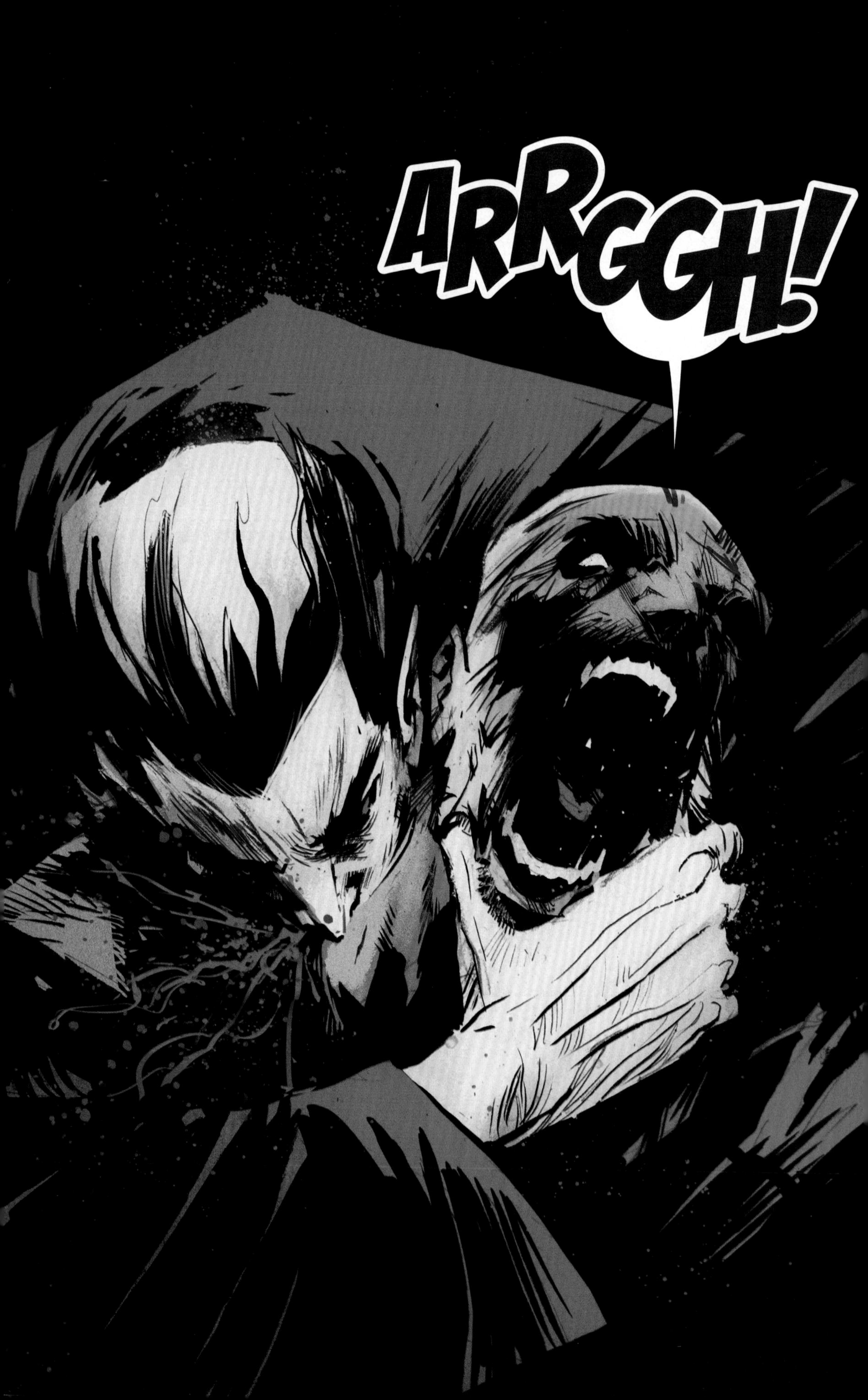
ARRGGH!

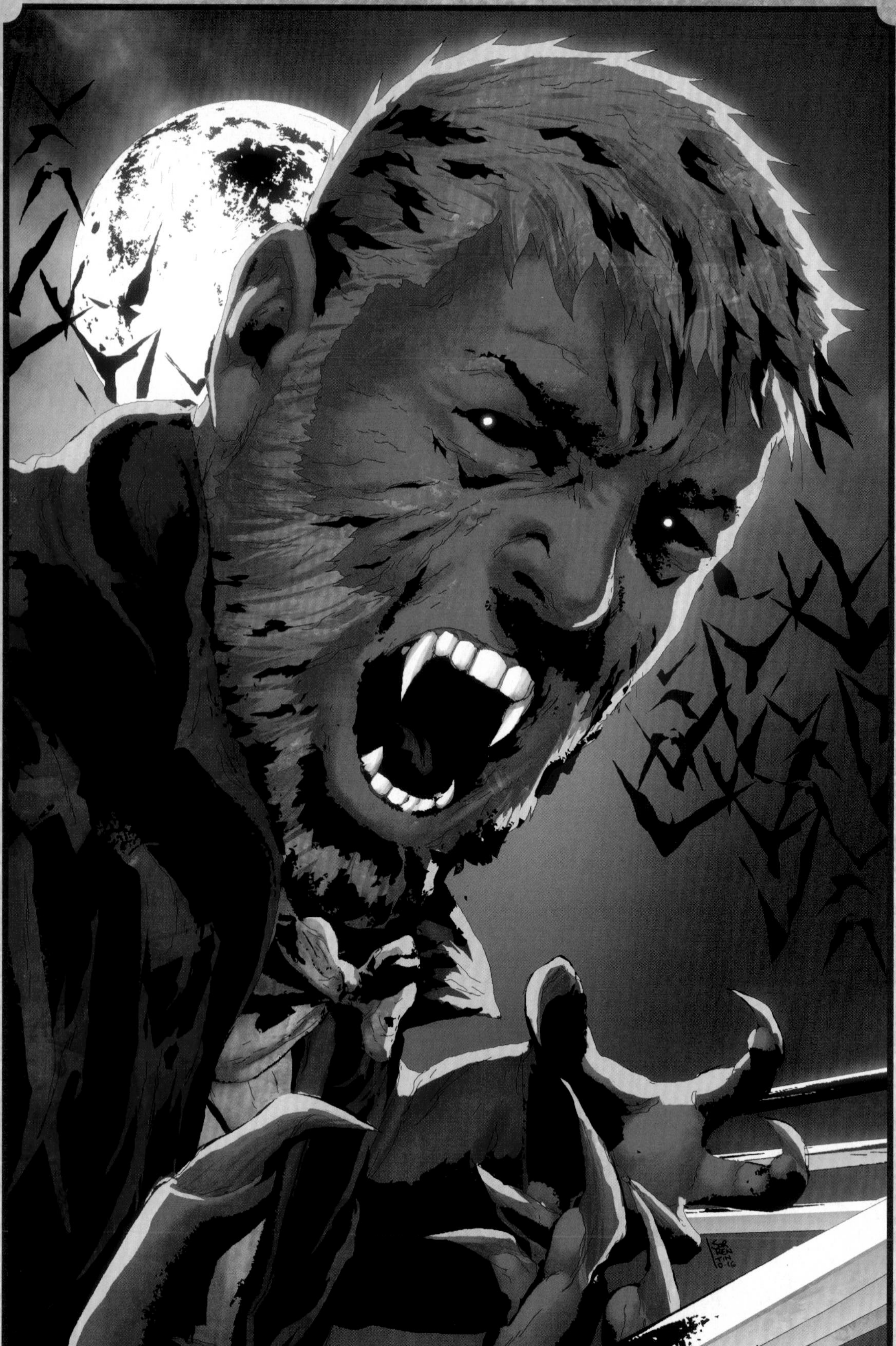

15

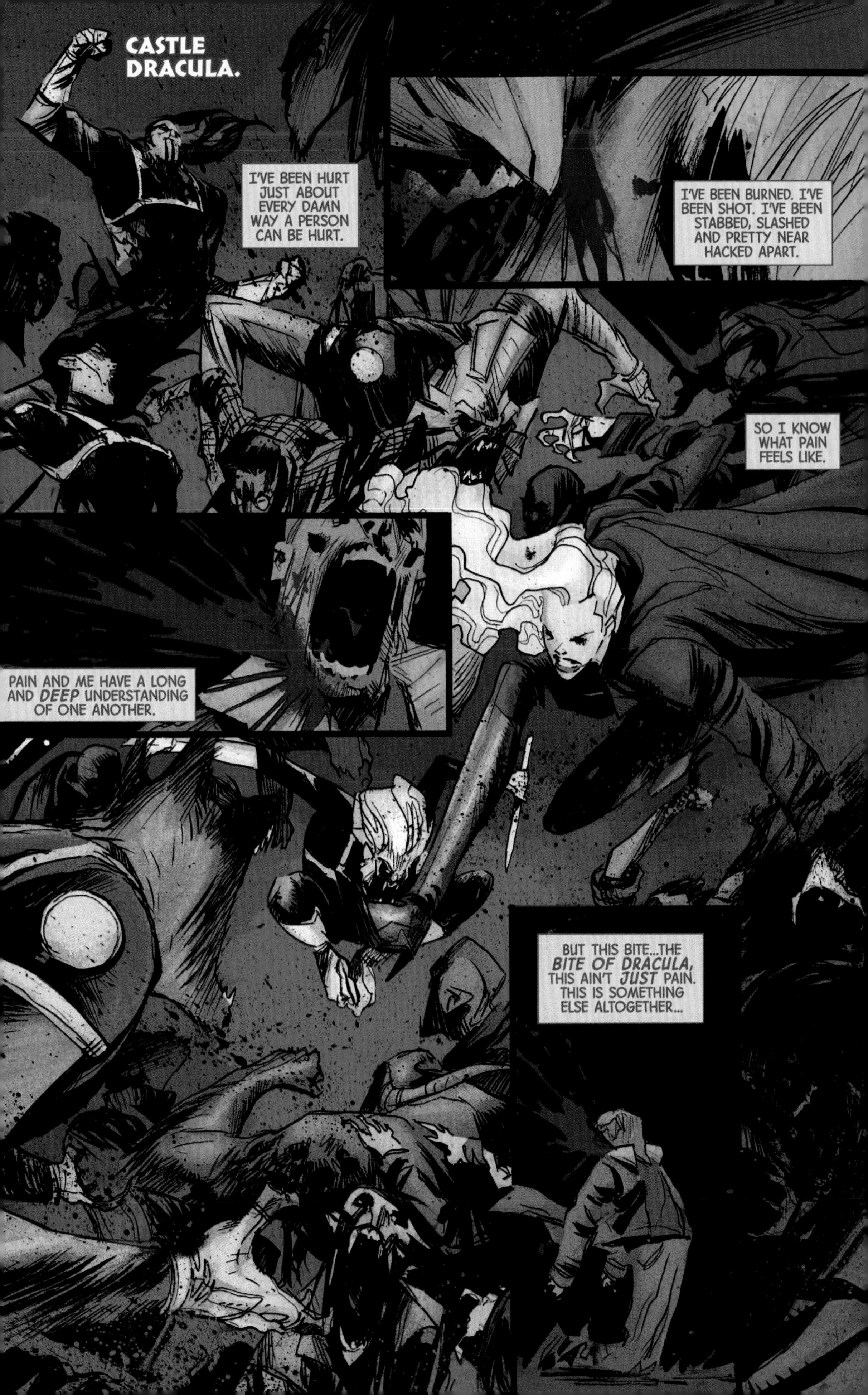
CASTLE DRACULA.
I'VE BEEN HURT JUST ABOUT EVERY DAMN WAY A PERSON CAN BE HURT.
I'VE BEEN BURNED. I'VE BEEN SHOT. I'VE BEEN STABBED, SLASHED AND PRETTY NEAR HACKED APART.
SO I KNOW WHAT PAIN FEELS LIKE.
PAIN AND ME HAVE A LONG AND *DEEP* UNDERSTANDING OF ONE ANOTHER.
BUT THIS BITE...THE *BITE OF DRACULA,* THIS AIN'T *JUST* PAIN. THIS IS SOMETHING ELSE ALTOGETHER...

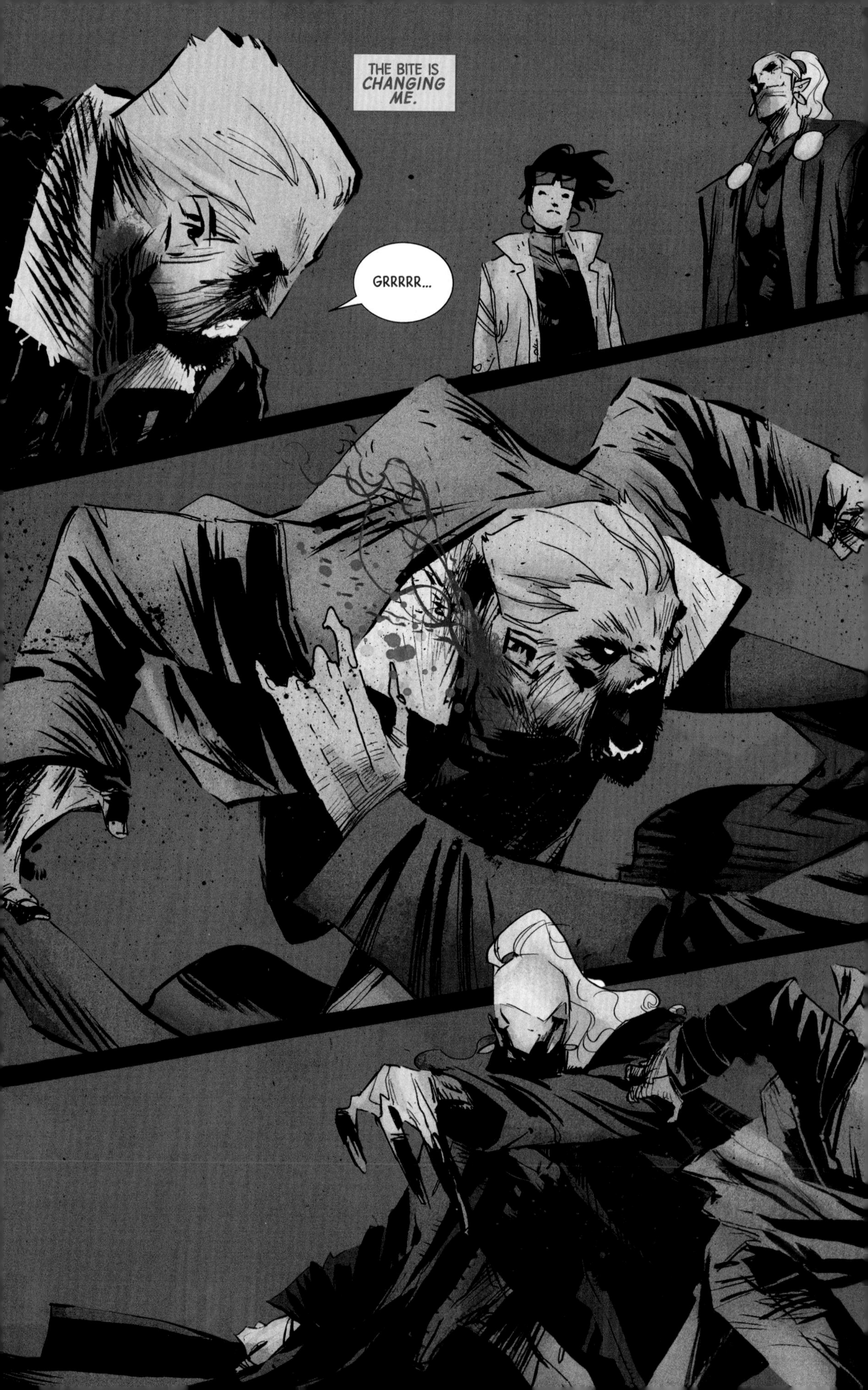
THE BITE IS CHANGING ME.
GRRRRR...

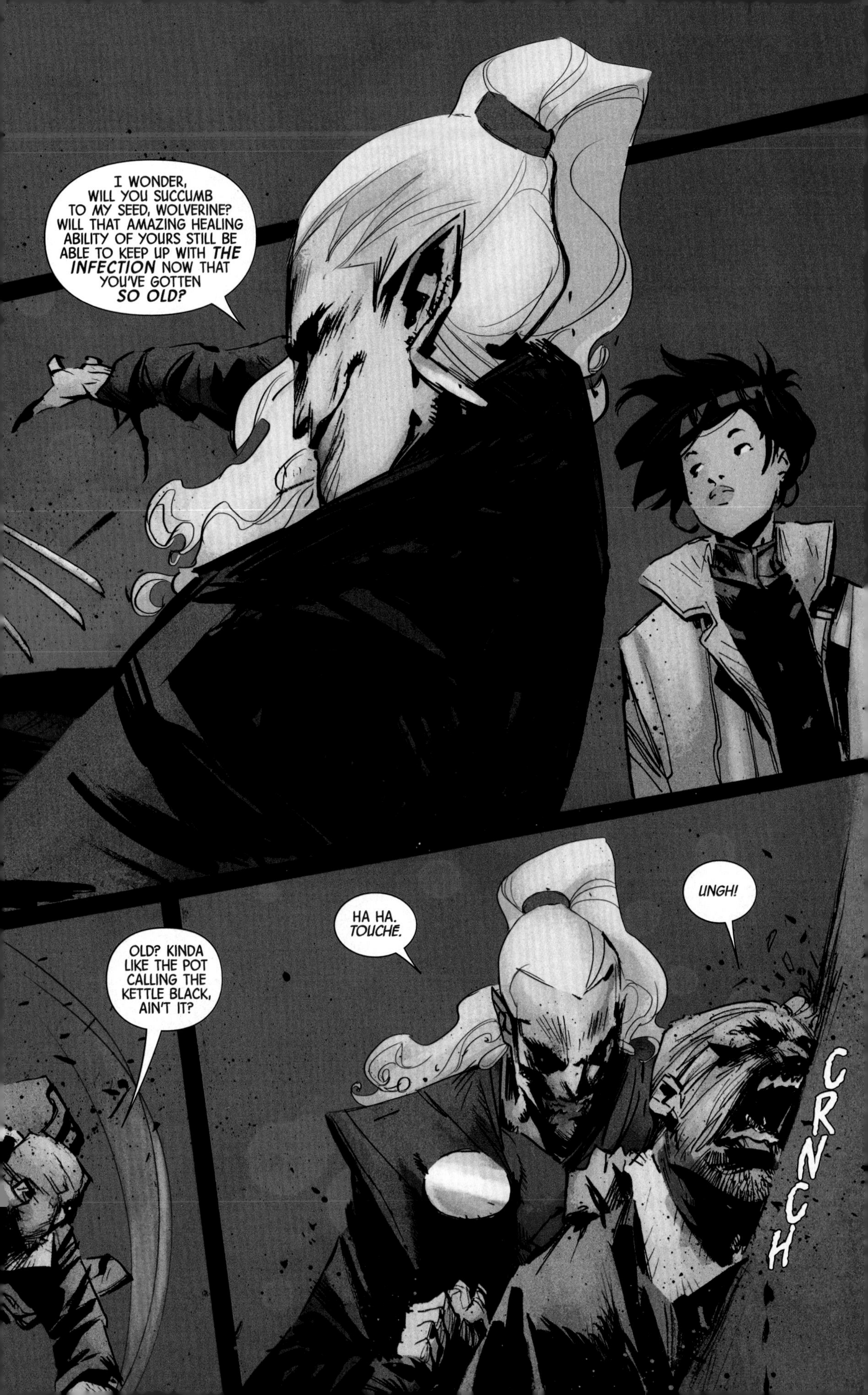
I WONDER, WILL YOU SUCCUMB TO MY SEED, WOLVERINE? WILL THAT AMAZING HEALING ABILITY OF YOURS STILL BE ABLE TO KEEP UP WITH THE INFECTION NOW THAT YOU'VE GOTTEN SO OLD?
OLD? KINDA LIKE THE POT CALLING THE KETTLE BLACK, AIN'T IT?
HA HA. TOUCHÉ.
UNGH!
CRNCH

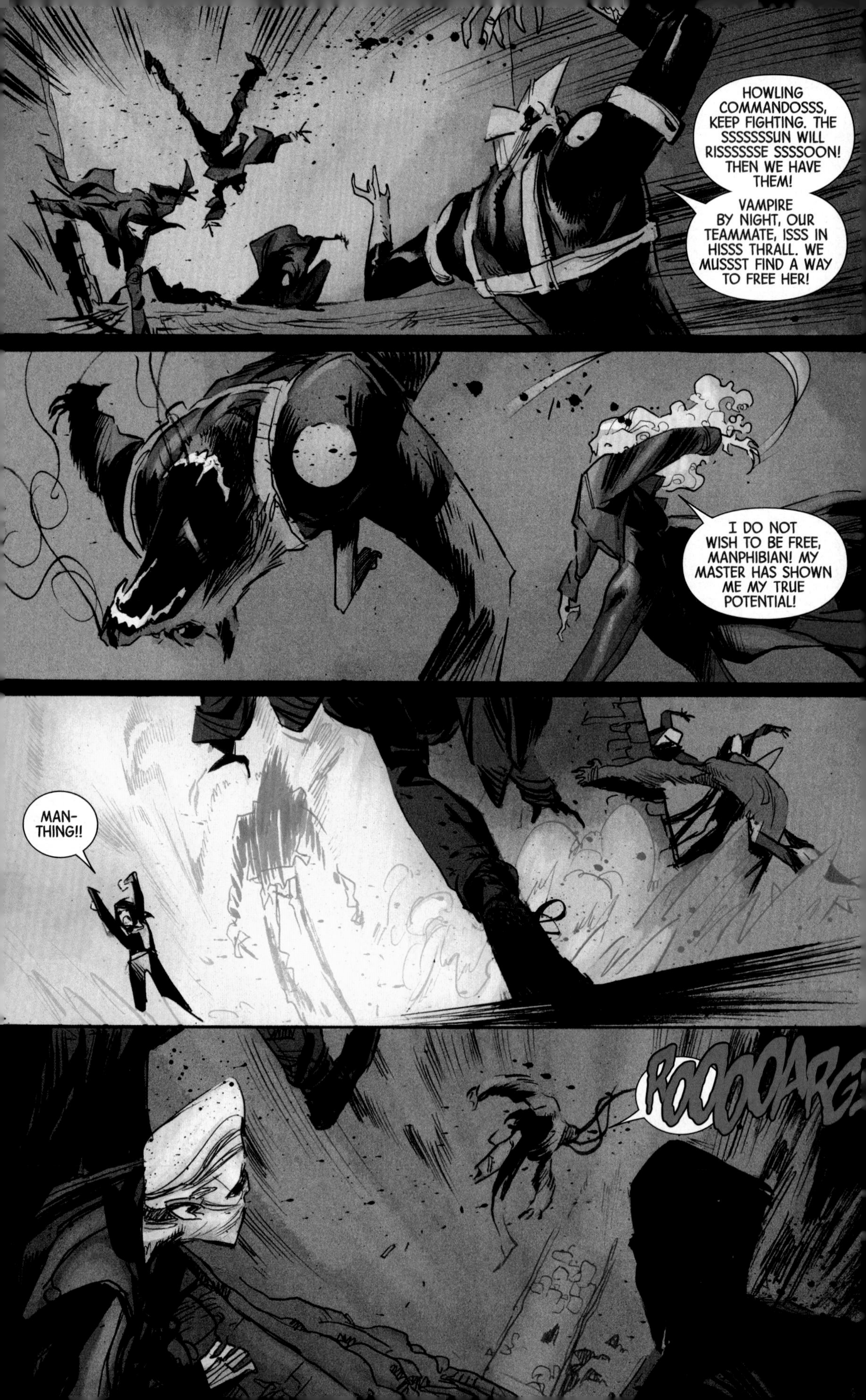
HOWLING COMMANDOSSS, KEEP FIGHTING. THE SSSSSSSUN WILL RISSSSSSE SSSSOON! THEN WE HAVE THEM!
VAMPIRE BY NIGHT, OUR TEAMMATE, ISSS IN HISSS THRALL. WE MUSSST FIND A WAY TO FREE HER!
I DO NOT WISH TO BE FREE, MANPHIBIAN! MY MASTER HAS SHOWN ME MY TRUE POTENTIAL!
MAN-THING!!

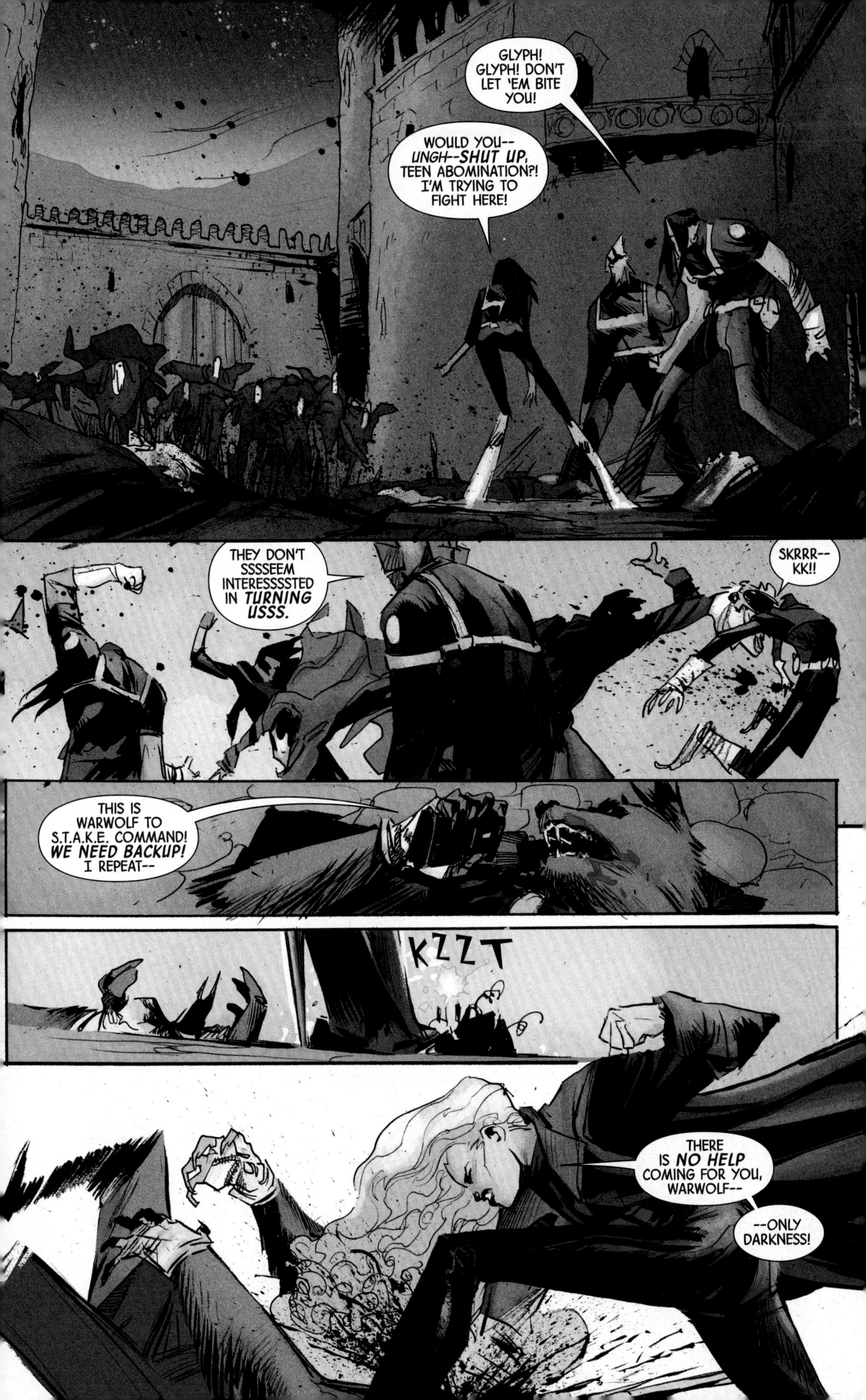
GLYPH! GLYPH! DON'T LET 'EM BITE YOU!
WOULD YOU-- UNGH--SHUT UP, TEEN ABOMINATION?! I'M TRYING TO FIGHT HERE!
THEY DON'T SSSSEEM INTERESSSSTED IN TURNING USSS.
SKRRR--KK!!
THIS IS WARWOLF TO S.T.A.K.E. COMMAND! WE NEED BACKUP! I REPEAT--
KZZT
THERE IS NO HELP COMING FOR YOU, WARWOLF--
--ONLY DARKNESS!

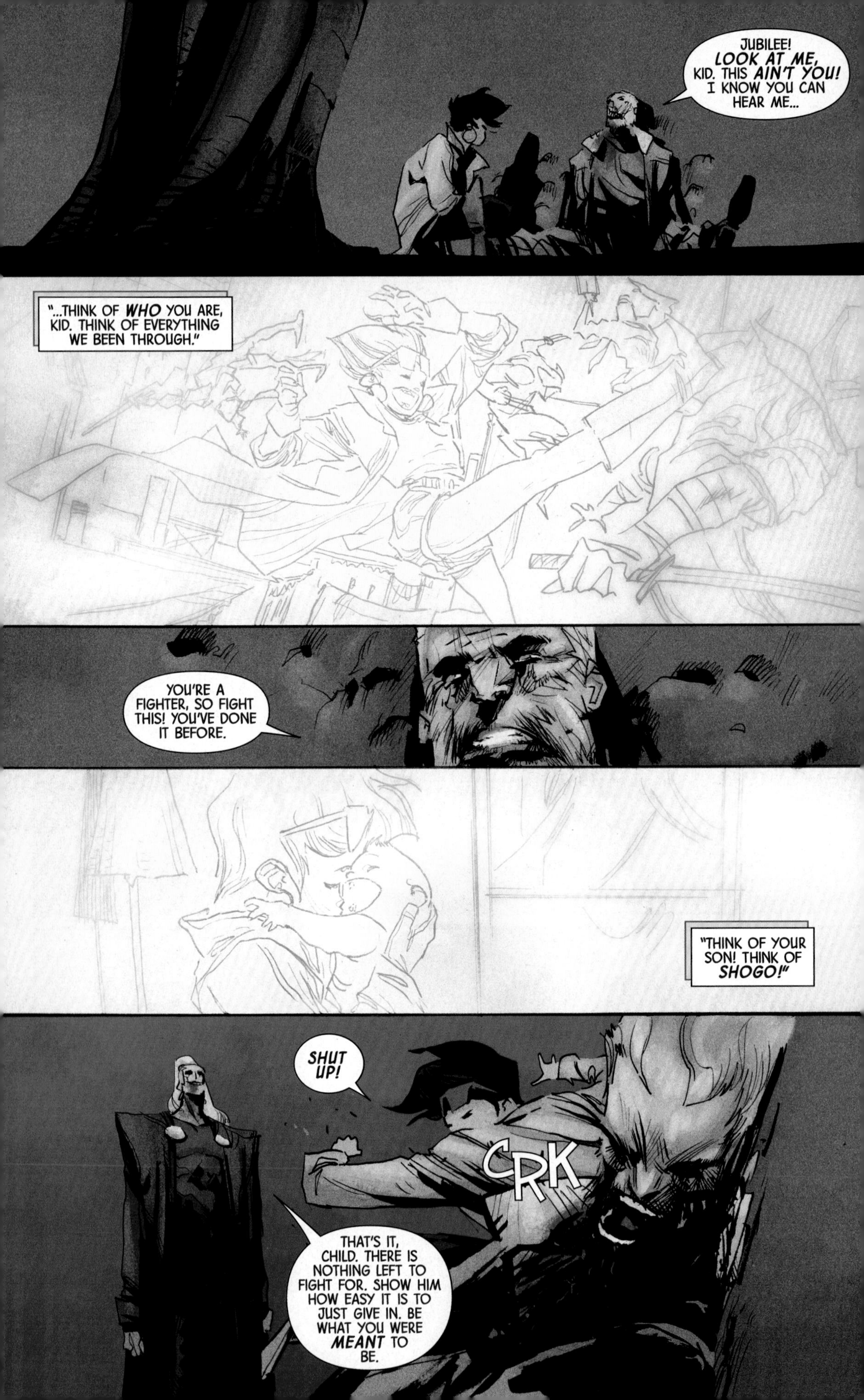
JUBILEE! LOOK AT ME, KID. THIS AIN'T YOU! I KNOW YOU CAN HEAR ME...
"...THINK OF WHO YOU ARE, KID. THINK OF EVERYTHING WE BEEN THROUGH."
YOU'RE A FIGHTER, SO FIGHT THIS! YOU'VE DONE IT BEFORE.
"THINK OF YOUR SON! THINK OF SHOGO!"
SHUT UP!
CRK
THAT'S IT, CHILD. THERE IS NOTHING LEFT TO FIGHT FOR. SHOW HIM HOW EASY IT IS TO JUST GIVE IN. BE WHAT YOU WERE MEANT TO BE.

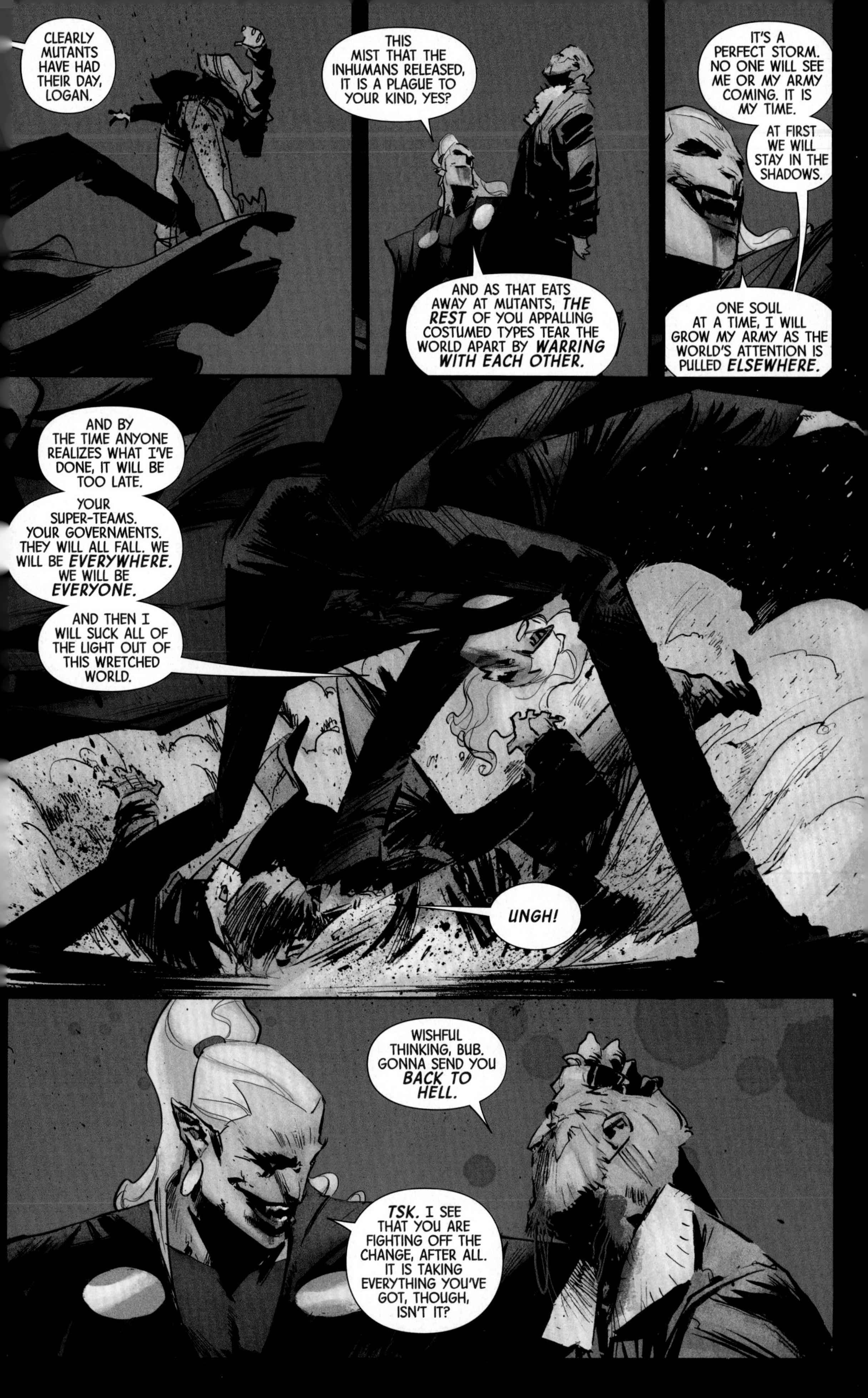
CLEARLY MUTANTS HAVE HAD THEIR DAY, LOGAN.
THIS MIST THAT THE INHUMANS RELEASED, IT IS A PLAGUE TO YOUR KIND, YES?
AND AS THAT EATS AWAY AT MUTANTS, THE REST OF YOU APPALLING COSTUMED TYPES TEAR THE WORLD APART BY WARRING WITH EACH OTHER.
IT'S A PERFECT STORM. NO ONE WILL SEE ME OR MY ARMY COMING. IT IS MY TIME.
AT FIRST WE WILL STAY IN THE SHADOWS.
ONE SOUL AT A TIME, I WILL GROW MY ARMY AS THE WORLD'S ATTENTION IS PULLED ELSEWHERE.
AND BY THE TIME ANYONE REALIZES WHAT I'VE DONE, IT WILL BE TOO LATE.
YOUR SUPER-TEAMS. YOUR GOVERNMENTS. THEY WILL ALL FALL. WE WILL BE EVERYWHERE. WE WILL BE EVERYONE.
AND THEN I WILL SUCK ALL OF THE LIGHT OUT OF THIS WRETCHED WORLD.
UNGH!
WISHFUL THINKING, BUB. GONNA SEND YOU BACK TO HELL.
TSK. I SEE THAT YOU ARE FIGHTING OFF THE CHANGE, AFTER ALL. IT IS TAKING EVERYTHING YOU'VE GOT, THOUGH, ISN'T IT?

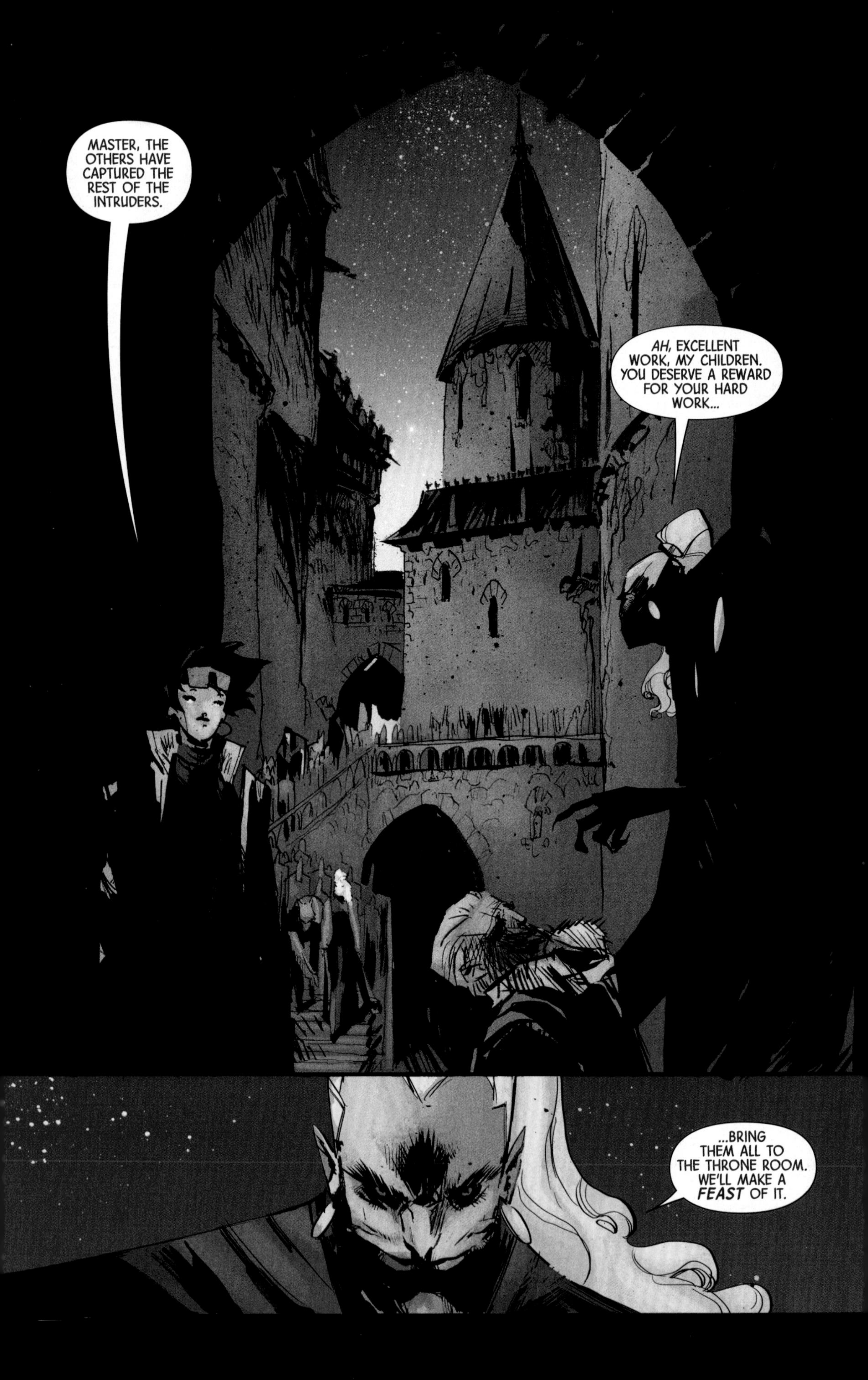
MASTER, THE OTHERS HAVE CAPTURED THE REST OF THE INTRUDERS.
AH, EXCELLENT WORK, MY CHILDREN. YOU DESERVE A REWARD FOR YOUR HARD WORK...
...BRING THEM ALL TO THE THRONE ROOM. WE'LL MAKE A FEAST OF IT.

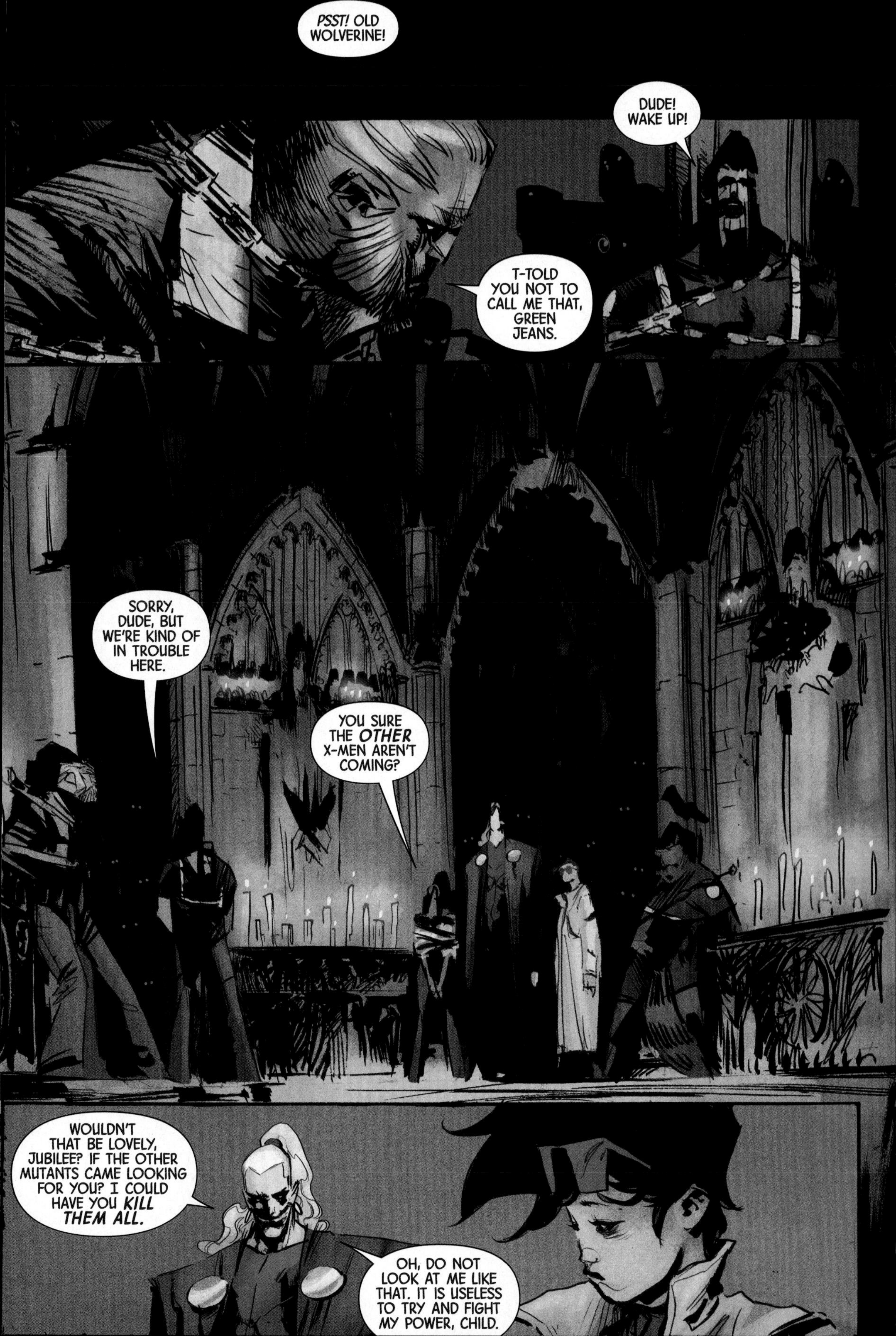
PSST! OLD WOLVERINE!
DUDE! WAKE UP!
T-TOLD YOU NOT TO CALL ME THAT, GREEN JEANS.
SORRY, DUDE, BUT WE'RE KIND OF IN TROUBLE HERE.
YOU SURE THE OTHER X-MEN AREN'T COMING?
WOULDN'T THAT BE LOVELY, JUBILEE? IF THE OTHER MUTANTS CAME LOOKING FOR YOU? I COULD HAVE YOU KILL THEM ALL.
OH, DO NOT LOOK AT ME LIKE THAT. IT IS USELESS TO TRY AND FIGHT MY POWER, CHILD.

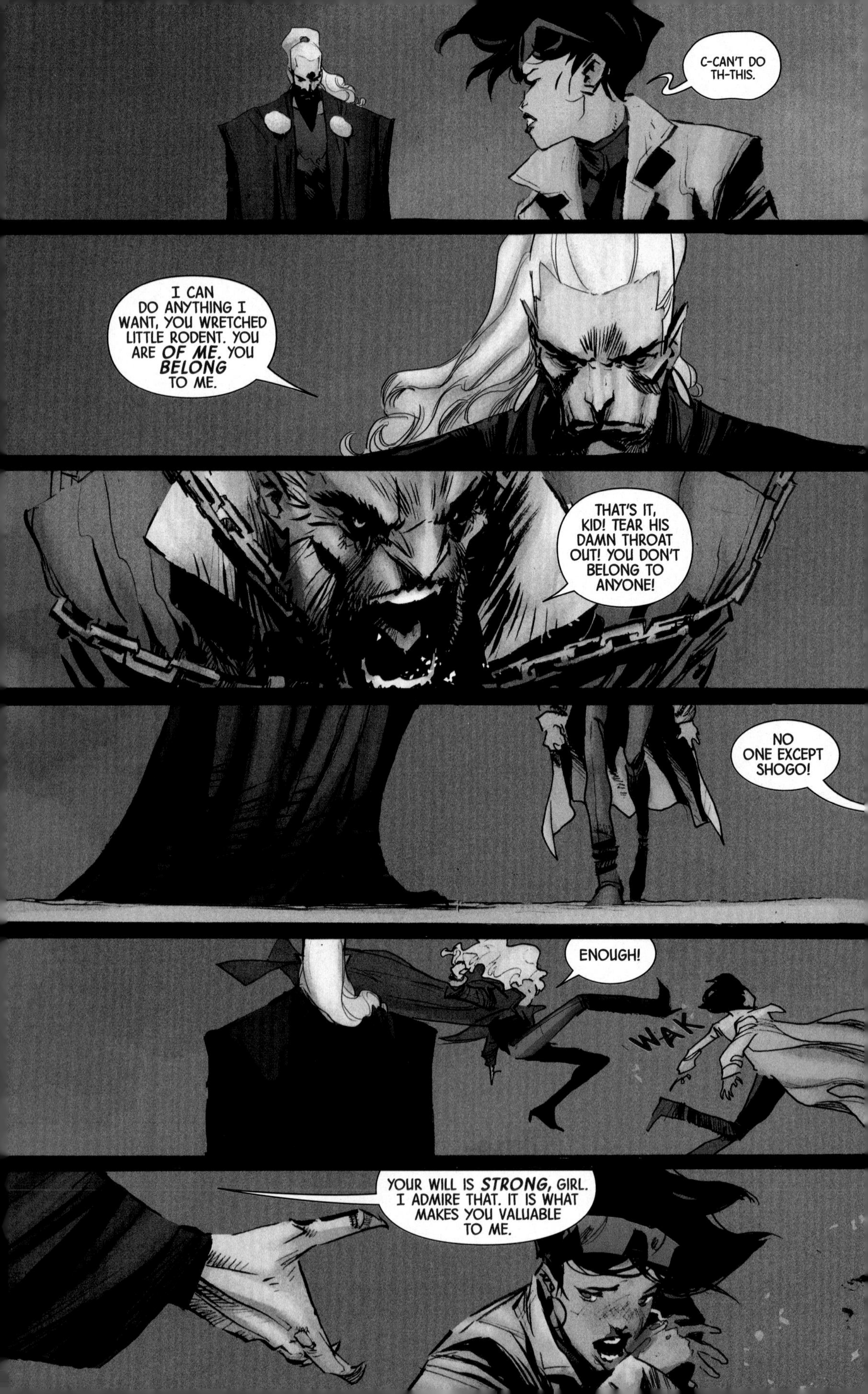
C-CAN'T DO TH-THIS.
I CAN DO ANYTHING I WANT, YOU WRETCHED LITTLE RODENT. YOU ARE *OF ME.* YOU *BELONG* TO ME.
THAT'S IT, KID! TEAR HIS DAMN THROAT OUT! YOU DON'T BELONG TO ANYONE!
NO ONE EXCEPT SHOGO!
ENOUGH!
WAK
YOUR WILL IS *STRONG,* GIRL. I ADMIRE THAT. IT IS WHAT MAKES YOU VALUABLE TO ME.

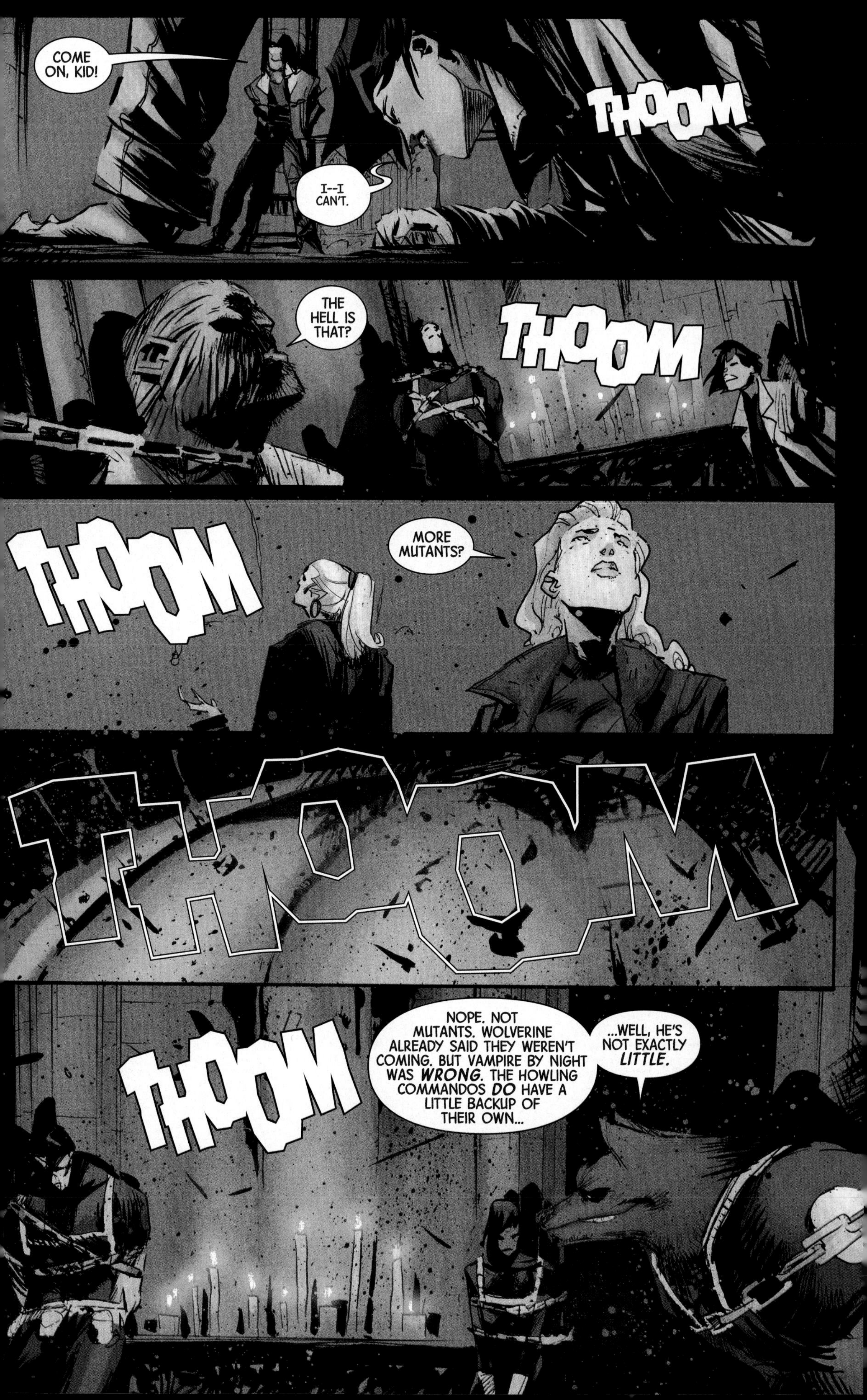
COME ON, KID!
THOOM
I--I CAN'T.
THE HELL IS THAT?
THOOM
THOOM
MORE MUTANTS?
THOOM
THOOM
NOPE. NOT MUTANTS. WOLVERINE ALREADY SAID THEY WEREN'T COMING. BUT VAMPIRE BY NIGHT WAS *WRONG*. THE HOWLING COMMANDOS *DO* HAVE A LITTLE BACKUP OF THEIR OWN...
...WELL, HE'S NOT EXACTLY *LITTLE*.

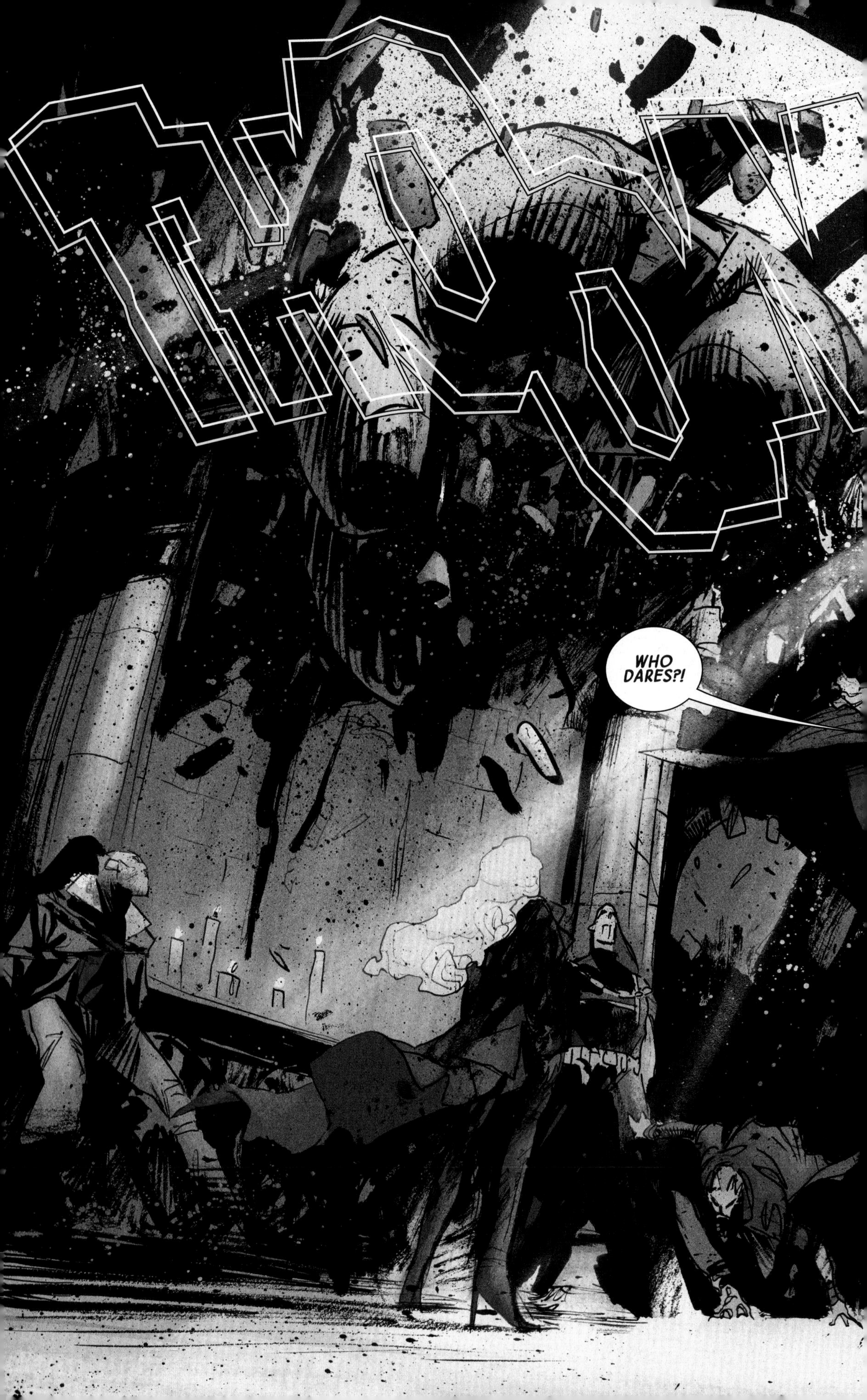
THOOM
WHO DARES?!

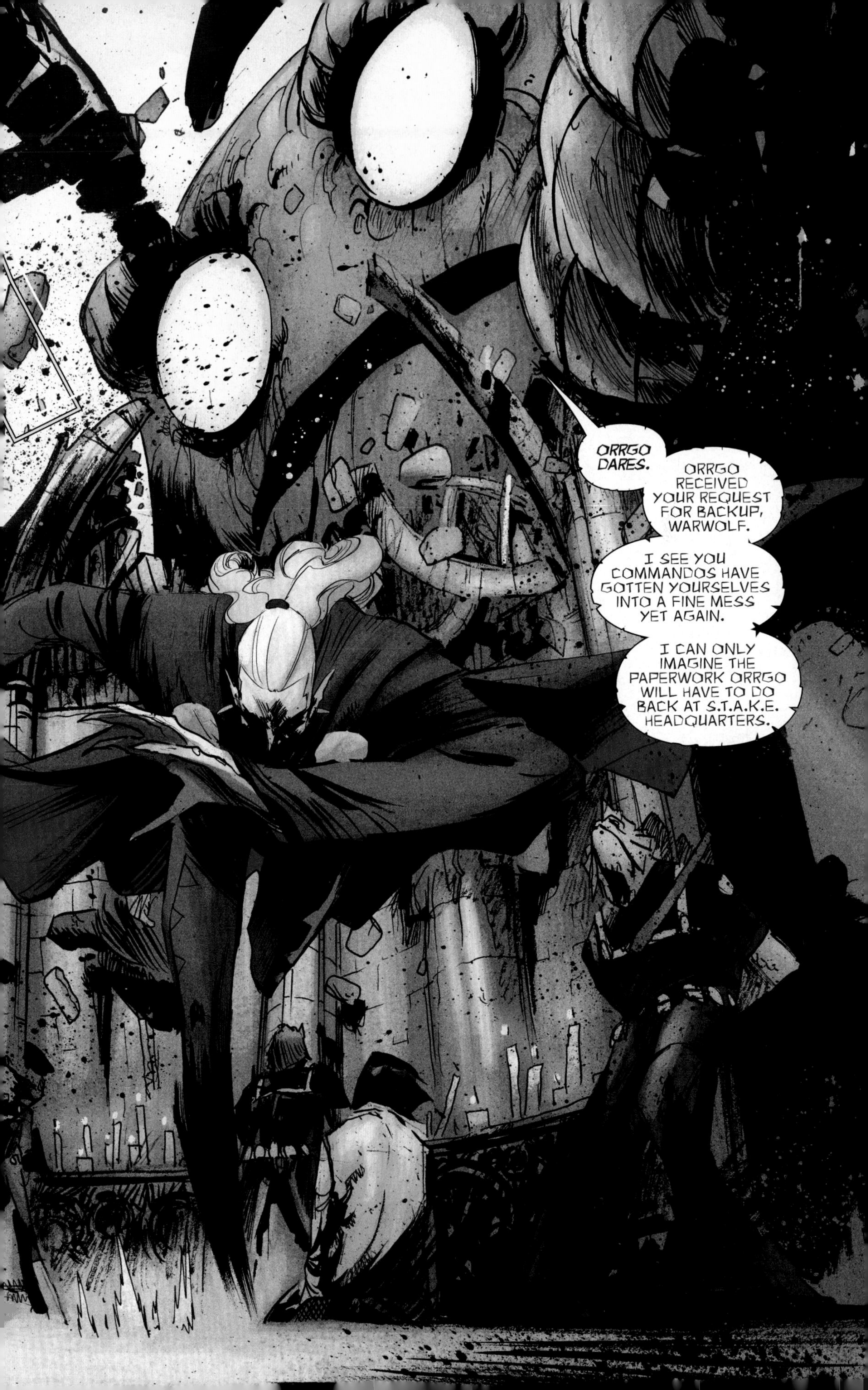
ORRGO DARES.
ORRGO RECEIVED YOUR REQUEST FOR BACKUP, WARWOLF.
I SEE YOU COMMANDOS HAVE GOTTEN YOURSELVES INTO A FINE MESS YET AGAIN.
I CAN ONLY IMAGINE THE PAPERWORK ORRGO WILL HAVE TO DO BACK AT S.T.A.K.E. HEADQUARTERS.

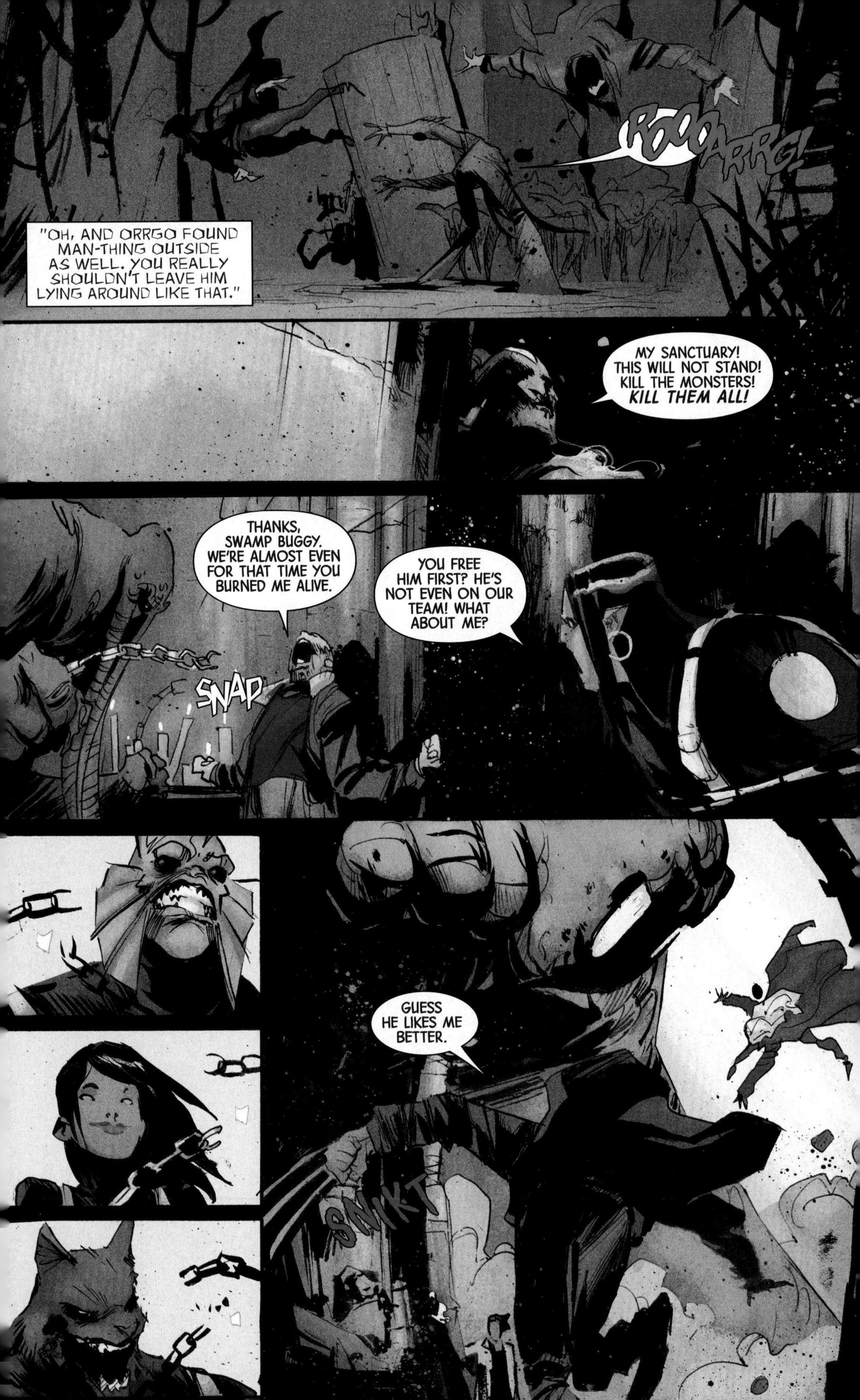
ROOOARRG!
"OH, AND ORRGO FOUND MAN-THING OUTSIDE AS WELL. YOU REALLY SHOULDN'T LEAVE HIM LYING AROUND LIKE THAT."
MY SANCTUARY! THIS WILL NOT STAND! KILL THE MONSTERS! KILL THEM ALL!
THANKS, SWAMP BUGGY. WE'RE ALMOST EVEN FOR THAT TIME YOU BURNED ME ALIVE.
YOU FREE HIM FIRST? HE'S NOT EVEN ON OUR TEAM! WHAT ABOUT ME?
SNAP
GUESS HE LIKES ME BETTER.
SNIKT

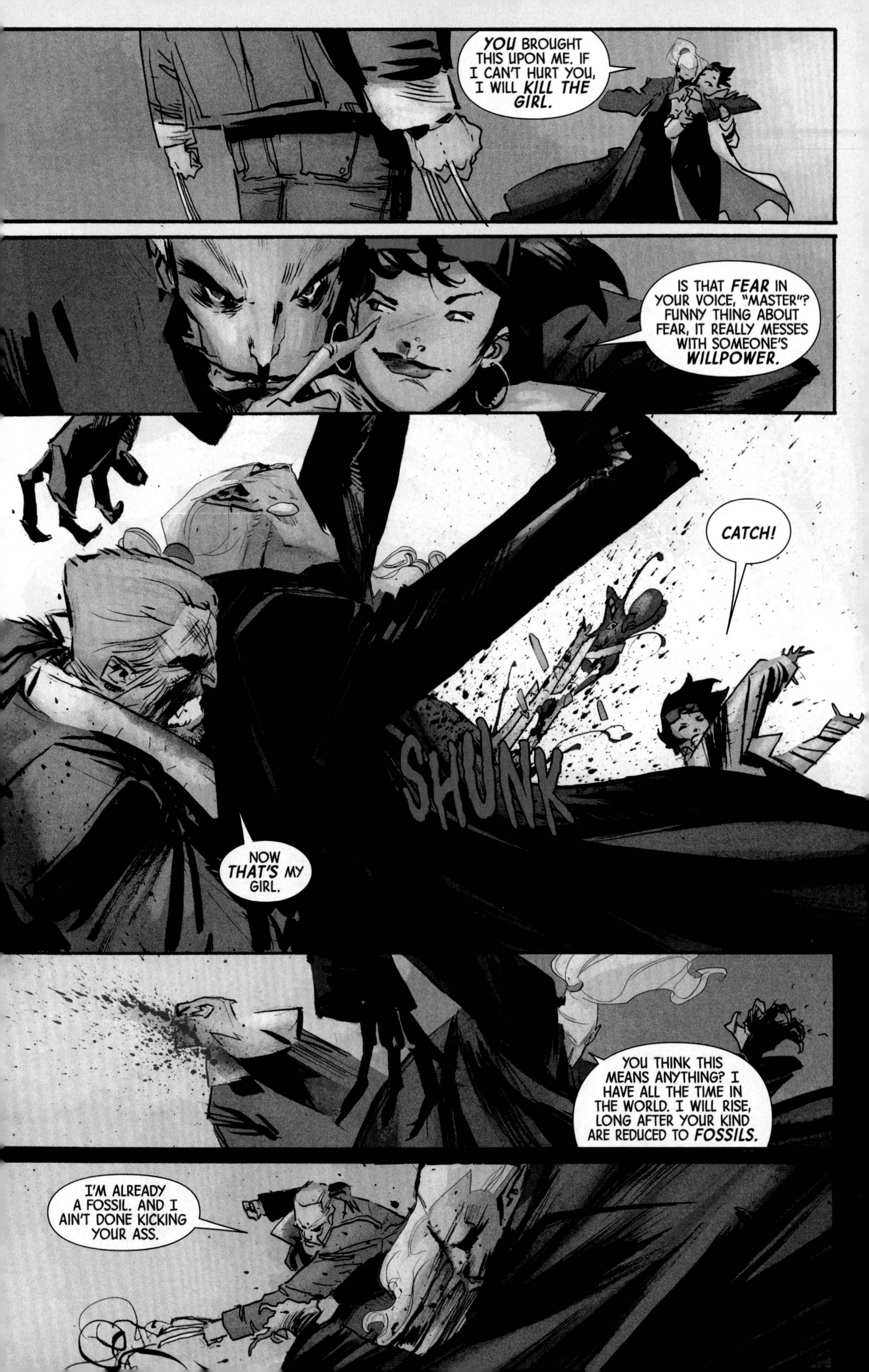
YOU BROUGHT THIS UPON ME. IF I CAN'T HURT YOU, I WILL KILL THE GIRL.
IS THAT FEAR IN YOUR VOICE, "MASTER"? FUNNY THING ABOUT FEAR, IT REALLY MESSES WITH SOMEONE'S WILLPOWER.
CATCH!
SHUNK
NOW THAT'S MY GIRL.
YOU THINK THIS MEANS ANYTHING? I HAVE ALL THE TIME IN THE WORLD. I WILL RISE, LONG AFTER YOUR KIND ARE REDUCED TO FOSSILS.
I'M ALREADY A FOSSIL. AND I AIN'T DONE KICKING YOUR ASS.

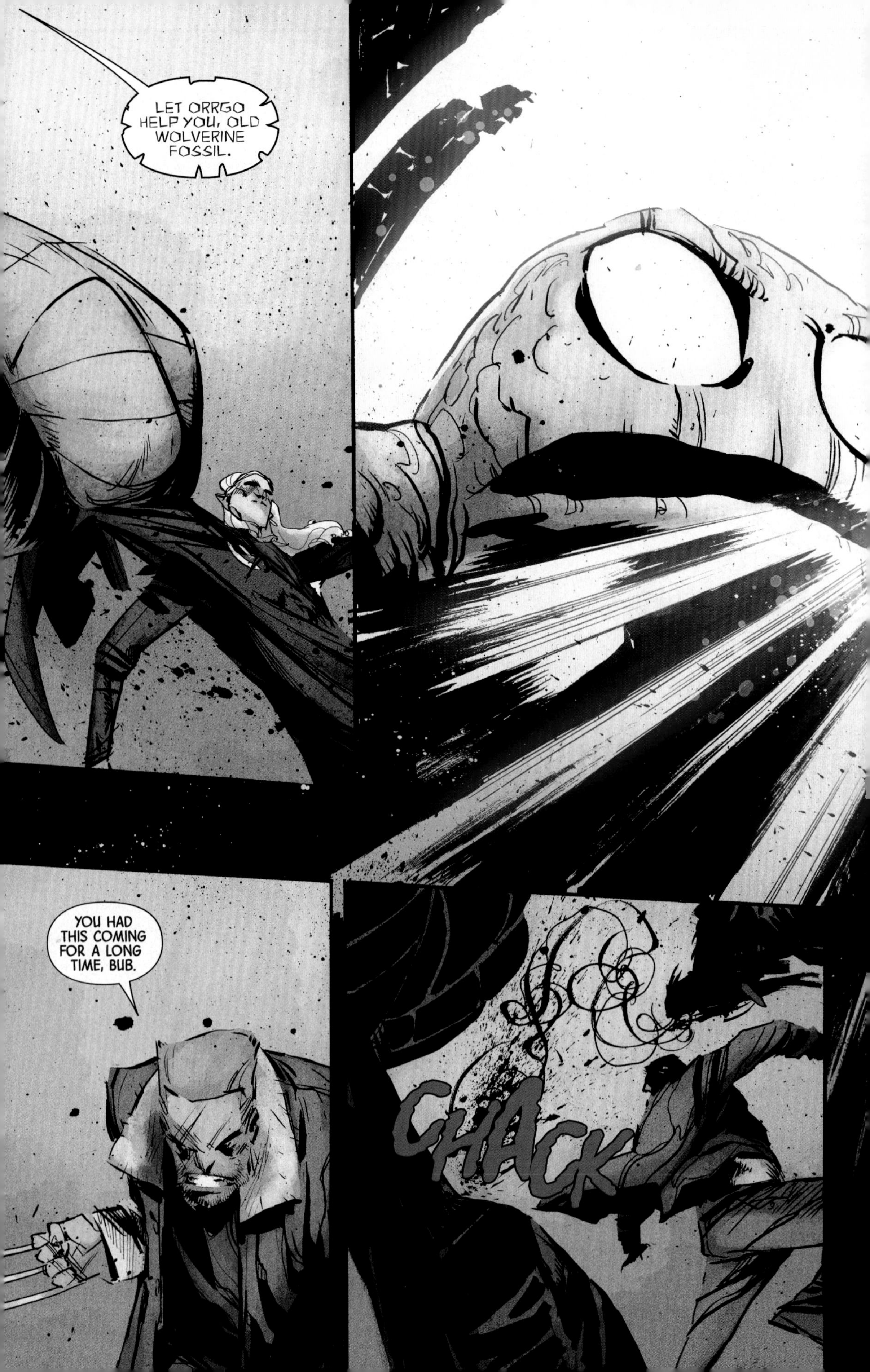
LET ORRGO HELP YOU, OLD WOLVERINE FOSSIL.
YOU HAD THIS COMING FOR A LONG TIME, BUB.
CHACK

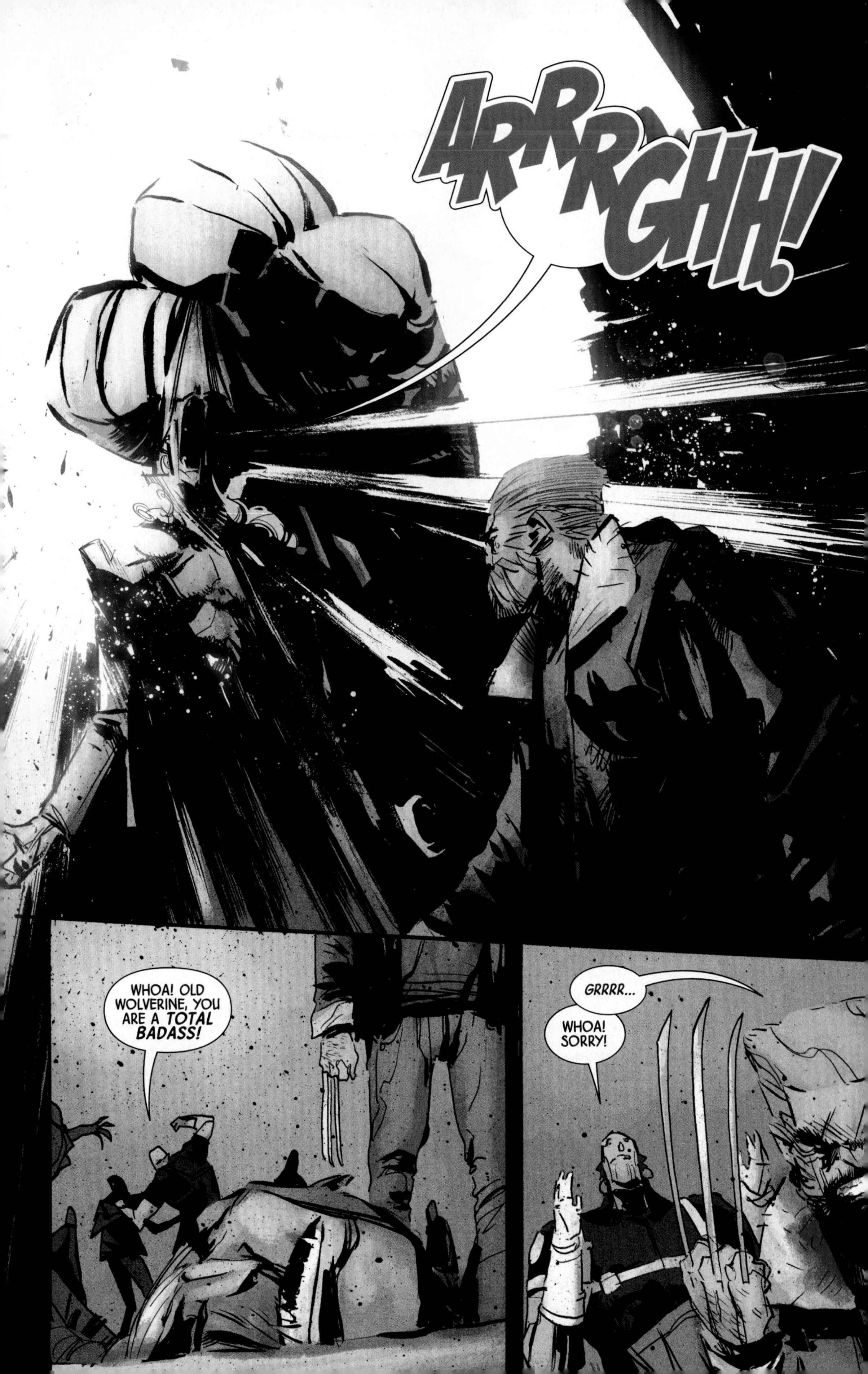
ARRRGHH!
WHOA! OLD WOLVERINE, YOU ARE A *TOTAL BADASS!*
GRRRR...
WHOA! SORRY!

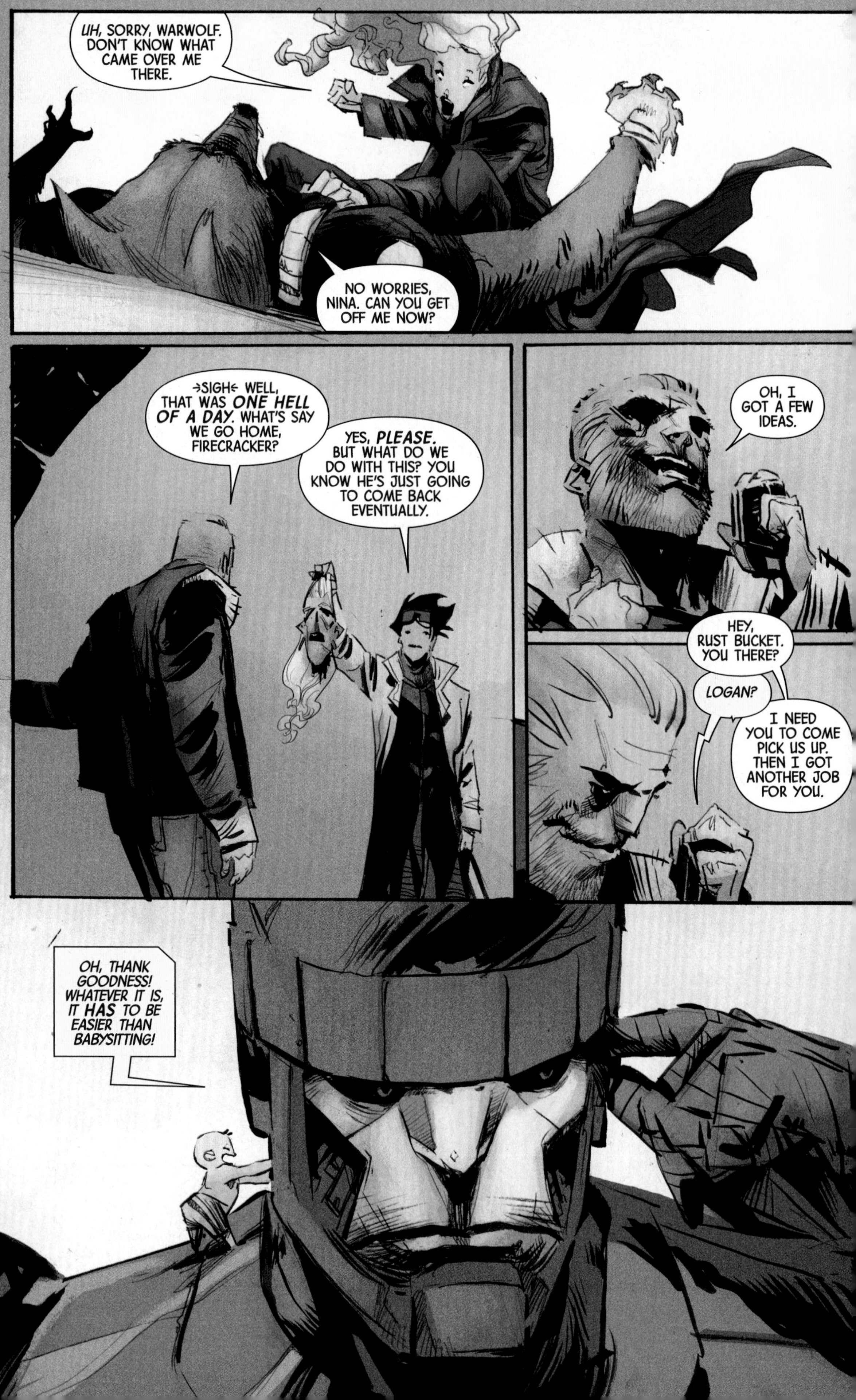
UH, SORRY, WARWOLF. DON'T KNOW WHAT CAME OVER ME THERE.
NO WORRIES, NINA. CAN YOU GET OFF ME NOW?
→SIGH← WELL, THAT WAS ONE HELL OF A DAY. WHAT'S SAY WE GO HOME, FIRECRACKER?
YES, PLEASE. BUT WHAT DO WE DO WITH THIS? YOU KNOW HE'S JUST GOING TO COME BACK EVENTUALLY.
OH, I GOT A FEW IDEAS.
HEY, RUST BUCKET. YOU THERE?
LOGAN?
I NEED YOU TO COME PICK US UP. THEN I GOT ANOTHER JOB FOR YOU.
OH, THANK GOODNESS! WHATEVER IT IS, IT HAS TO BE EASIER THAN BABYSITTING!

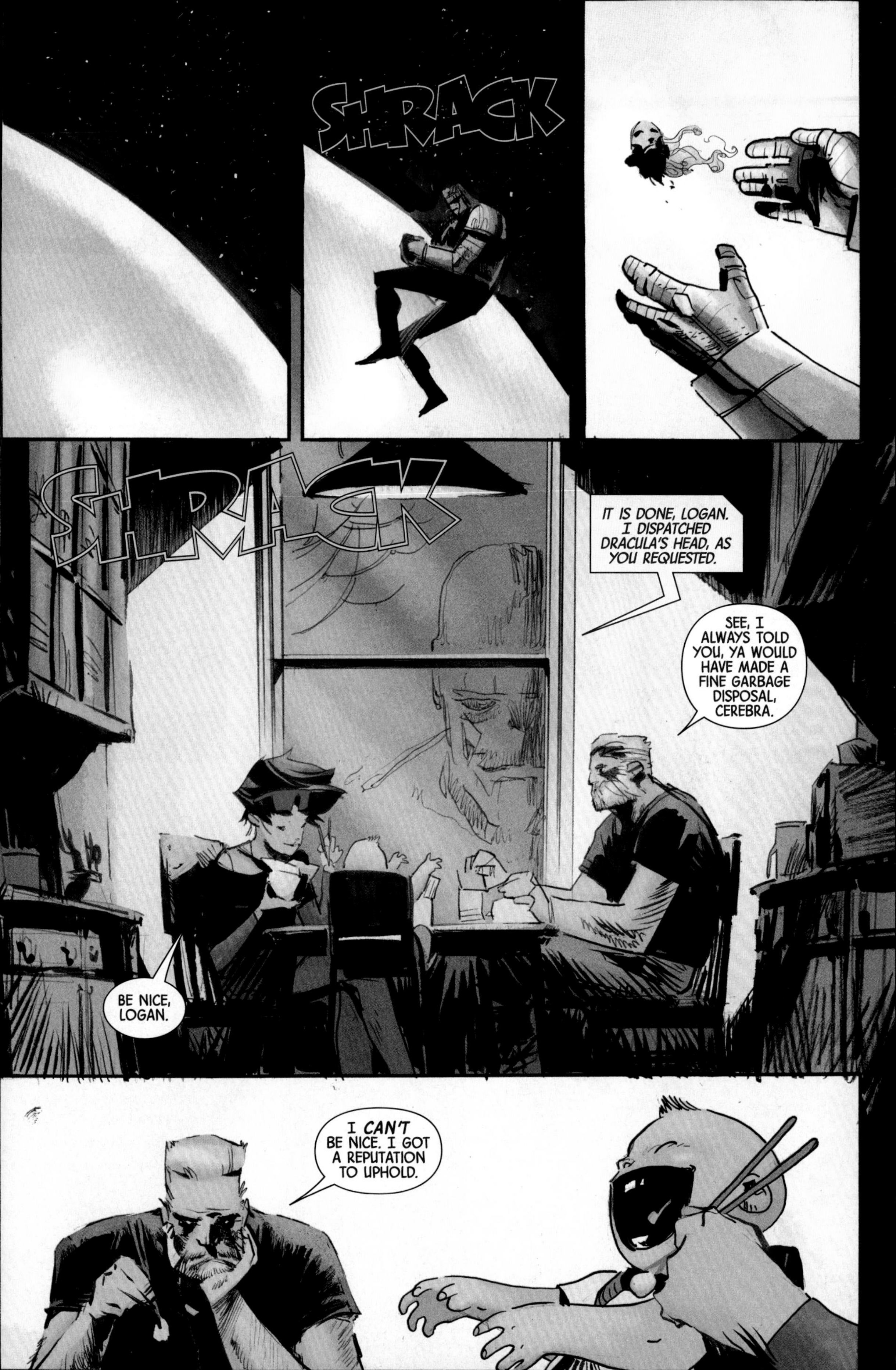
SHRACK
SHRACK
IT IS DONE, LOGAN. I DISPATCHED DRACULA'S HEAD, AS YOU REQUESTED.
SEE, I ALWAYS TOLD YOU, YA WOULD HAVE MADE A FINE GARBAGE DISPOSAL, CEREBRA.
BE NICE, LOGAN.
I *CAN'T* BE NICE. I GOT A REPUTATION TO UPHOLD.

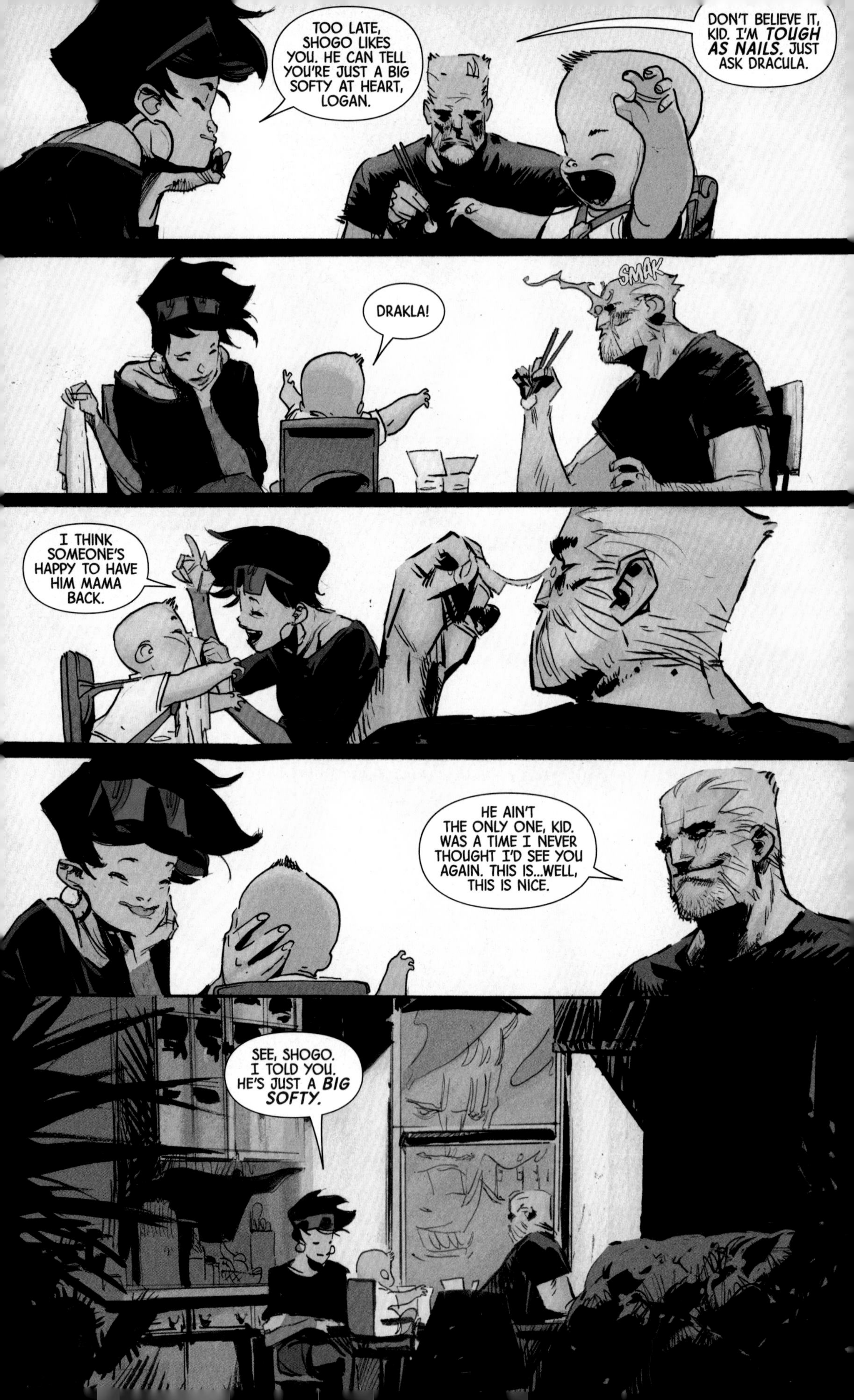

TOO LATE, SHOGO LIKES YOU. HE CAN TELL YOU'RE JUST A BIG SOFTY AT HEART, LOGAN.
DON'T BELIEVE IT, KID. I'M TOUGH AS NAILS. JUST ASK DRACULA.
DRAKLA!
SMAK
I THINK SOMEONE'S HAPPY TO HAVE HIM MAMA BACK.
HE AIN'T THE ONLY ONE, KID. WAS A TIME I NEVER THOUGHT I'D SEE YOU AGAIN. THIS IS...WELL, THIS IS NICE.
SEE, SHOGO. I TOLD YOU. HE'S JUST A BIG SOFTY.

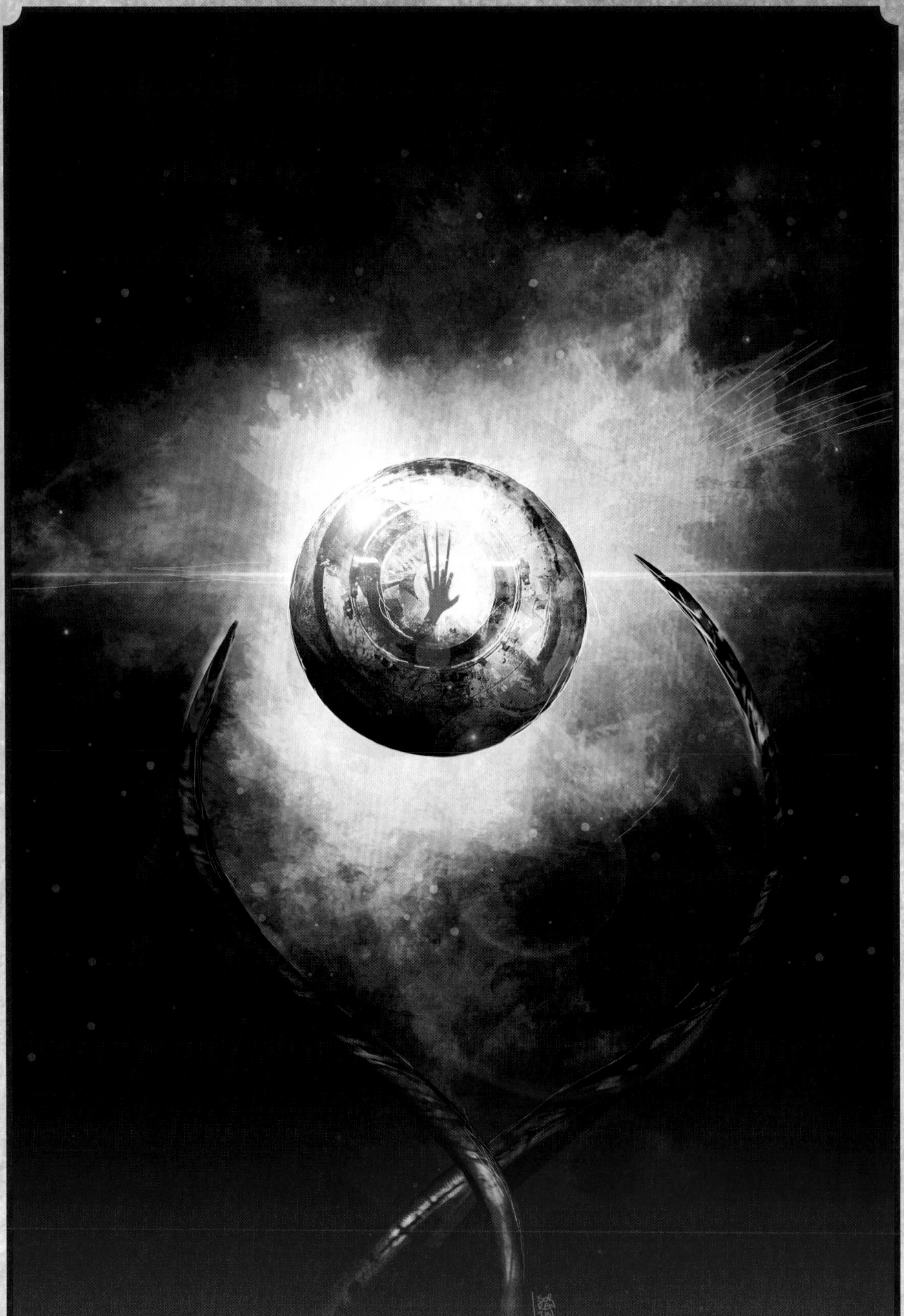

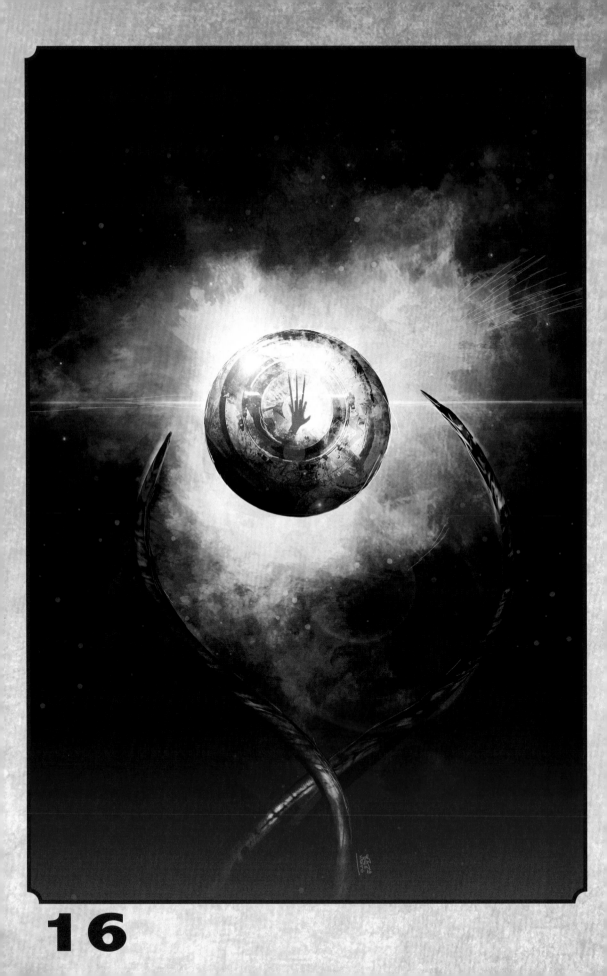

16

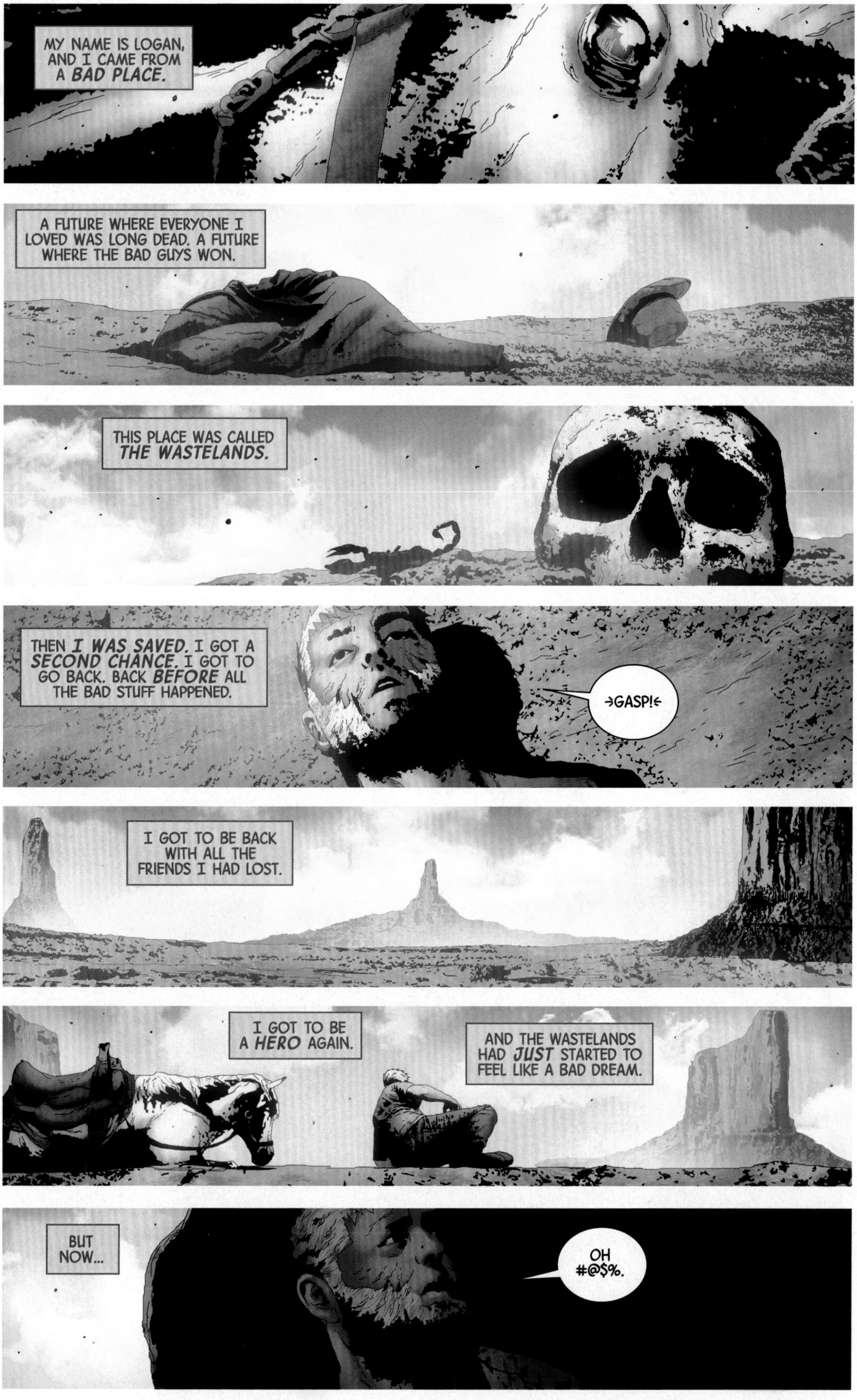

MY NAME IS LOGAN, AND I CAME FROM A BAD PLACE.
A FUTURE WHERE EVERYONE I LOVED WAS LONG DEAD. A FUTURE WHERE THE BAD GUYS WON.
THIS PLACE WAS CALLED THE WASTELANDS.
THEN I WAS SAVED. I GOT A SECOND CHANCE. I GOT TO GO BACK. BACK BEFORE ALL THE BAD STUFF HAPPENED.
GASP!
I GOT TO BE BACK WITH ALL THE FRIENDS I HAD LOST.
I GOT TO BE A HERO AGAIN.
AND THE WASTELANDS HAD JUST STARTED TO FEEL LIKE A BAD DREAM.
BUT NOW...
OH #@$%.

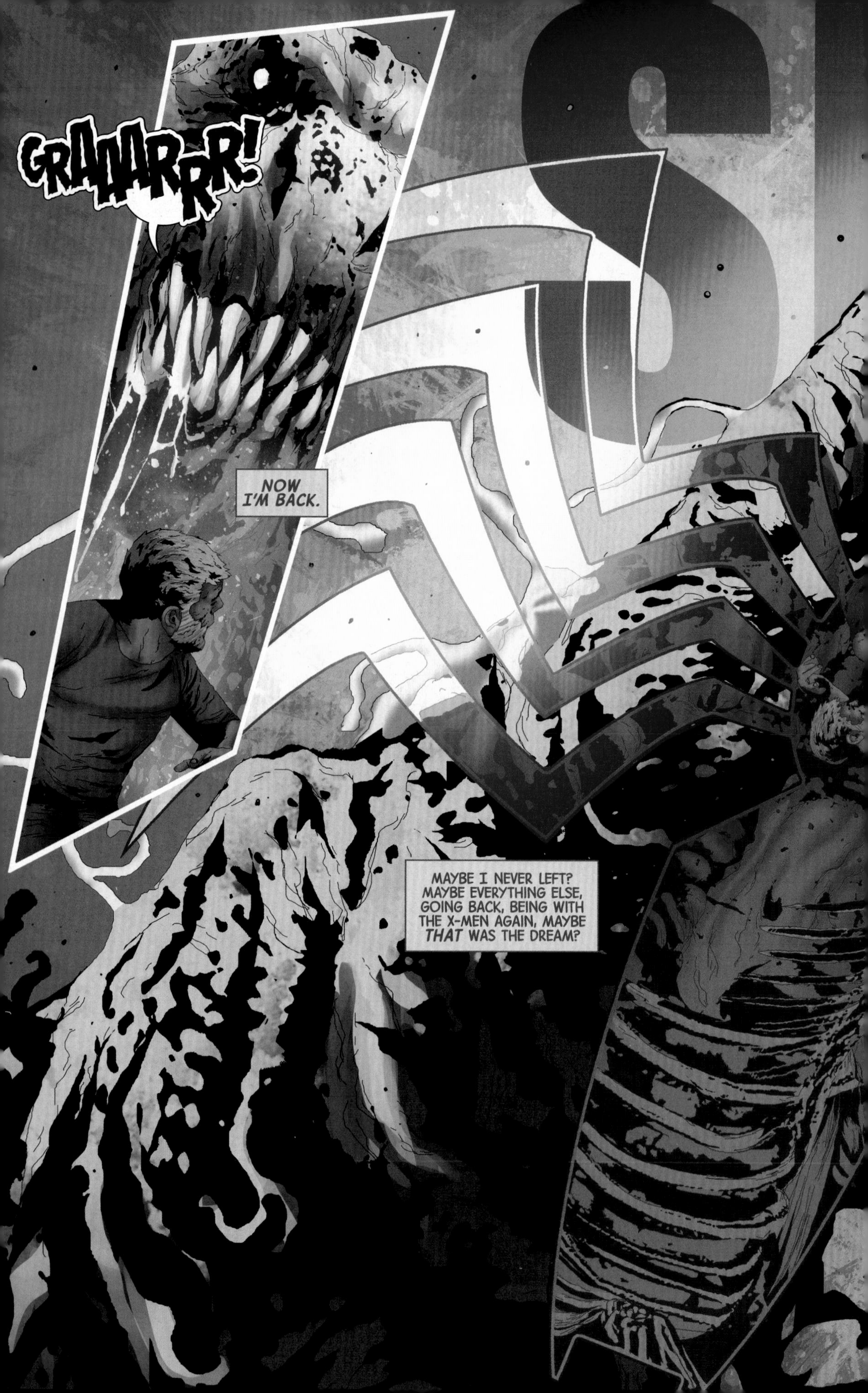
GRAAARRR!
NOW I'M BACK.
MAYBE I NEVER LEFT? MAYBE EVERYTHING ELSE, GOING BACK, BEING WITH THE X-MEN AGAIN, MAYBE *THAT* WAS THE DREAM?

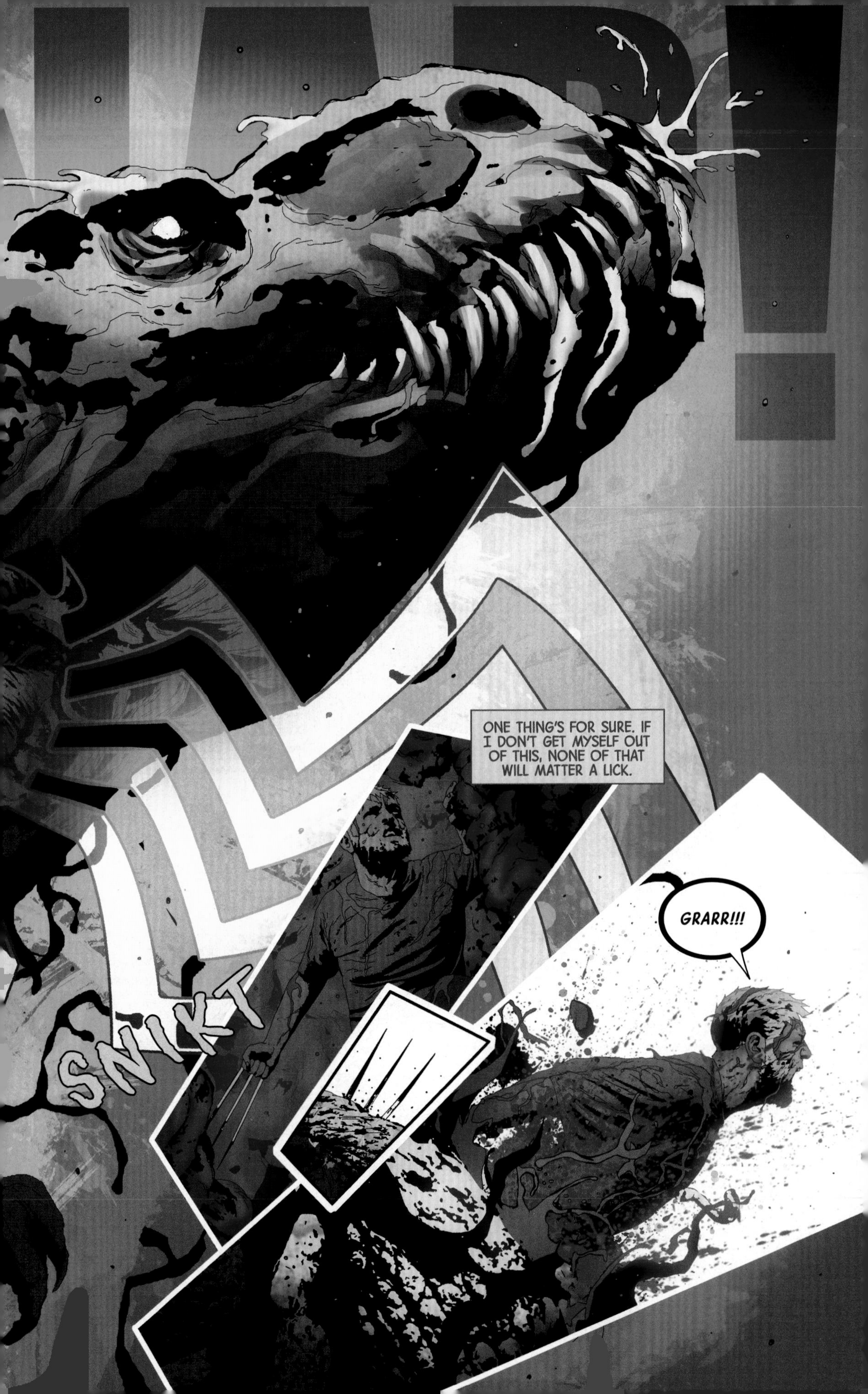
ONE THING'S FOR SURE. IF I DON'T GET MYSELF OUT OF THIS, NONE OF THAT WILL MATTER A LICK.
SNIKT
GRARR!!!

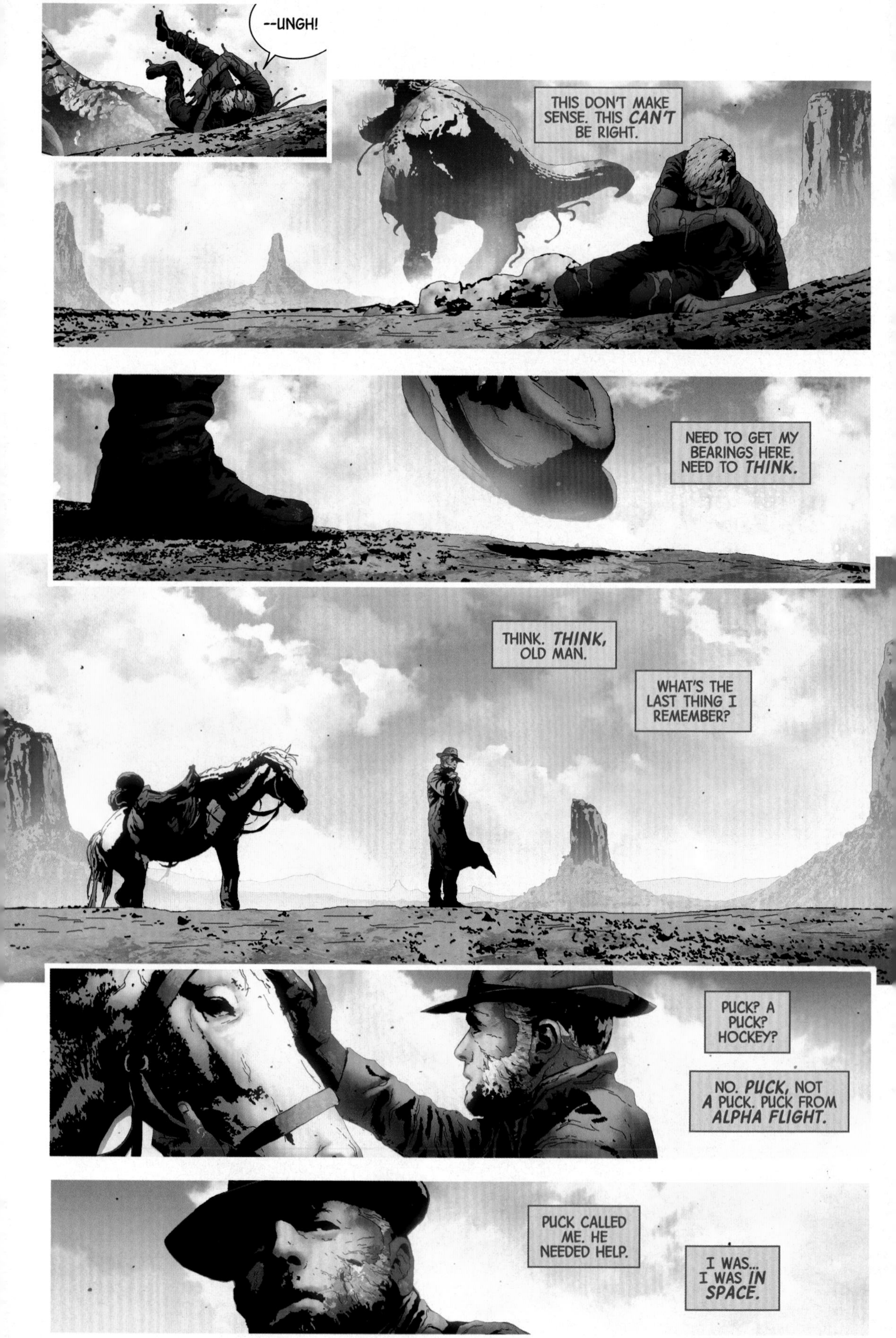
--UNGH!
THIS DON'T MAKE SENSE. THIS CAN'T BE RIGHT.
NEED TO GET MY BEARINGS HERE. NEED TO THINK.
THINK. THINK, OLD MAN.
WHAT'S THE LAST THING I REMEMBER?
PUCK? A PUCK? HOCKEY?
NO. PUCK, NOT A PUCK. PUCK FROM ALPHA FLIGHT.
PUCK CALLED ME. HE NEEDED HELP.
I WAS... I WAS IN SPACE.

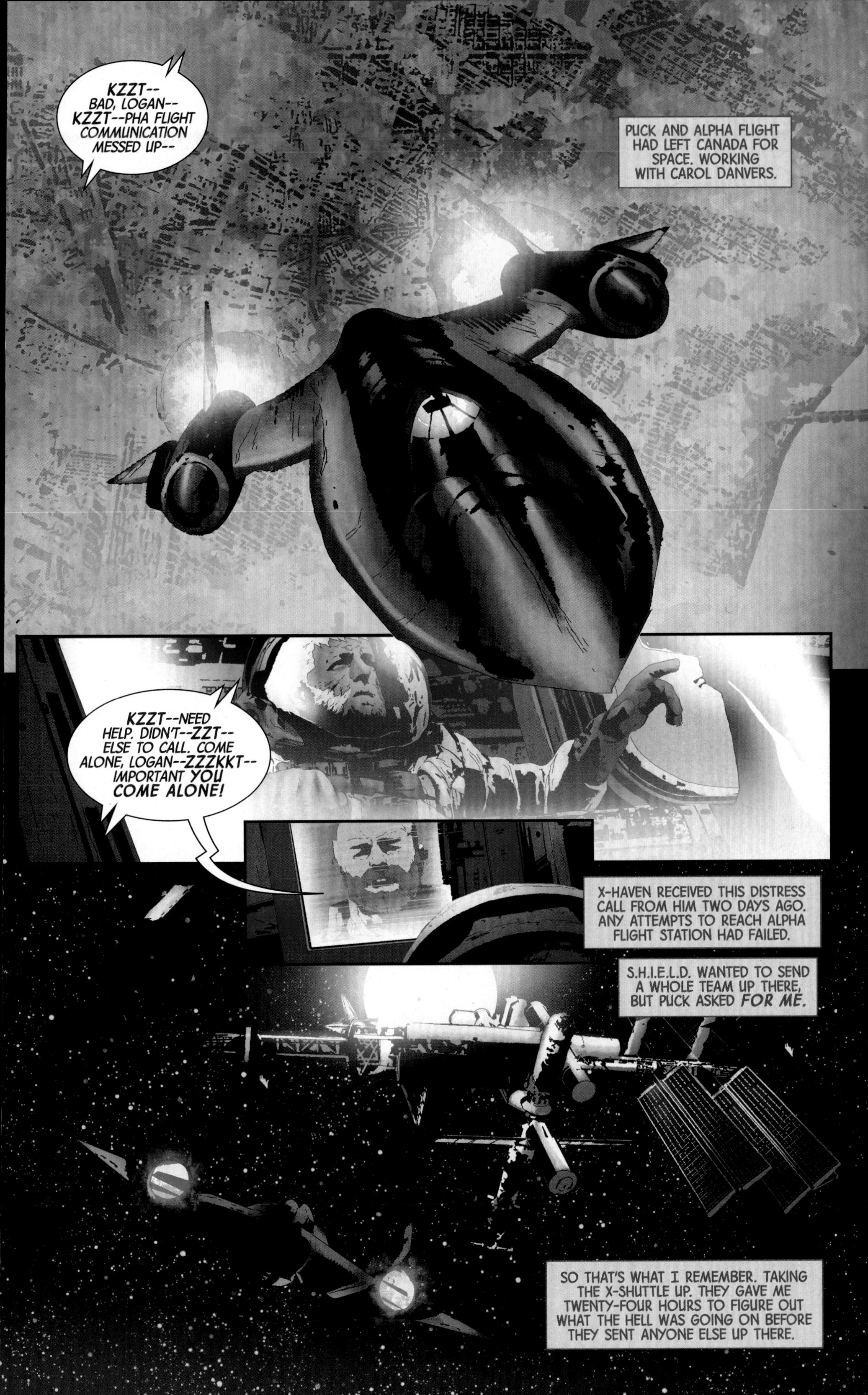
KZZT-- BAD, LOGAN-- KZZT--PHA FLIGHT COMMUNICATION MESSED UP--
PUCK AND ALPHA FLIGHT HAD LEFT CANADA FOR SPACE. WORKING WITH CAROL DANVERS.
KZZT--NEED HELP. DIDN'T--ZZT-- ELSE TO CALL. COME ALONE, LOGAN--ZZZKKT-- IMPORTANT YOU COME ALONE!
X-HAVEN RECEIVED THIS DISTRESS CALL FROM HIM TWO DAYS AGO. ANY ATTEMPTS TO REACH ALPHA FLIGHT STATION HAD FAILED.
S.H.I.E.L.D. WANTED TO SEND A WHOLE TEAM UP THERE, BUT PUCK ASKED FOR ME.
SO THAT'S WHAT I REMEMBER. TAKING THE X-SHUTTLE UP. THEY GAVE ME TWENTY-FOUR HOURS TO FIGURE OUT WHAT THE HELL WAS GOING ON BEFORE THEY SENT ANYONE ELSE UP THERE.

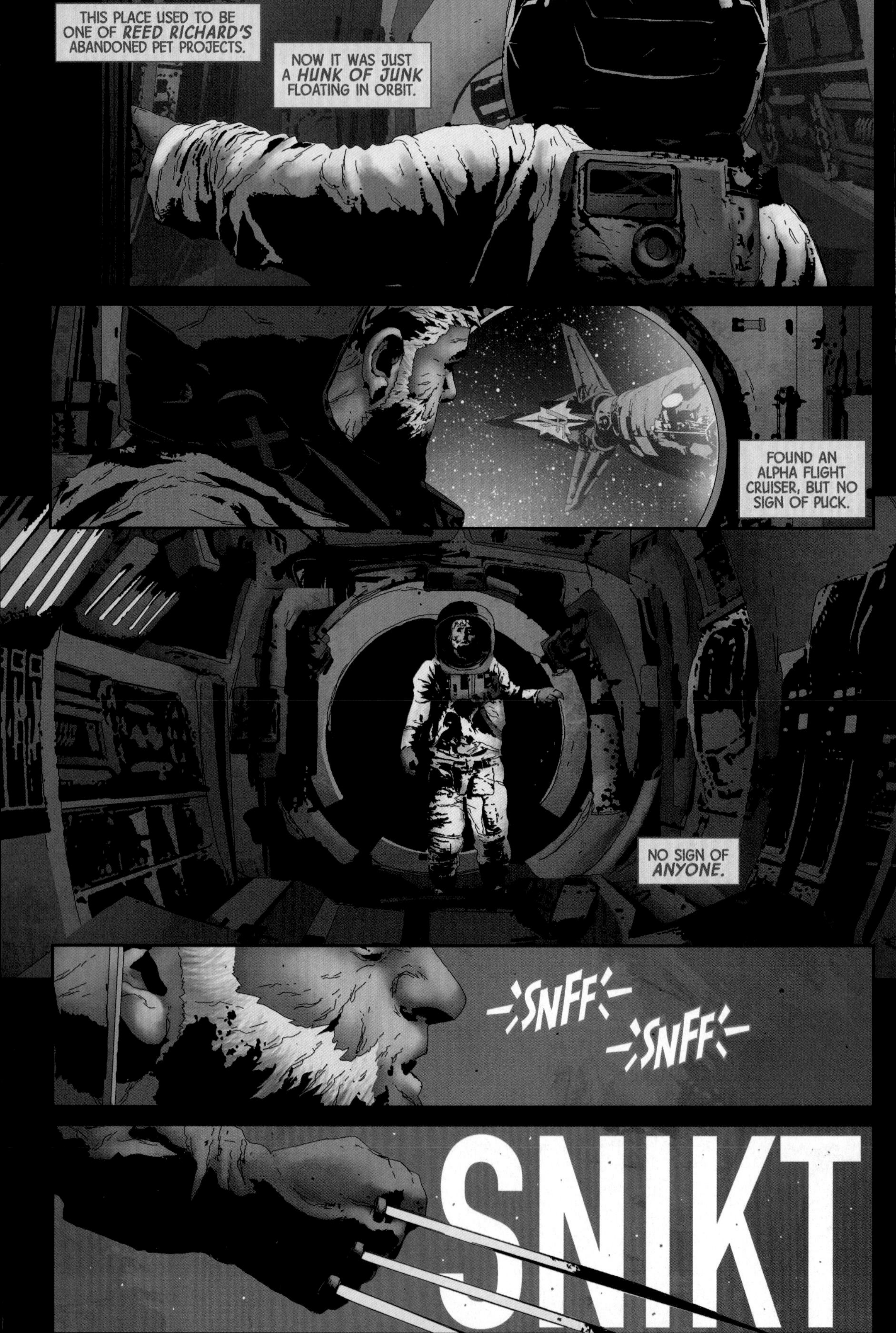
THIS PLACE USED TO BE ONE OF REED RICHARD'S ABANDONED PET PROJECTS.
NOW IT WAS JUST A HUNK OF JUNK FLOATING IN ORBIT.
FOUND AN ALPHA FLIGHT CRUISER, BUT NO SIGN OF PUCK.
NO SIGN OF ANYONE.
SNFF
SNFF
SNIKT

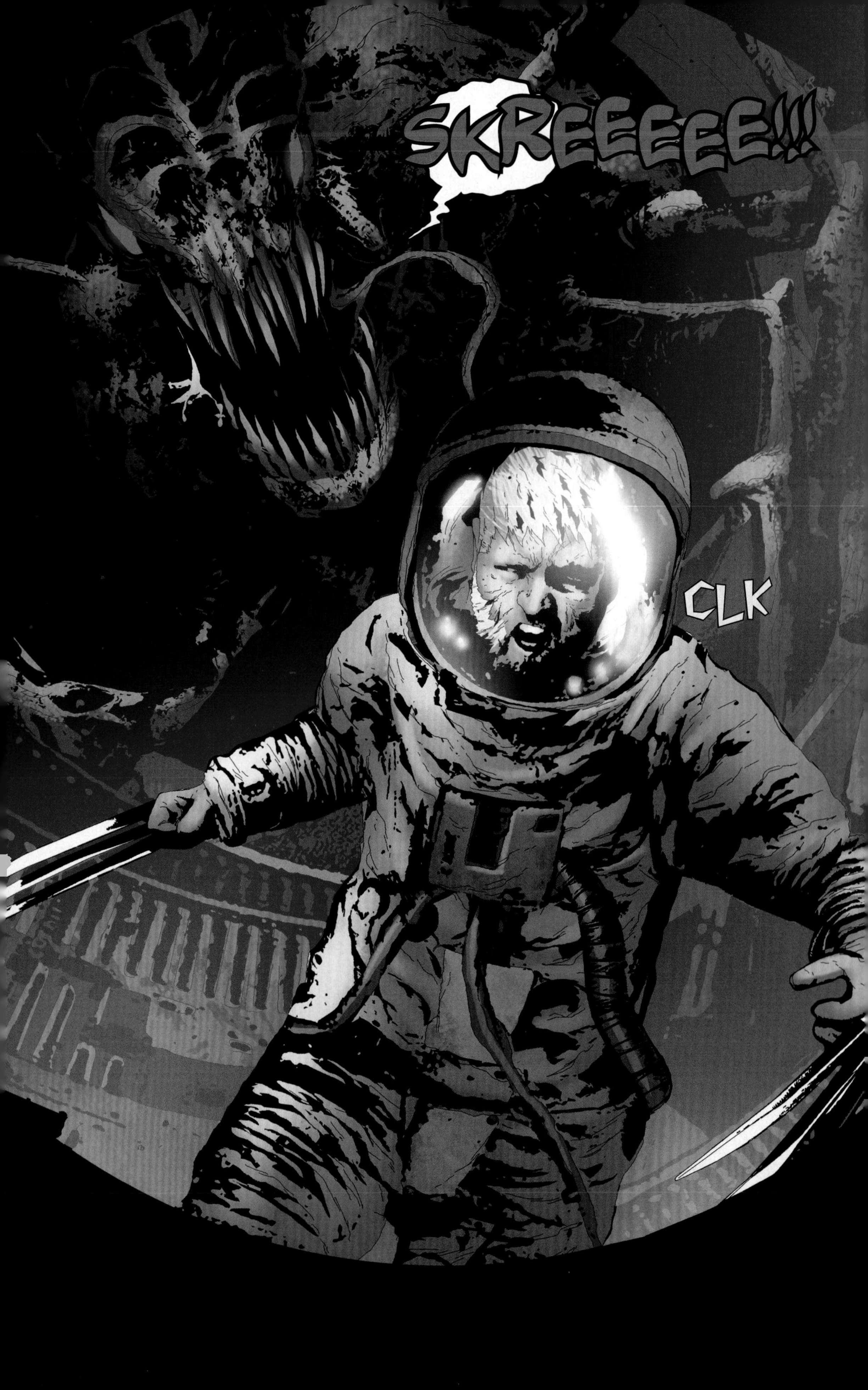
SKREEEEEE!!!
CLK

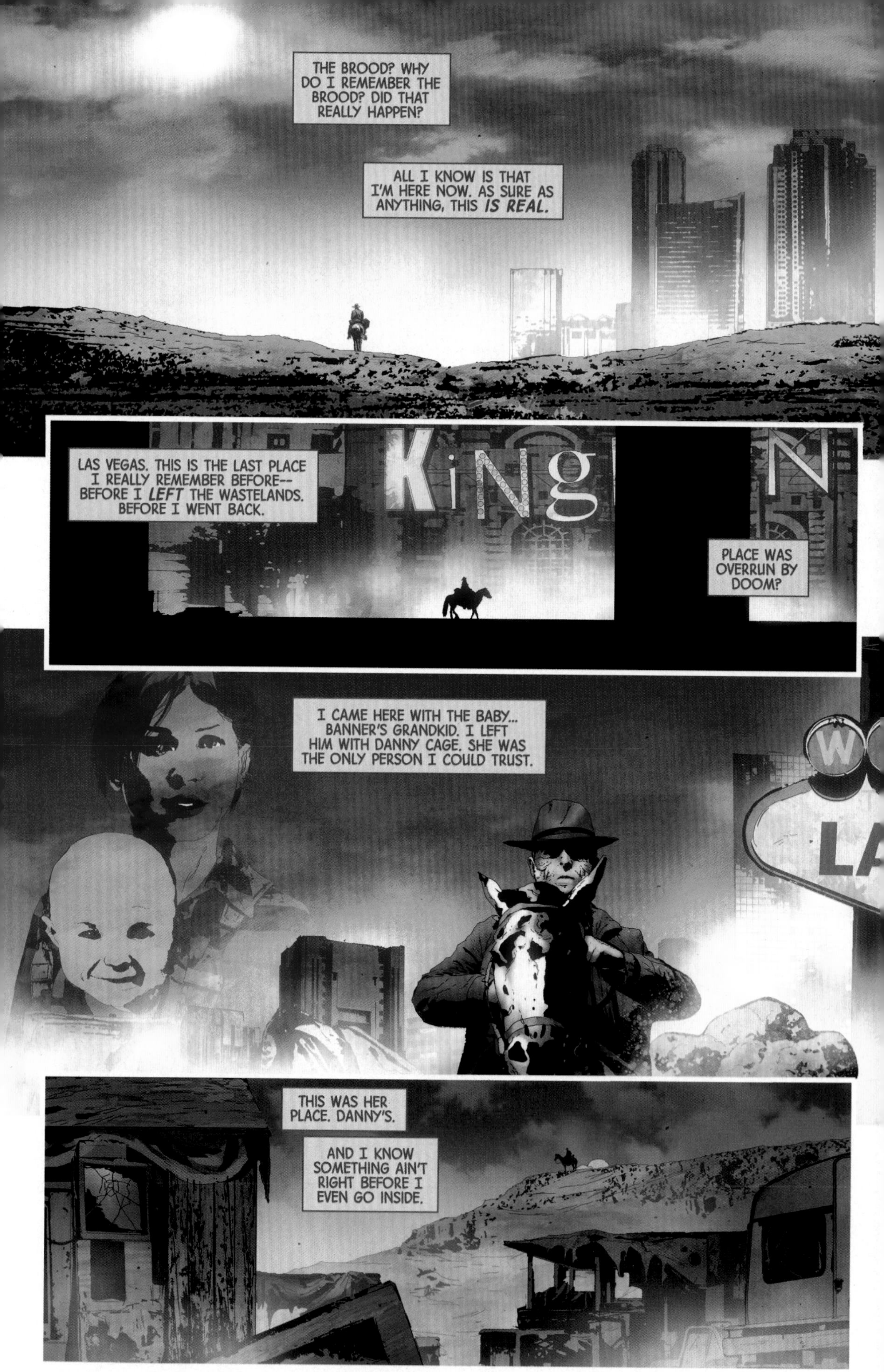
THE BROOD? WHY DO I REMEMBER THE BROOD? DID THAT REALLY HAPPEN?
ALL I KNOW IS THAT I'M HERE NOW. AS SURE AS ANYTHING, THIS IS REAL.
LAS VEGAS. THIS IS THE LAST PLACE I REALLY REMEMBER BEFORE-- BEFORE I LEFT THE WASTELANDS. BEFORE I WENT BACK.
King
PLACE WAS OVERRUN BY DOOM?
I CAME HERE WITH THE BABY... BANNER'S GRANDKID. I LEFT HIM WITH DANNY CAGE. SHE WAS THE ONLY PERSON I COULD TRUST.
THIS WAS HER PLACE. DANNY'S.
AND I KNOW SOMETHING AIN'T RIGHT BEFORE I EVEN GO INSIDE.

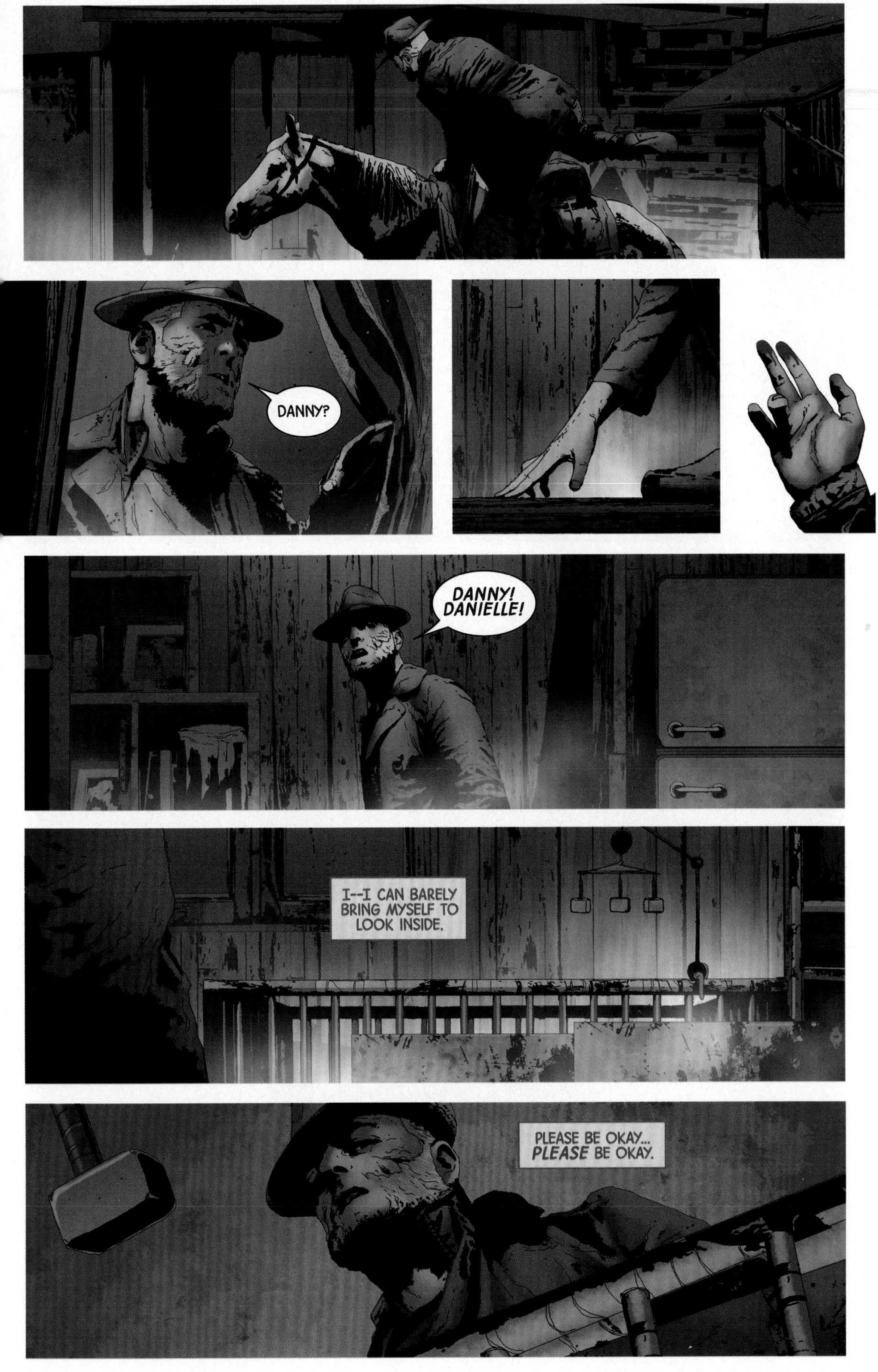
DANNY?
DANNY! DANIELLE!
I--I CAN BARELY BRING MYSELF TO LOOK INSIDE.
PLEASE BE OKAY... *PLEASE* BE OKAY.

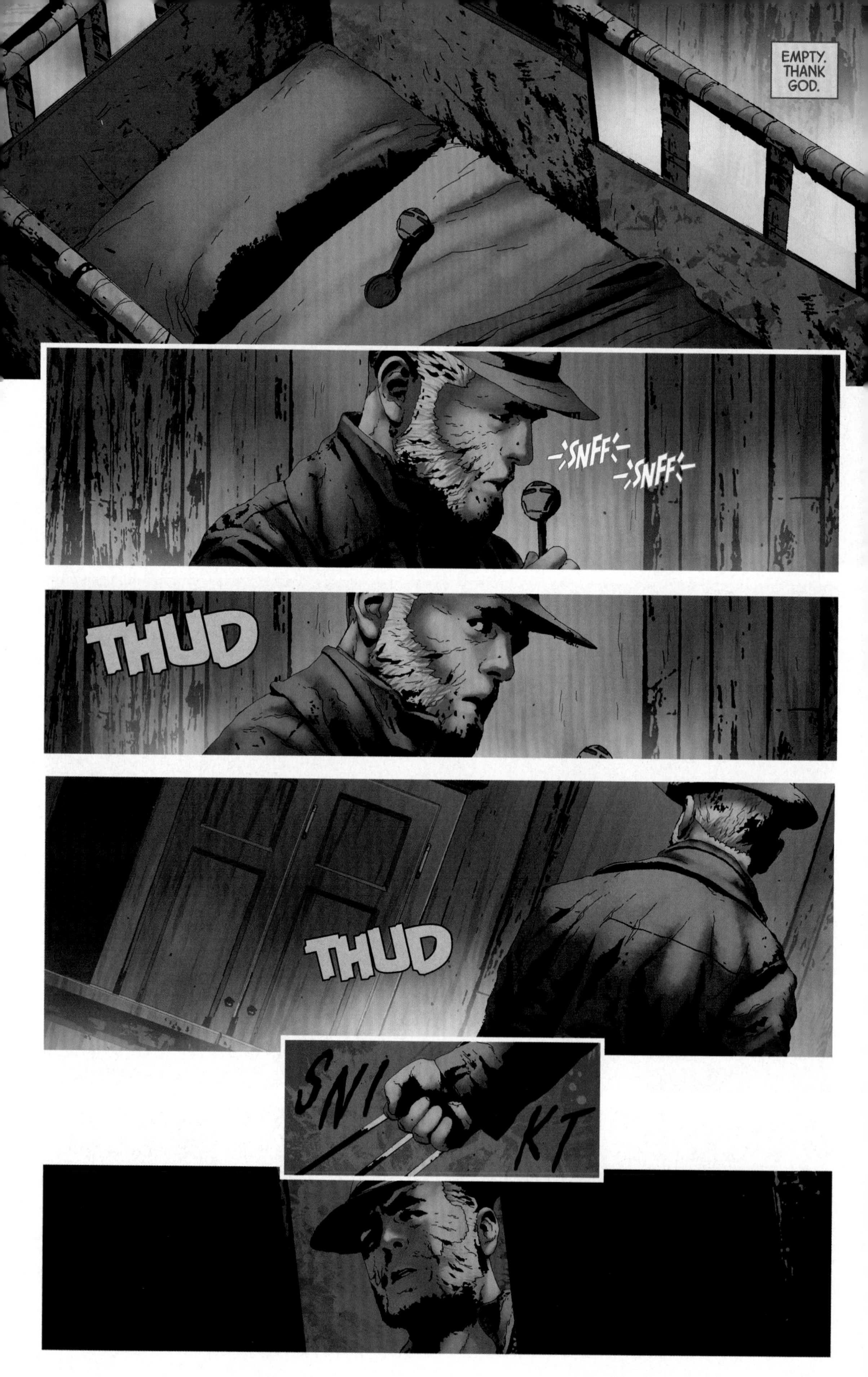
EMPTY. THANK GOD.
SNFF
SNFF
THUD
THUD
SNI KT

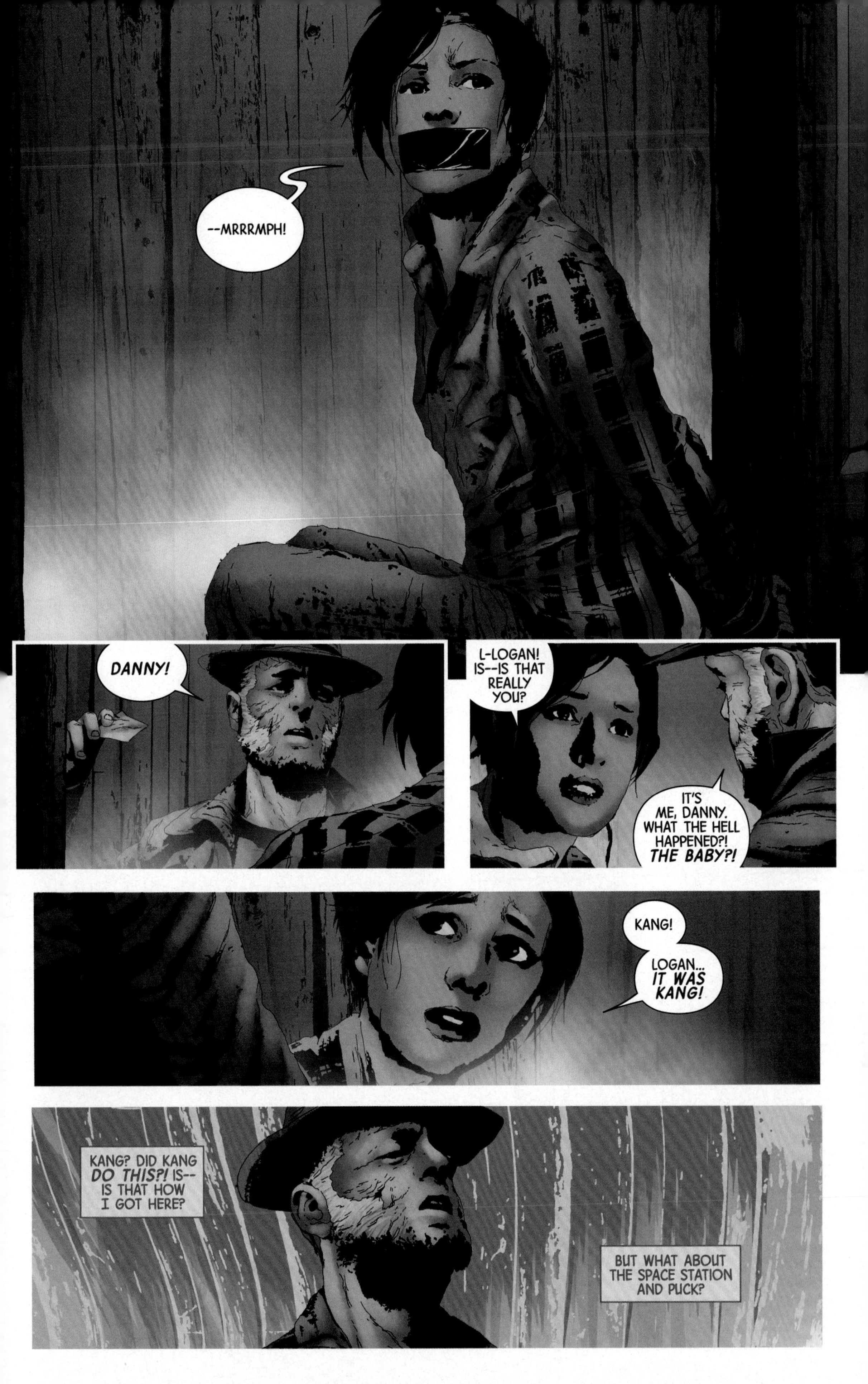

--MRRRMPH!
DANNY!
L-LOGAN! IS--IS THAT REALLY YOU?
IT'S ME, DANNY. WHAT THE HELL HAPPENED?! THE BABY?!
KANG!
LOGAN... IT WAS KANG!
KANG? DID KANG DO THIS?! IS--IS THAT HOW I GOT HERE?
BUT WHAT ABOUT THE SPACE STATION AND PUCK?

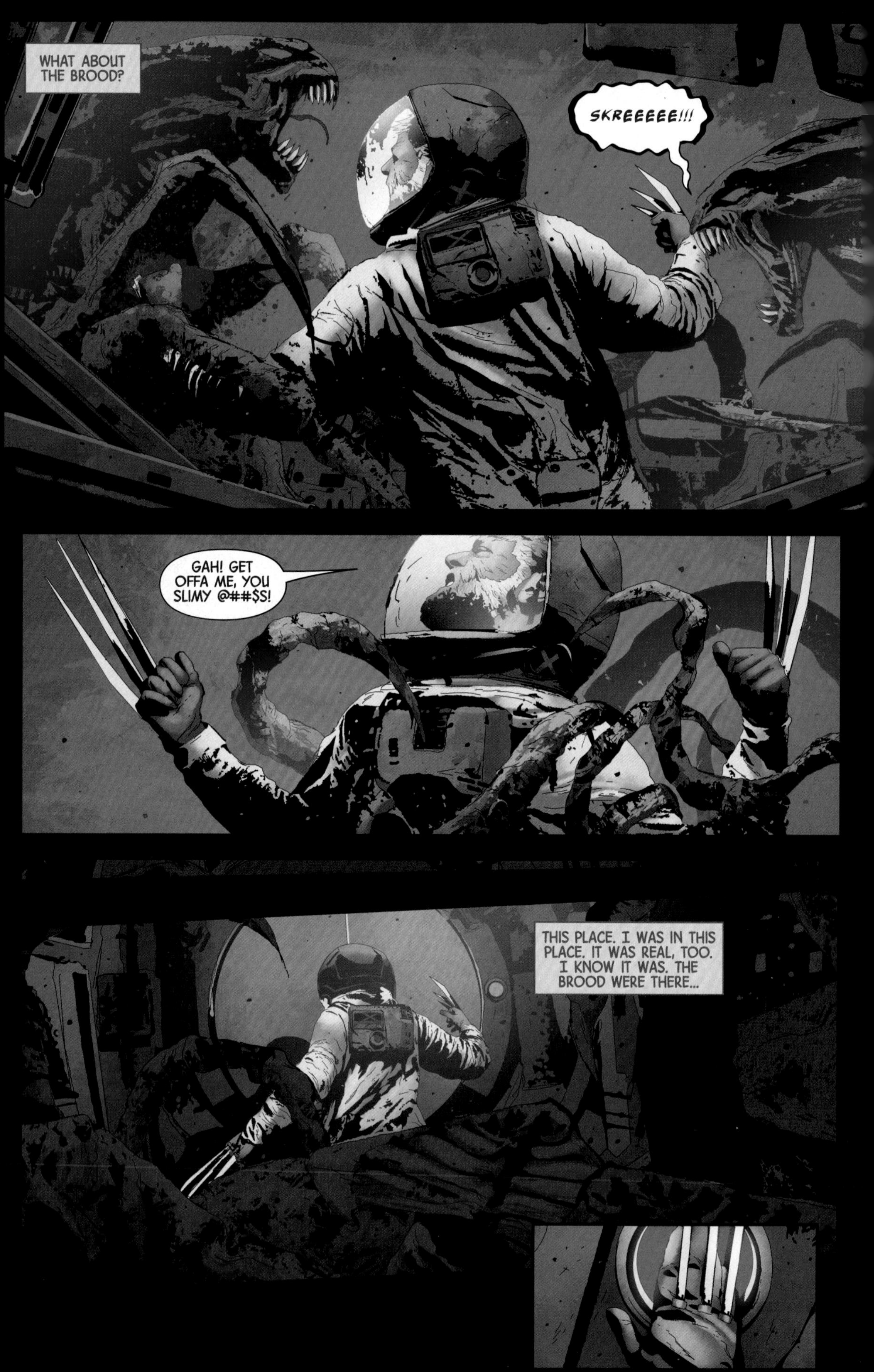
WHAT ABOUT THE BROOD?
SKREEEEEE!!!
GAH! GET OFFA ME, YOU SLIMY @##$S!
THIS PLACE. I WAS IN THIS PLACE. IT WAS REAL, TOO. I KNOW IT WAS. THE BROOD WERE THERE...

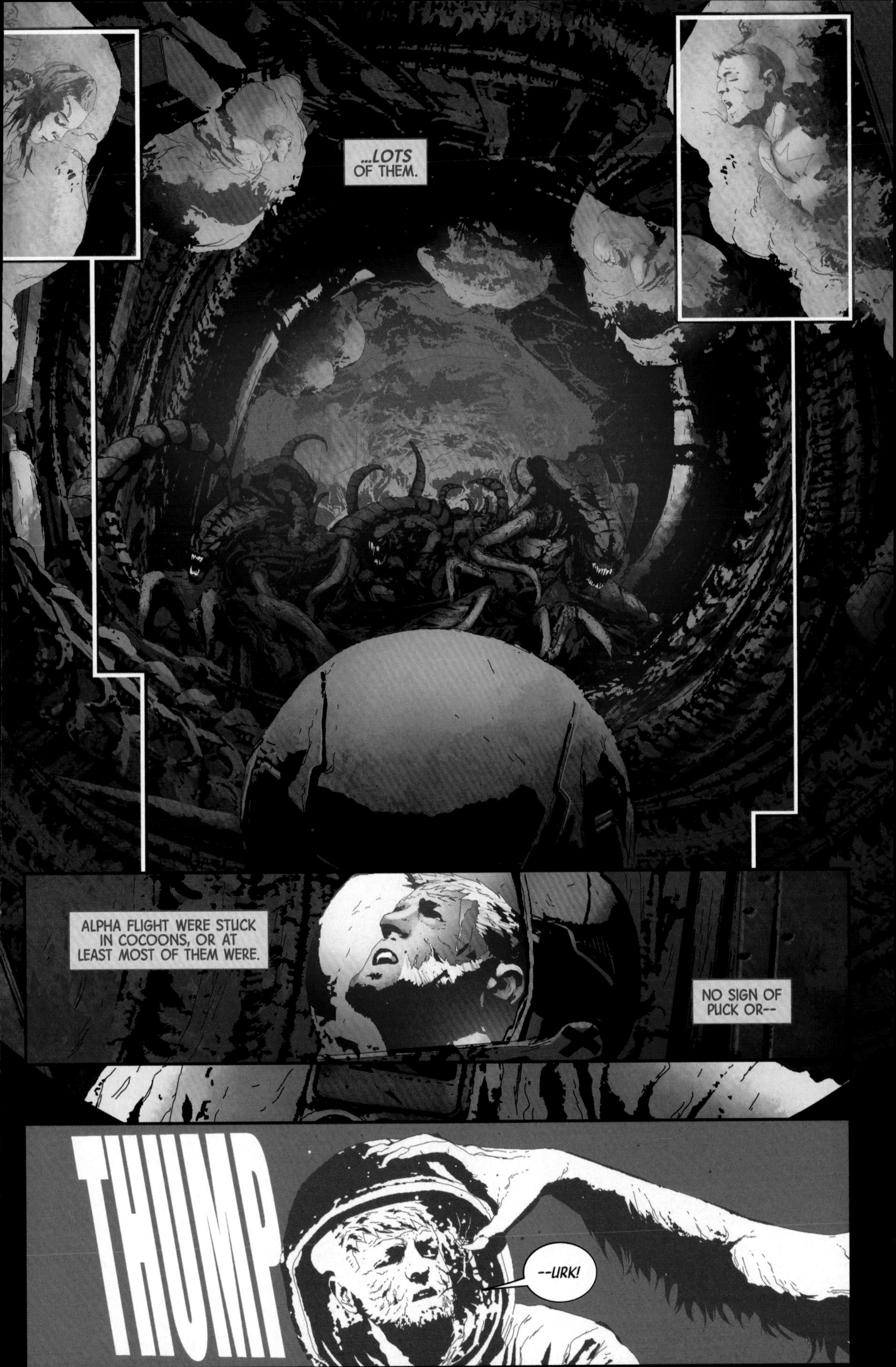

...LOTS OF THEM.
ALPHA FLIGHT WERE STUCK IN COCOONS, OR AT LEAST MOST OF THEM WERE.
NO SIGN OF PUCK OR--
THUMP
--URK!

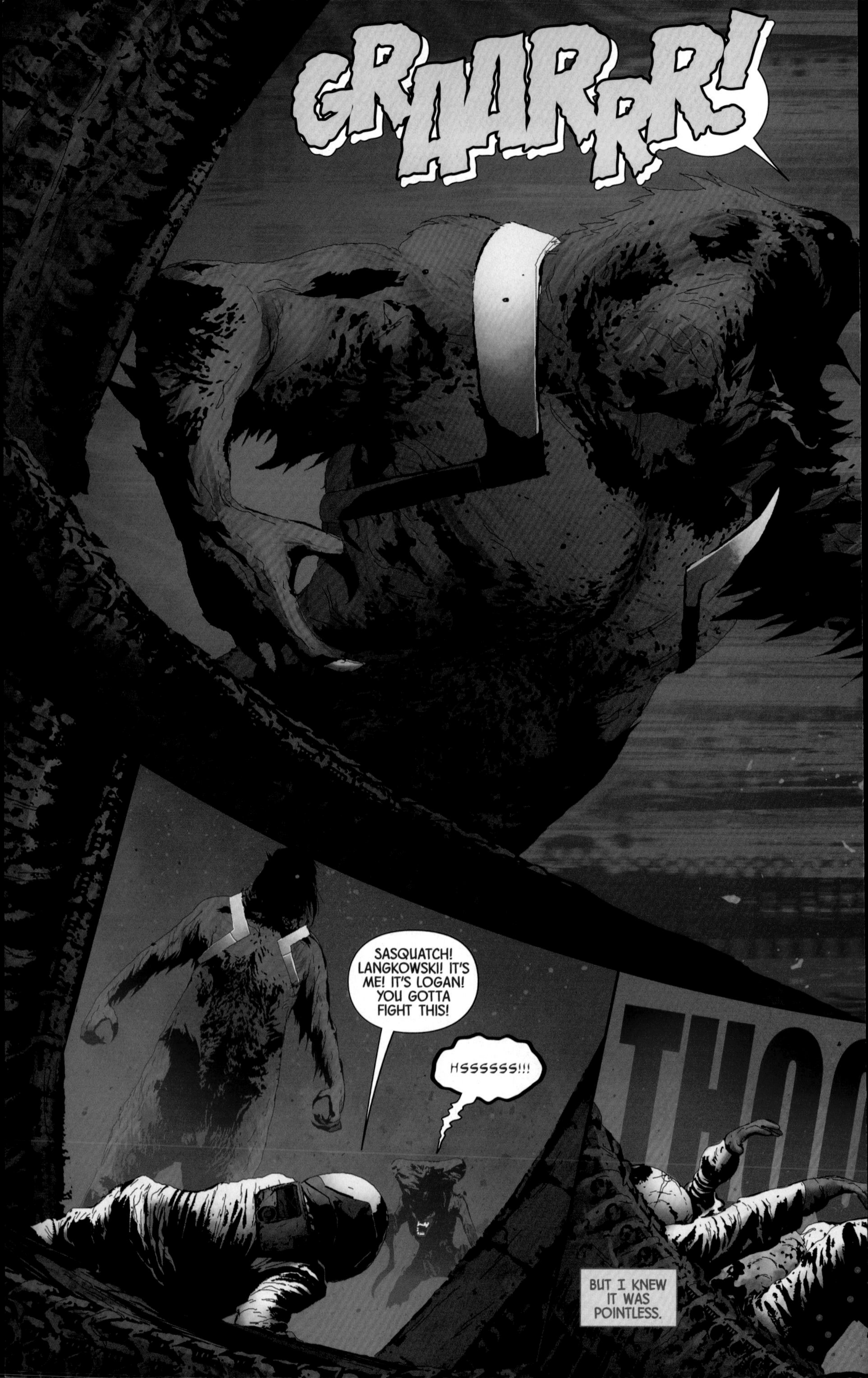
GRWARRR!
SASQUATCH! LANGKOWSKI! IT'S ME! IT'S LOGAN! YOU GOTTA FIGHT THIS!
HSSSSSS!!!
BUT I KNEW IT WAS POINTLESS.

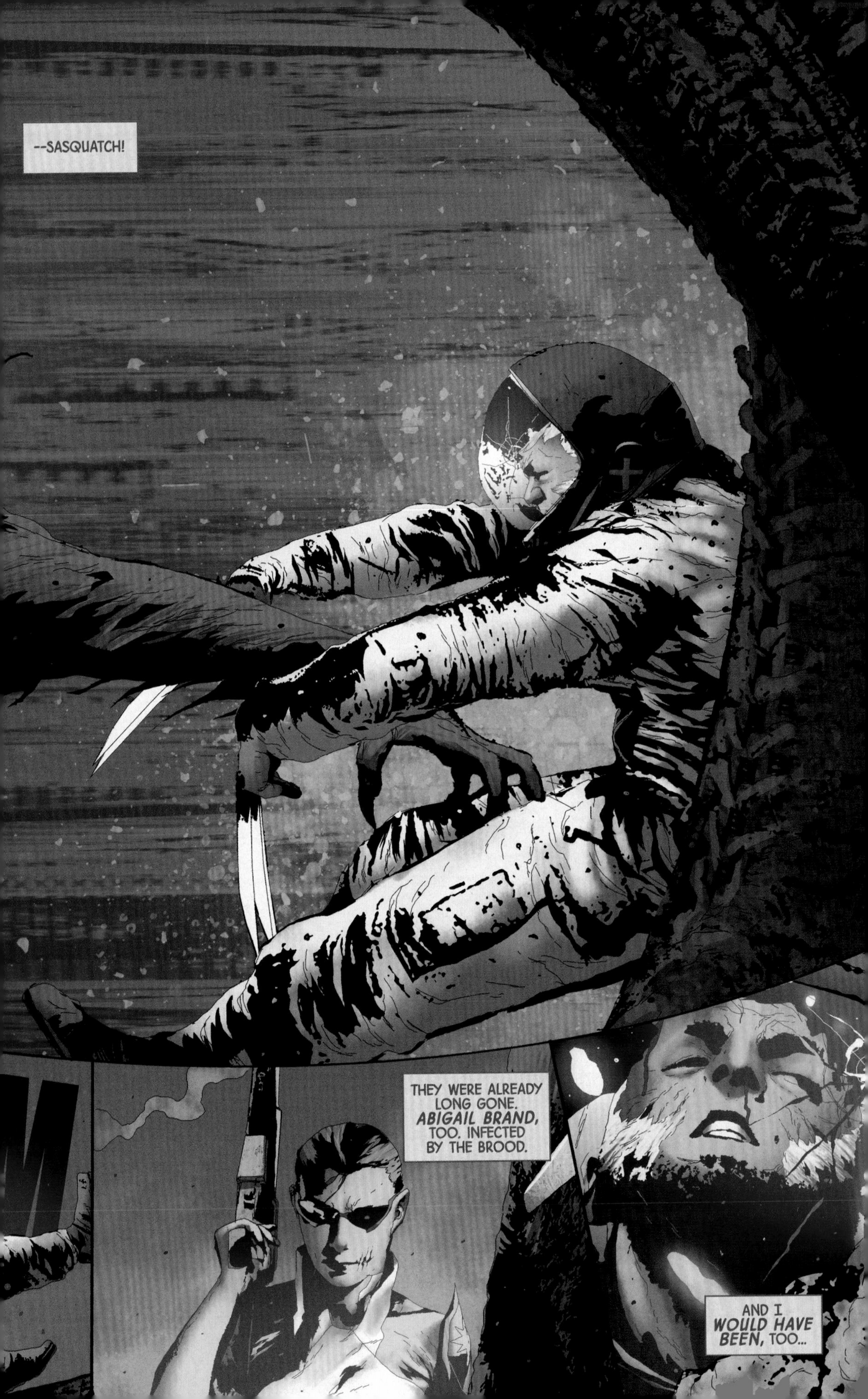
--SASQUATCH!
THEY WERE ALREADY LONG GONE. ABIGAIL BRAND, TOO. INFECTED BY THE BROOD.
AND I WOULD HAVE BEEN, TOO...

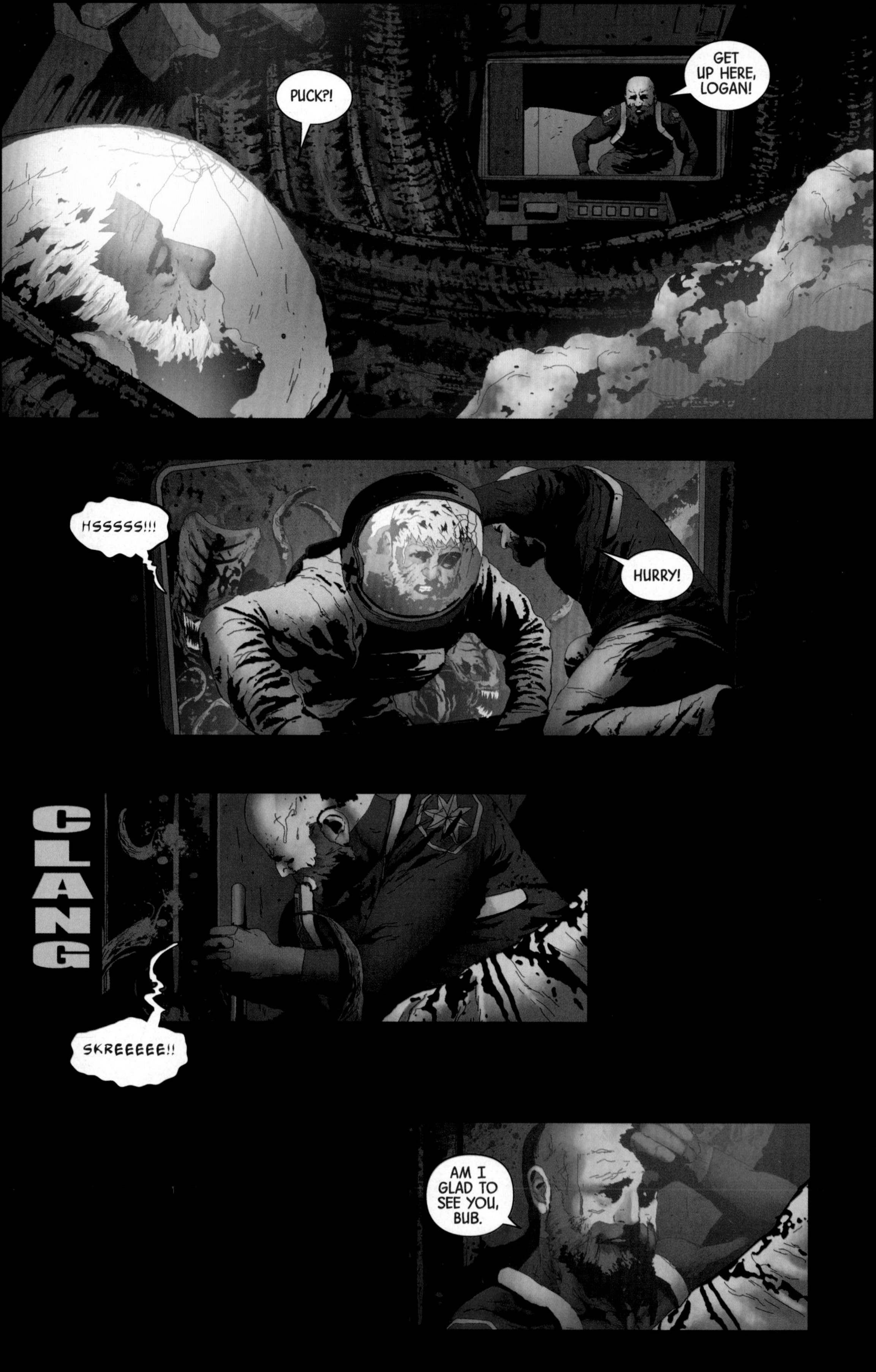
PUCK?!
GET UP HERE, LOGAN!
HSSSSS!!!
HURRY!
CLANG
SKREEEEE!!
AM I GLAD TO SEE YOU, BUB.

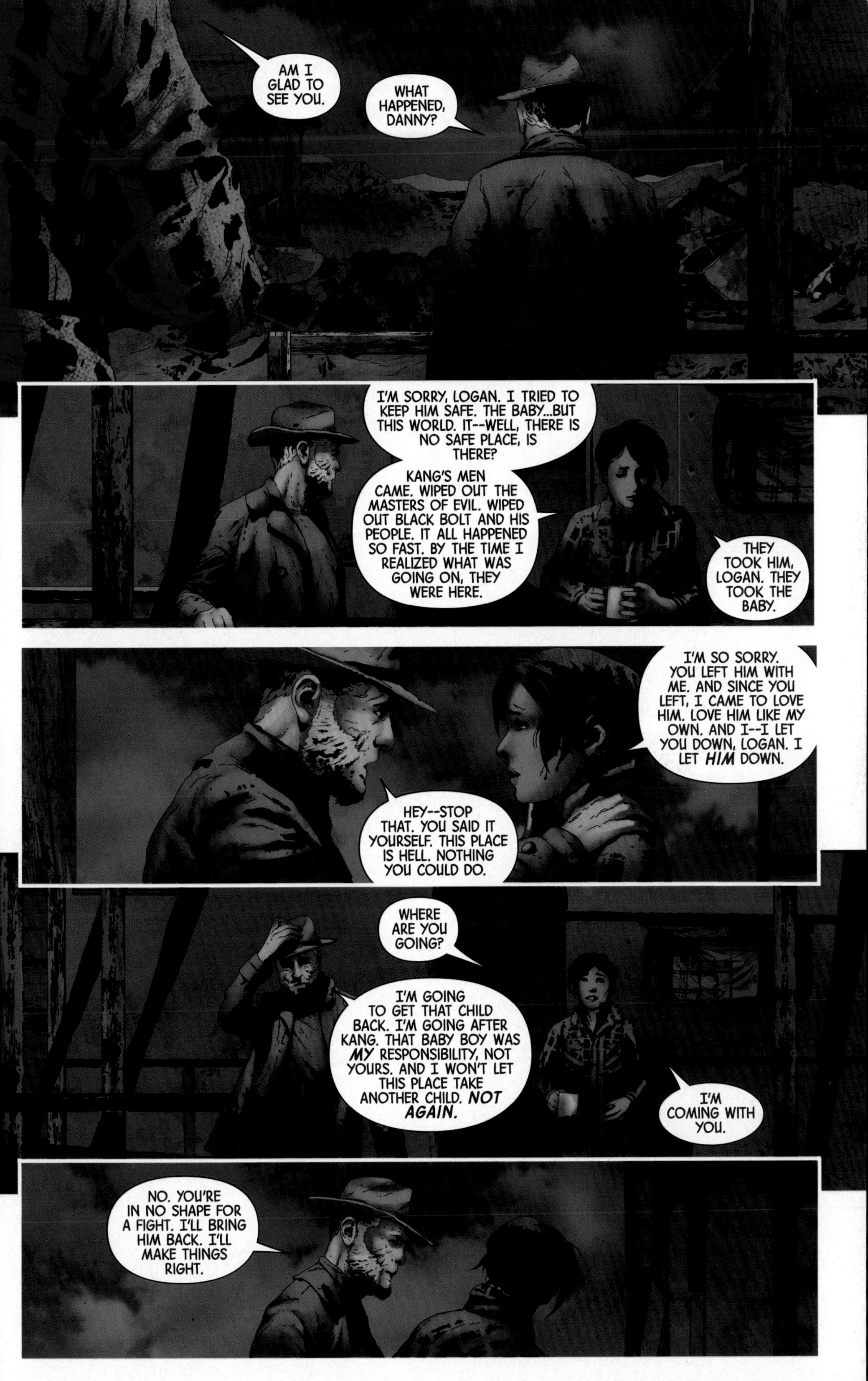
AM I GLAD TO SEE YOU.
WHAT HAPPENED, DANNY?
I'M SORRY, LOGAN. I TRIED TO KEEP HIM SAFE. THE BABY...BUT THIS WORLD. IT--WELL, THERE IS NO SAFE PLACE, IS THERE?
KANG'S MEN CAME. WIPED OUT THE MASTERS OF EVIL. WIPED OUT BLACK BOLT AND HIS PEOPLE. IT ALL HAPPENED SO FAST. BY THE TIME I REALIZED WHAT WAS GOING ON, THEY WERE HERE.
THEY TOOK HIM, LOGAN. THEY TOOK THE BABY.
I'M SO SORRY. YOU LEFT HIM WITH ME. AND SINCE YOU LEFT, I CAME TO LOVE HIM. LOVE HIM LIKE MY OWN. AND I--I LET YOU DOWN, LOGAN. I LET HIM DOWN.
HEY--STOP THAT. YOU SAID IT YOURSELF. THIS PLACE IS HELL. NOTHING YOU COULD DO.
WHERE ARE YOU GOING?
I'M GOING TO GET THAT CHILD BACK. I'M GOING AFTER KANG. THAT BABY BOY WAS MY RESPONSIBILITY, NOT YOURS. AND I WON'T LET THIS PLACE TAKE ANOTHER CHILD. NOT AGAIN.
I'M COMING WITH YOU.
NO. YOU'RE IN NO SHAPE FOR A FIGHT. I'LL BRING HIM BACK. I'LL MAKE THINGS RIGHT.

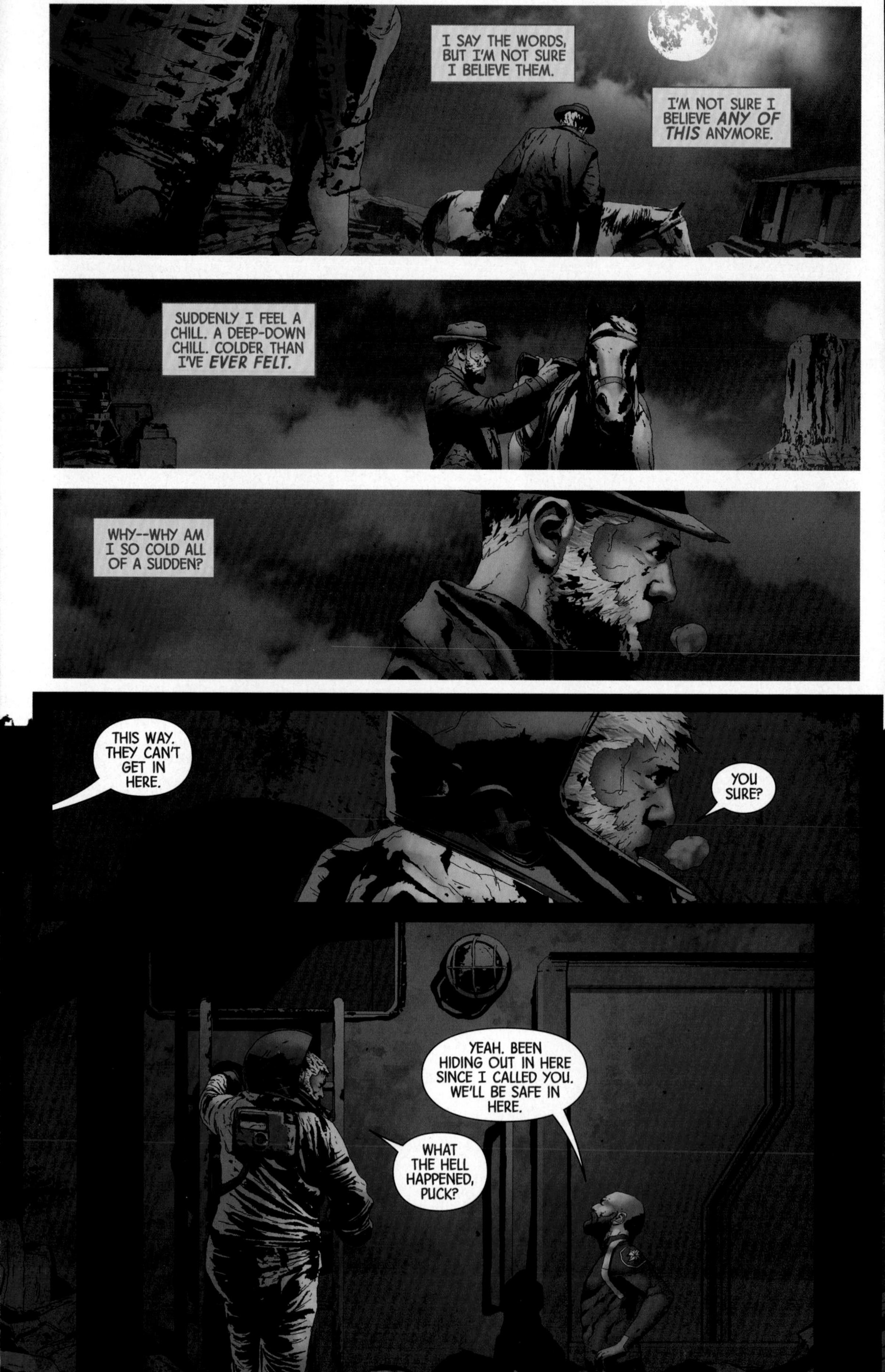
I SAY THE WORDS, BUT I'M NOT SURE I BELIEVE THEM.
I'M NOT SURE I BELIEVE ANY OF THIS ANYMORE.
SUDDENLY I FEEL A CHILL. A DEEP-DOWN CHILL. COLDER THAN I'VE EVER FELT.
WHY--WHY AM I SO COLD ALL OF A SUDDEN?
THIS WAY. THEY CAN'T GET IN HERE.
YOU SURE?
YEAH. BEEN HIDING OUT IN HERE SINCE I CALLED YOU. WE'LL BE SAFE IN HERE.
WHAT THE HELL HAPPENED, PUCK?

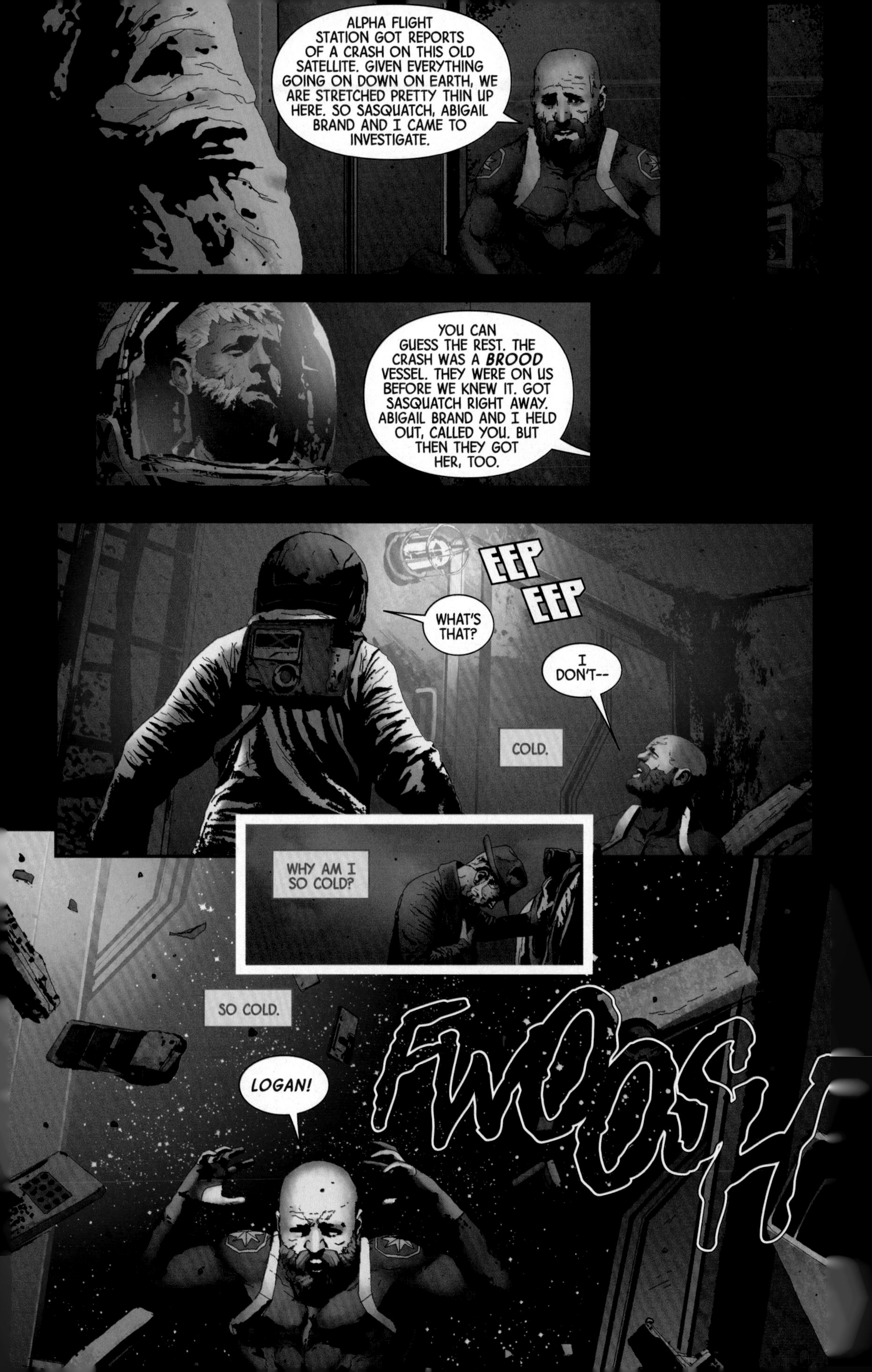
ALPHA FLIGHT STATION GOT REPORTS OF A CRASH ON THIS OLD SATELLITE. GIVEN EVERYTHING GOING ON DOWN ON EARTH, WE ARE STRETCHED PRETTY THIN UP HERE. SO SASQUATCH, ABIGAIL BRAND AND I CAME TO INVESTIGATE.
YOU CAN GUESS THE REST. THE CRASH WAS A *BROOD* VESSEL. THEY WERE ON US BEFORE WE KNEW IT. GOT SASQUATCH RIGHT AWAY. ABIGAIL BRAND AND I HELD OUT, CALLED YOU. BUT THEN THEY GOT HER, TOO.
EEP EEP
WHAT'S THAT?
I DON'T--
COLD.
WHY AM I SO COLD?
SO COLD.
LOGAN!
FWOOSH

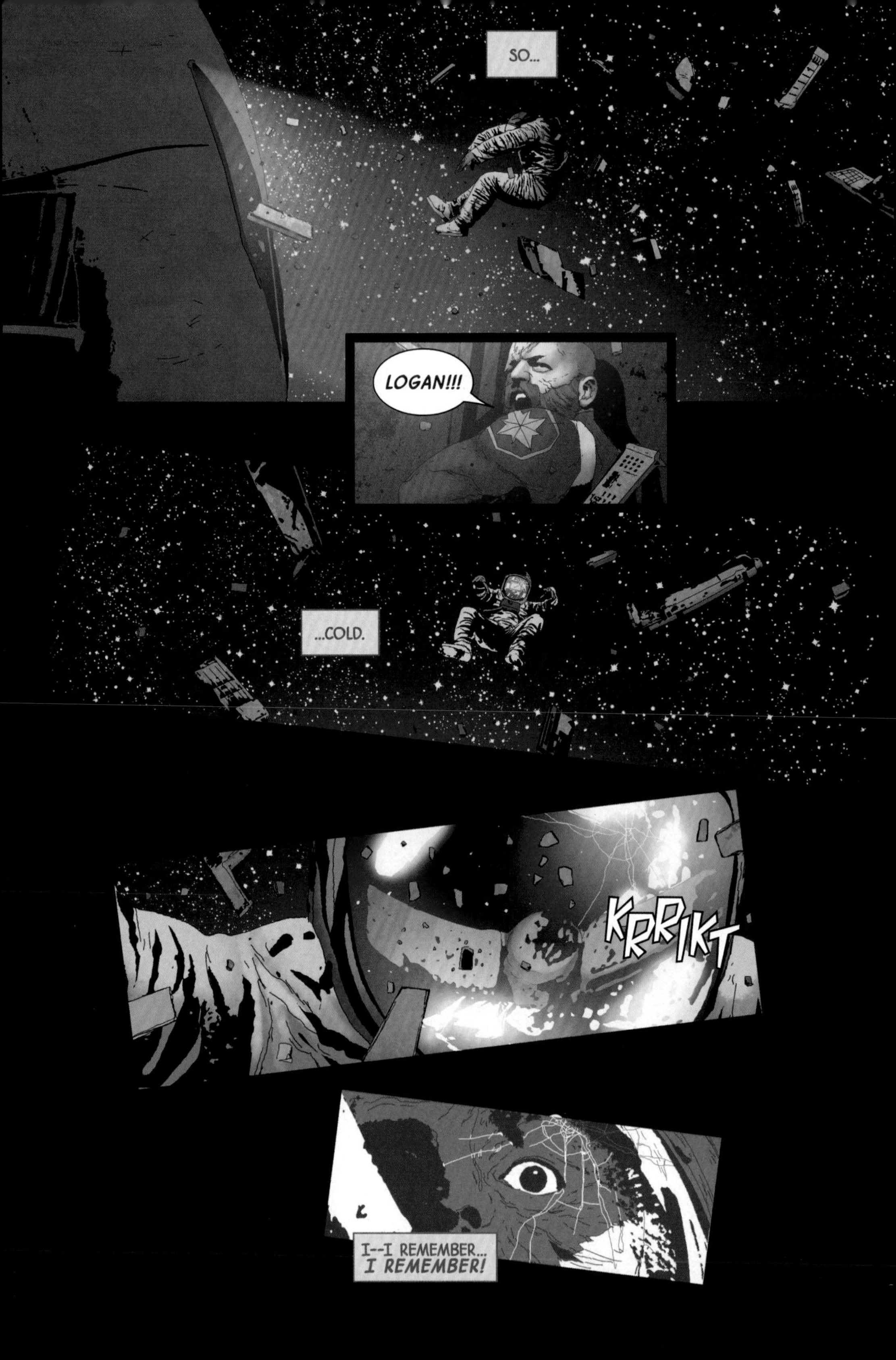
SO...
LOGAN!!!
...COLD.
KRRIKT
I--I REMEMBER...
I REMEMBER!

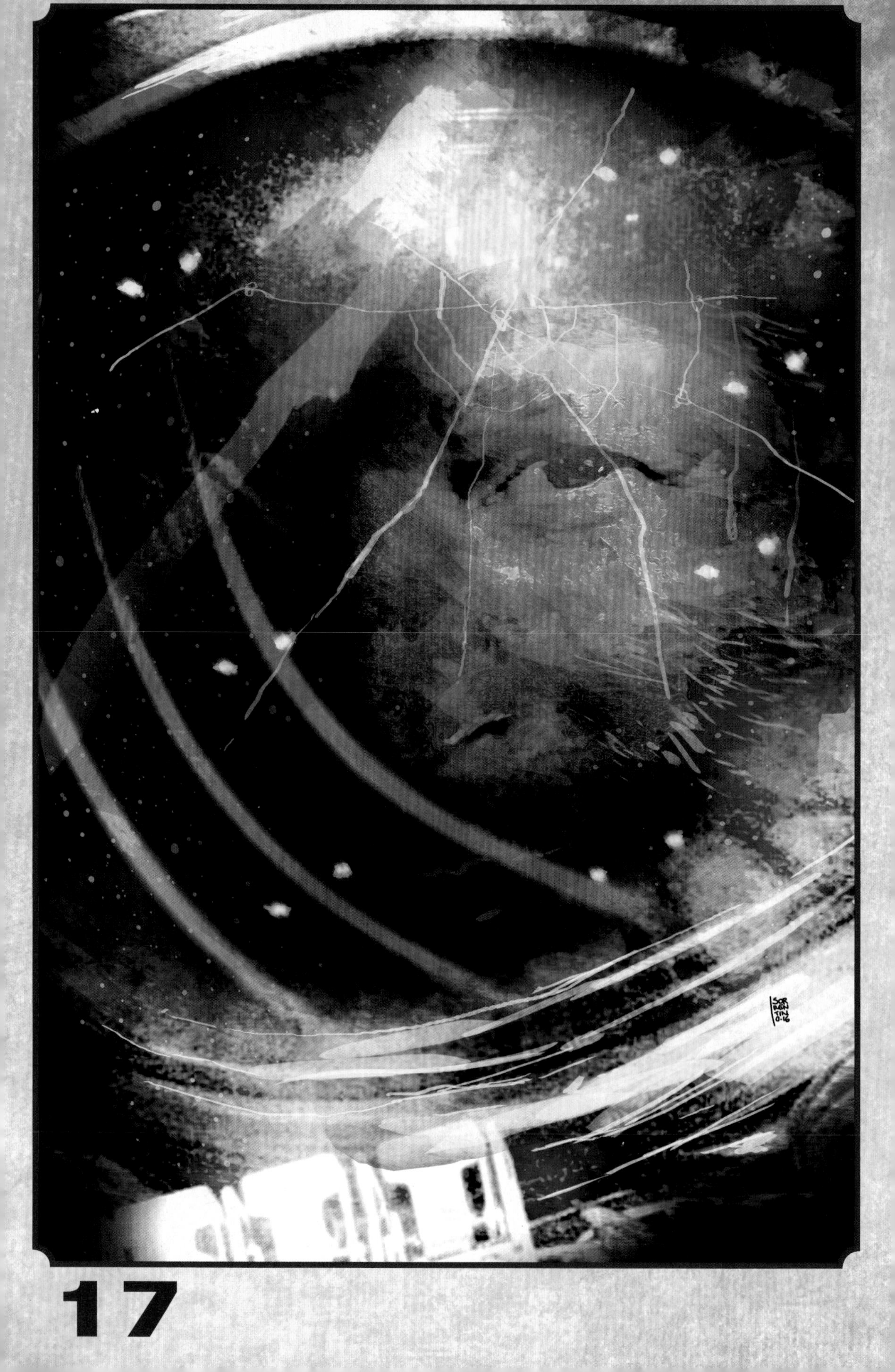

17

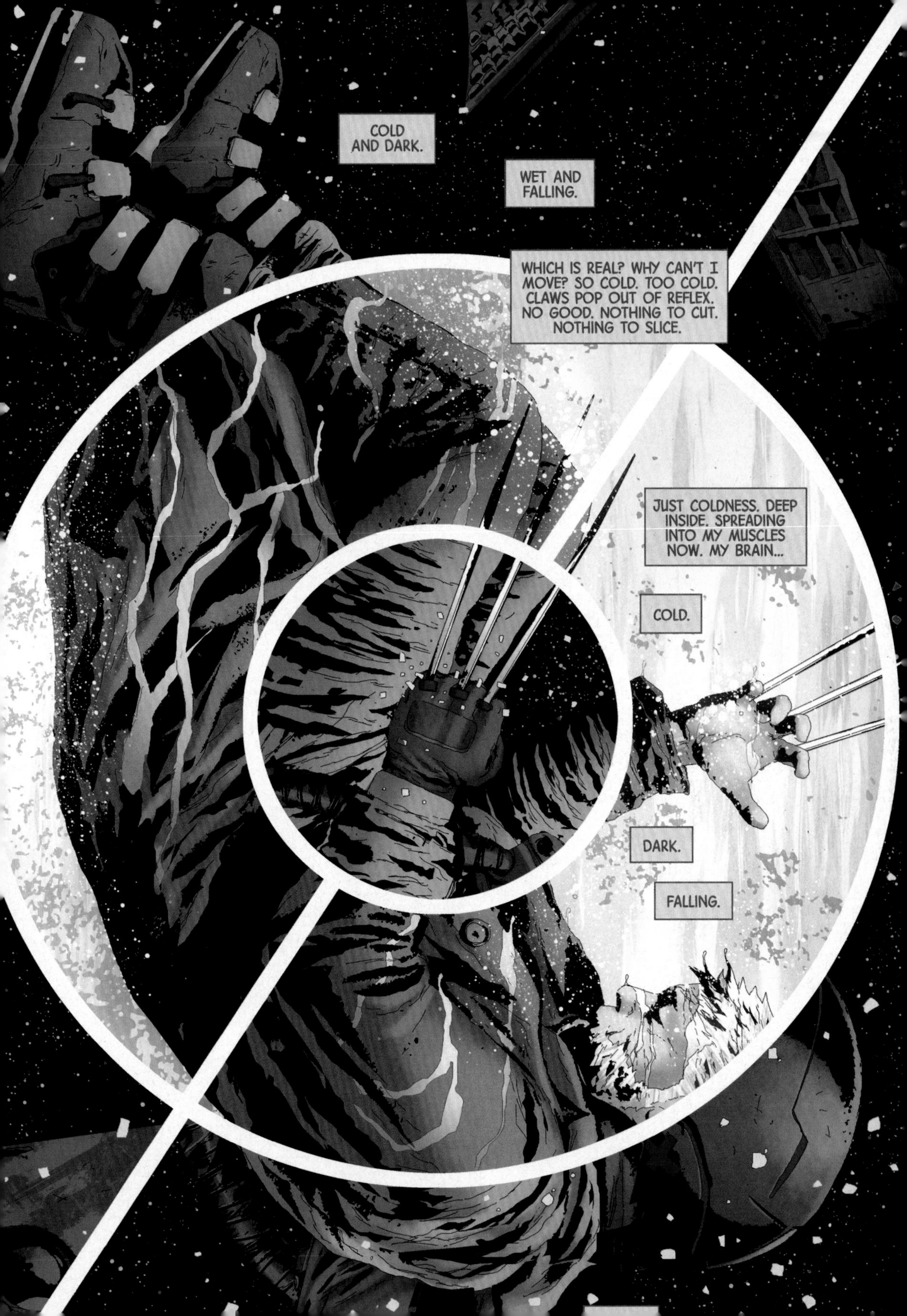
COLD AND DARK.
WET AND FALLING.
WHICH IS REAL? WHY CAN'T I MOVE? SO COLD. TOO COLD. CLAWS POP OUT OF REFLEX. NO GOOD. NOTHING TO CUT. NOTHING TO SLICE.
JUST COLDNESS. DEEP INSIDE. SPREADING INTO MY MUSCLES NOW. MY BRAIN...
COLD.
DARK.
FALLING.

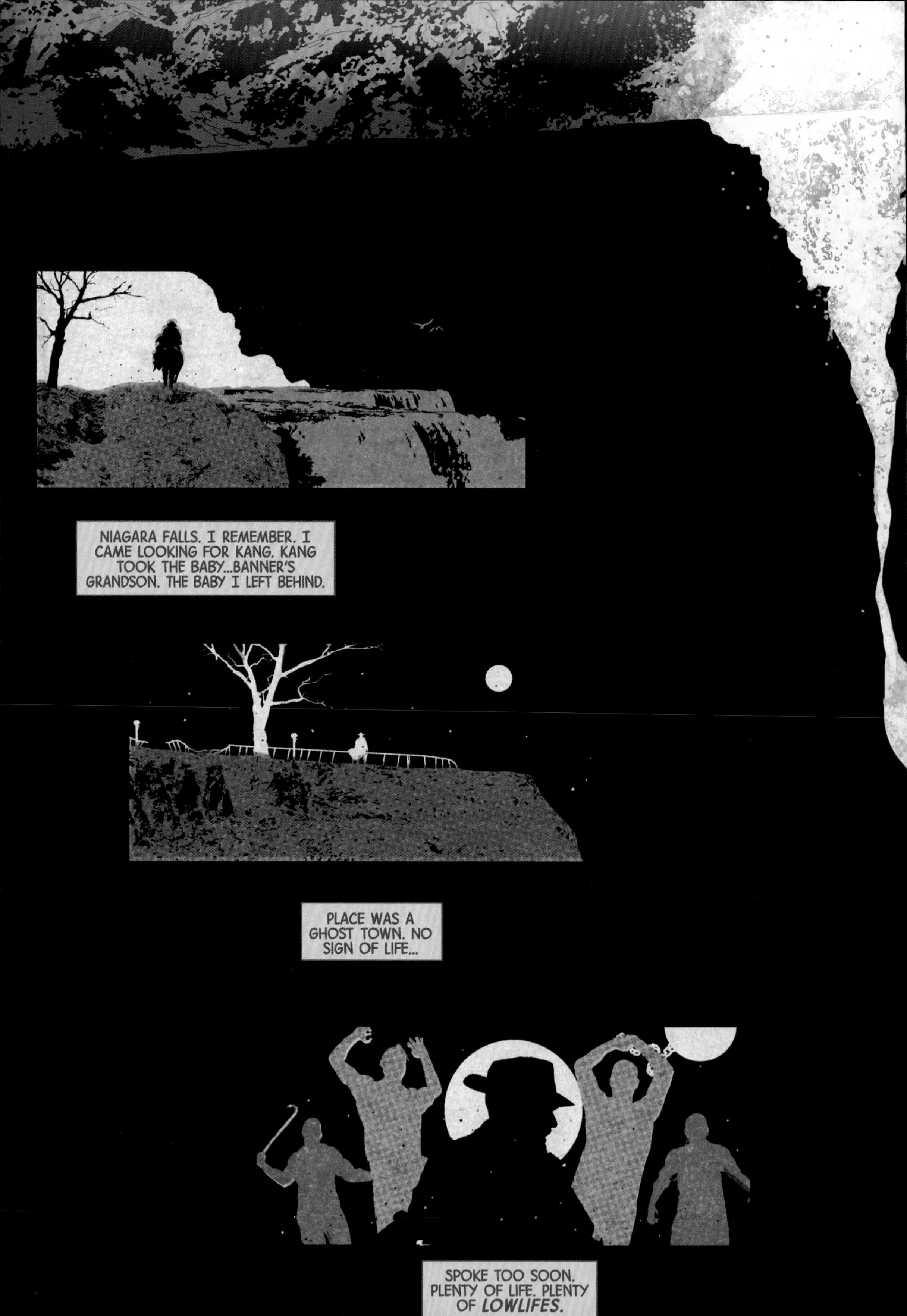
NIAGARA FALLS. I REMEMBER. I CAME LOOKING FOR KANG. KANG TOOK THE BABY...BANNER'S GRANDSON. THE BABY I LEFT BEHIND.
PLACE WAS A GHOST TOWN. NO SIGN OF LIFE...
SPOKE TOO SOON. PLENTY OF LIFE. PLENTY OF *LOWLIFES.*

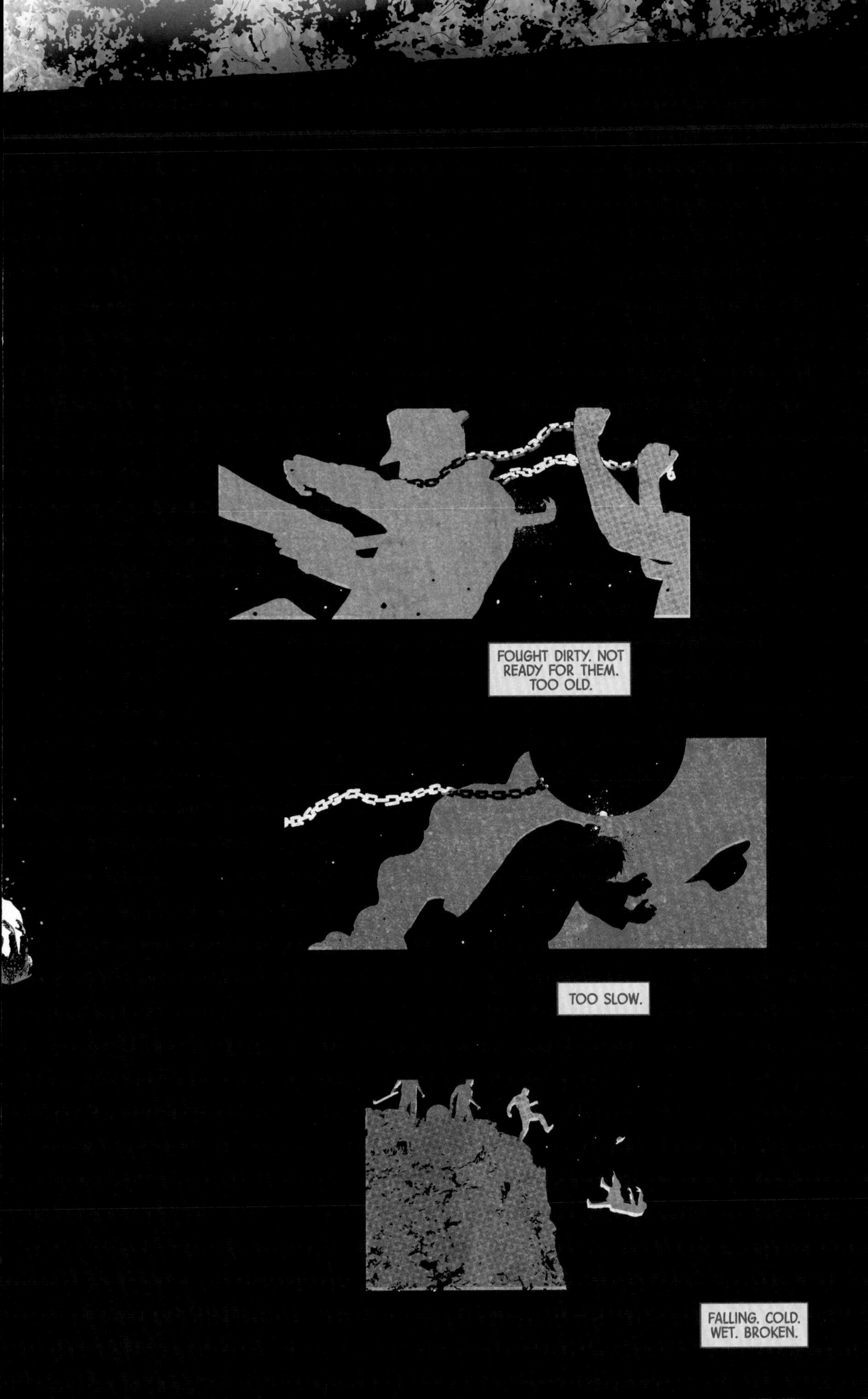
FOUGHT DIRTY. NOT READY FOR THEM. TOO OLD.
TOO SLOW.
FALLING. COLD. WET. BROKEN.

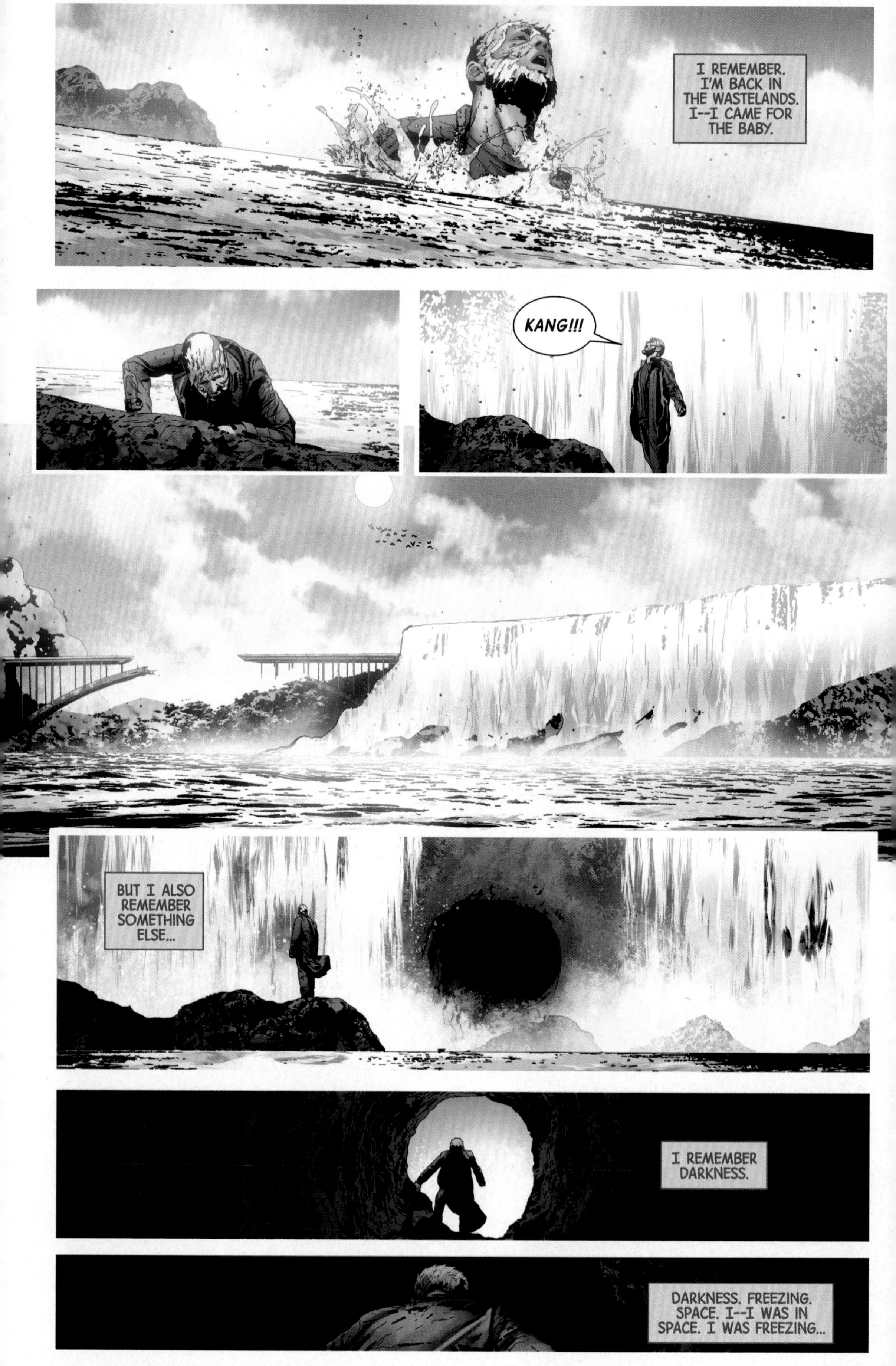
I REMEMBER. I'M BACK IN THE WASTELANDS. I--I CAME FOR THE BABY.
KANG!!!
BUT I ALSO REMEMBER SOMETHING ELSE...
I REMEMBER DARKNESS.
DARKNESS. FREEZING. SPACE. I--I WAS IN SPACE. I WAS FREEZING...

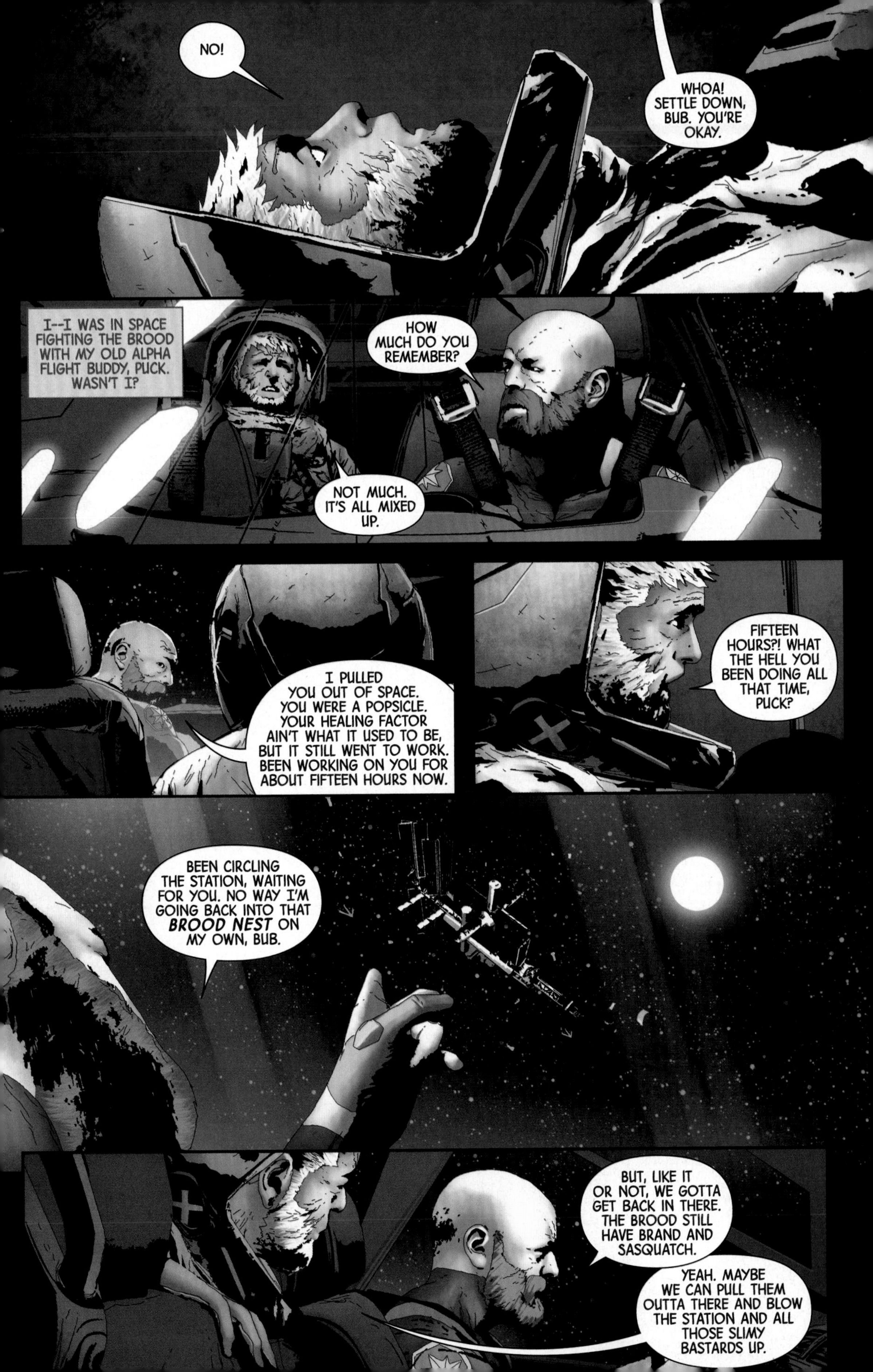
NO!
WHOA! SETTLE DOWN, BUB. YOU'RE OKAY.
I--I WAS IN SPACE FIGHTING THE BROOD WITH MY OLD ALPHA FLIGHT BUDDY, PUCK. WASN'T I?
HOW MUCH DO YOU REMEMBER?
NOT MUCH. IT'S ALL MIXED UP.
I PULLED YOU OUT OF SPACE. YOU WERE A POPSICLE. YOUR HEALING FACTOR AIN'T WHAT IT USED TO BE, BUT IT STILL WENT TO WORK. BEEN WORKING ON YOU FOR ABOUT FIFTEEN HOURS NOW.
FIFTEEN HOURS?! WHAT THE HELL YOU BEEN DOING ALL THAT TIME, PUCK?
BEEN CIRCLING THE STATION, WAITING FOR YOU. NO WAY I'M GOING BACK INTO THAT BROOD NEST ON MY OWN, BUB.
BUT, LIKE IT OR NOT, WE GOTTA GET BACK IN THERE. THE BROOD STILL HAVE BRAND AND SASQUATCH.
YEAH. MAYBE WE CAN PULL THEM OUTTA THERE AND BLOW THE STATION AND ALL THOSE SLIMY BASTARDS UP.

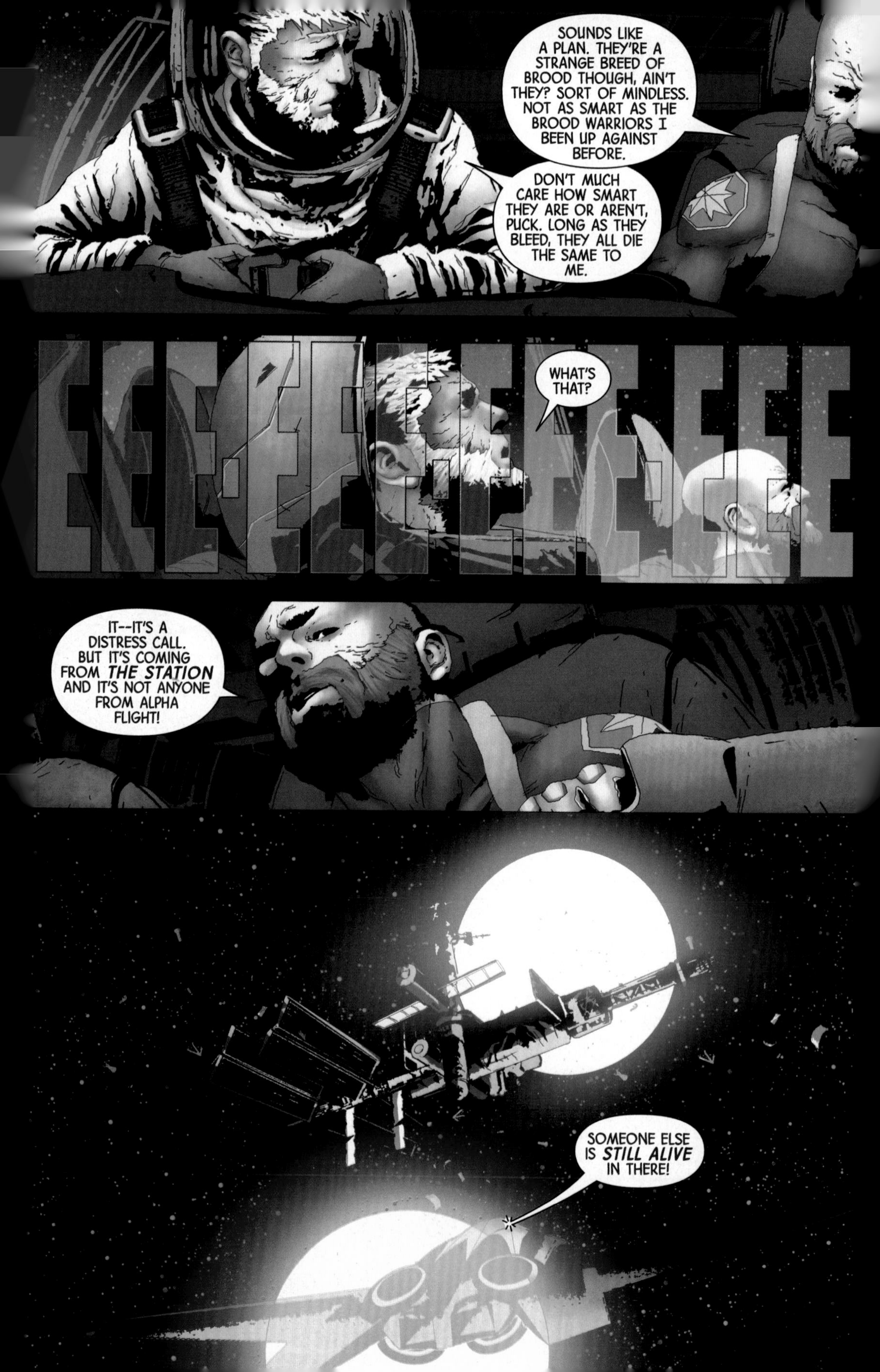
SOUNDS LIKE A PLAN. THEY'RE A STRANGE BREED OF BROOD THOUGH, AIN'T THEY? SORT OF MINDLESS. NOT AS SMART AS THE BROOD WARRIORS I BEEN UP AGAINST BEFORE.
DON'T MUCH CARE HOW SMART THEY ARE OR AREN'T, PUCK. LONG AS THEY BLEED, THEY ALL DIE THE SAME TO ME.
EEEEEEEEEEEE
WHAT'S THAT?
IT--IT'S A DISTRESS CALL. BUT IT'S COMING FROM THE STATION AND IT'S NOT ANYONE FROM ALPHA FLIGHT!
SOMEONE ELSE IS STILL ALIVE IN THERE!

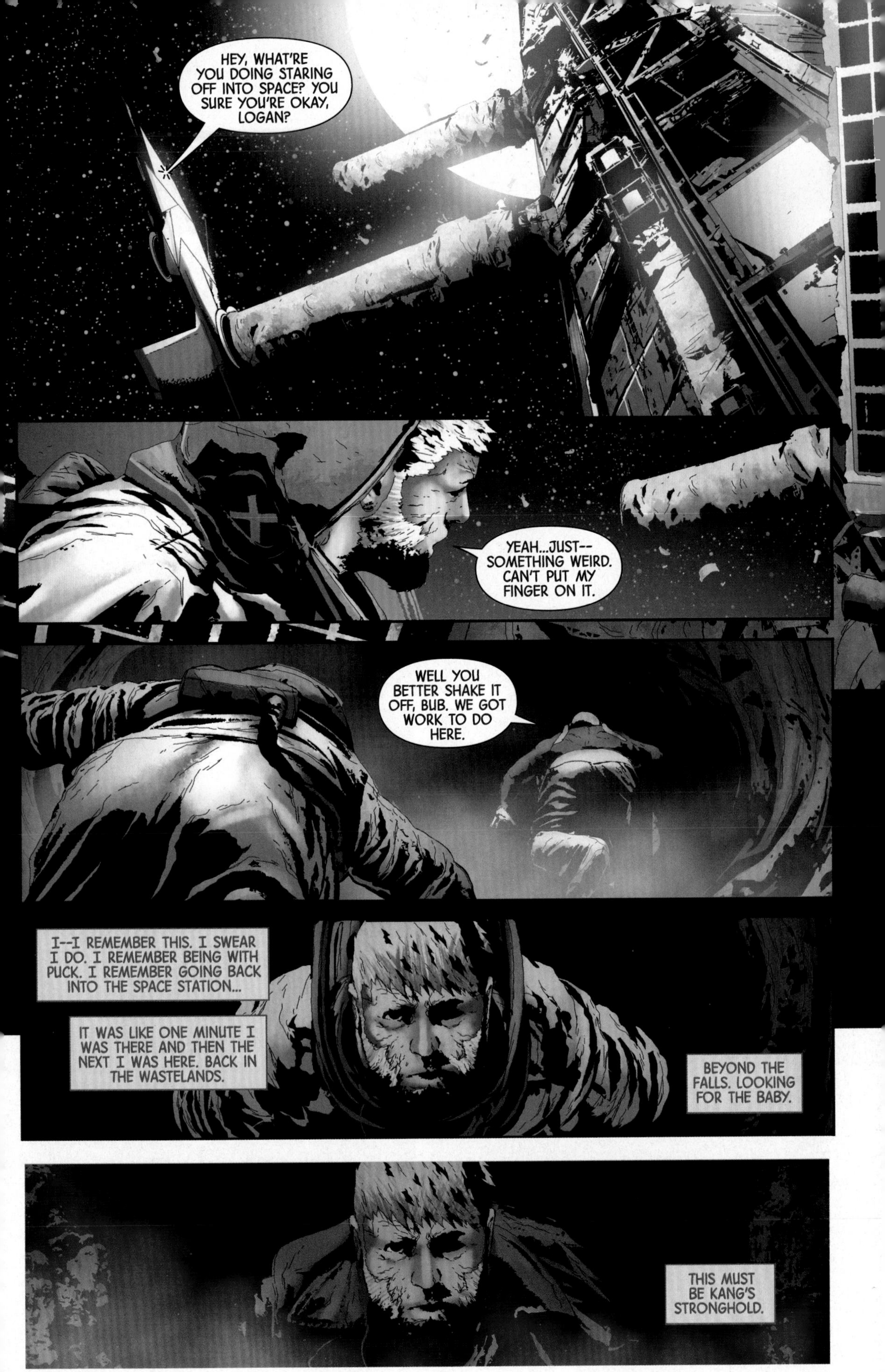
HEY, WHAT'RE YOU DOING STARING OFF INTO SPACE? YOU SURE YOU'RE OKAY, LOGAN?
YEAH...JUST-- SOMETHING WEIRD. CAN'T PUT MY FINGER ON IT.
WELL YOU BETTER SHAKE IT OFF, BUB. WE GOT WORK TO DO HERE.
I--I REMEMBER THIS. I SWEAR I DO. I REMEMBER BEING WITH PUCK. I REMEMBER GOING BACK INTO THE SPACE STATION...
IT WAS LIKE ONE MINUTE I WAS THERE AND THEN THE NEXT I WAS HERE. BACK IN THE WASTELANDS.
BEYOND THE FALLS. LOOKING FOR THE BABY.
THIS MUST BE KANG'S STRONGHOLD.

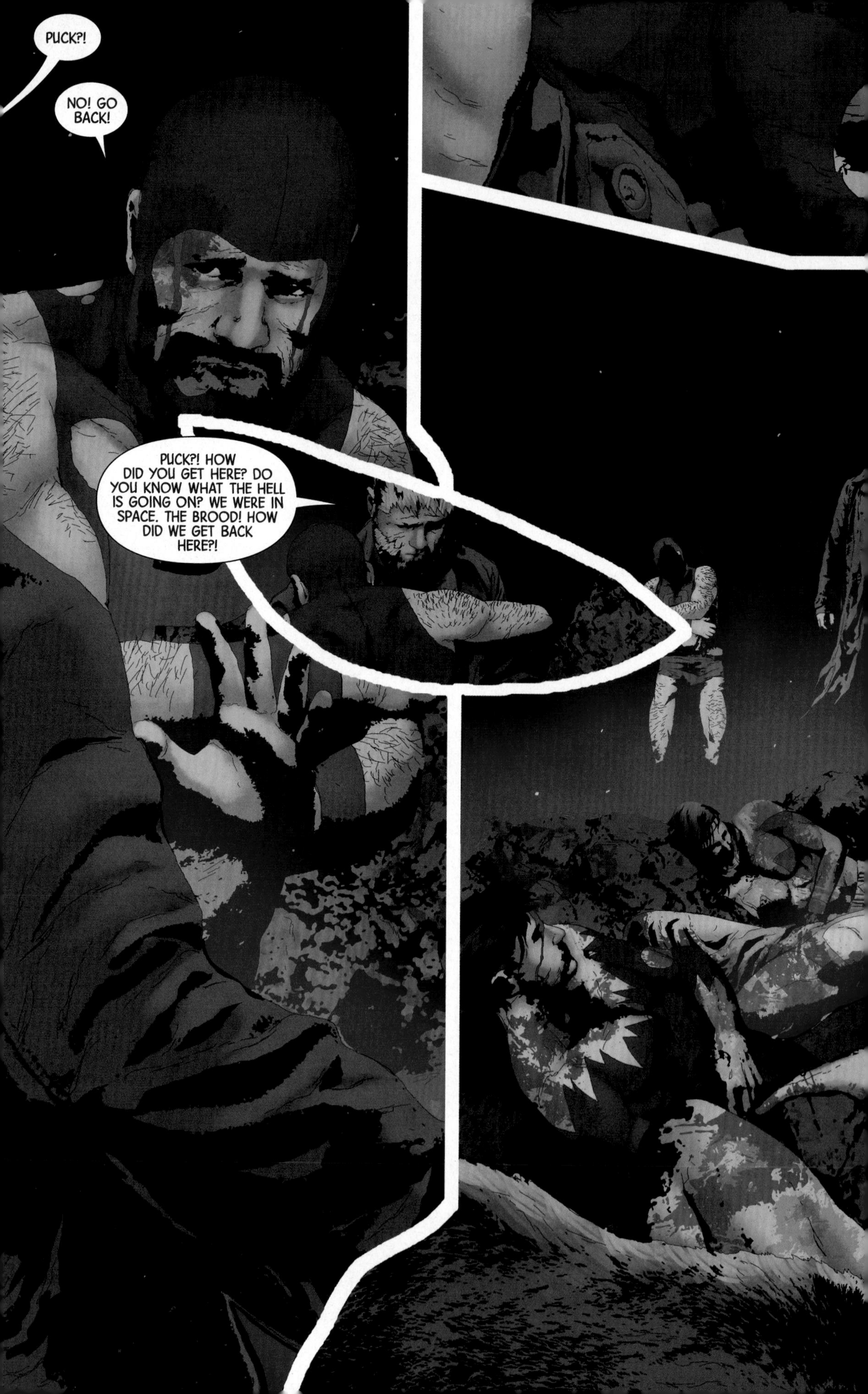
PUCK?!
NO! GO BACK!
PUCK?! HOW DID YOU GET HERE? DO YOU KNOW WHAT THE HELL IS GOING ON? WE WERE IN SPACE. THE BROOD! HOW DID WE GET BACK HERE?!

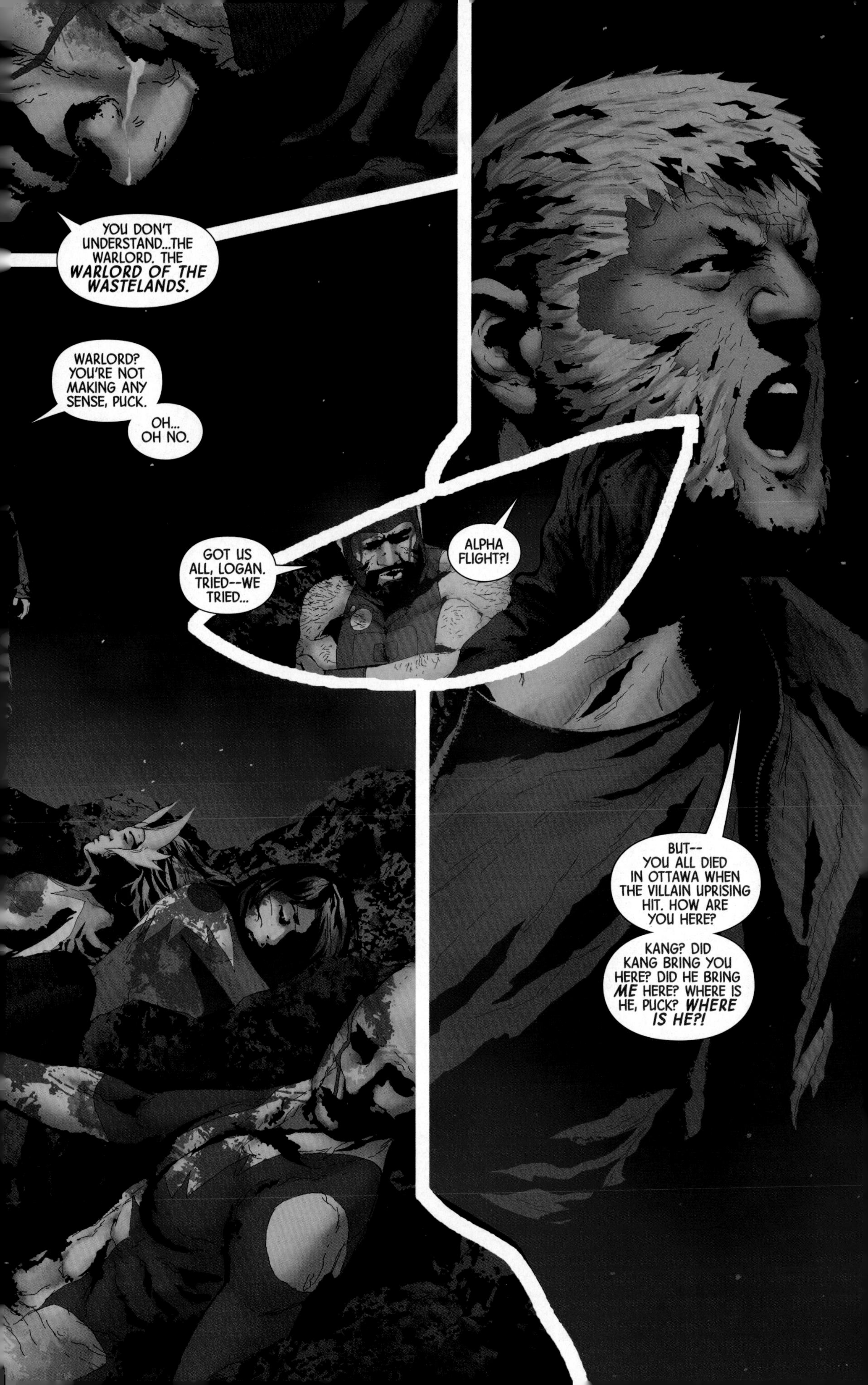
YOU DON'T UNDERSTAND...THE WARLORD. THE *WARLORD OF THE WASTELANDS.*
WARLORD? YOU'RE NOT MAKING ANY SENSE, PUCK.
OH... OH NO.
GOT US ALL, LOGAN. TRIED--WE TRIED...
ALPHA FLIGHT?!
BUT-- YOU ALL DIED IN OTTAWA WHEN THE VILLAIN UPRISING HIT. HOW ARE YOU HERE?
KANG? DID KANG BRING YOU HERE? DID HE BRING *ME* HERE? WHERE IS HE, PUCK? *WHERE IS HE?!*

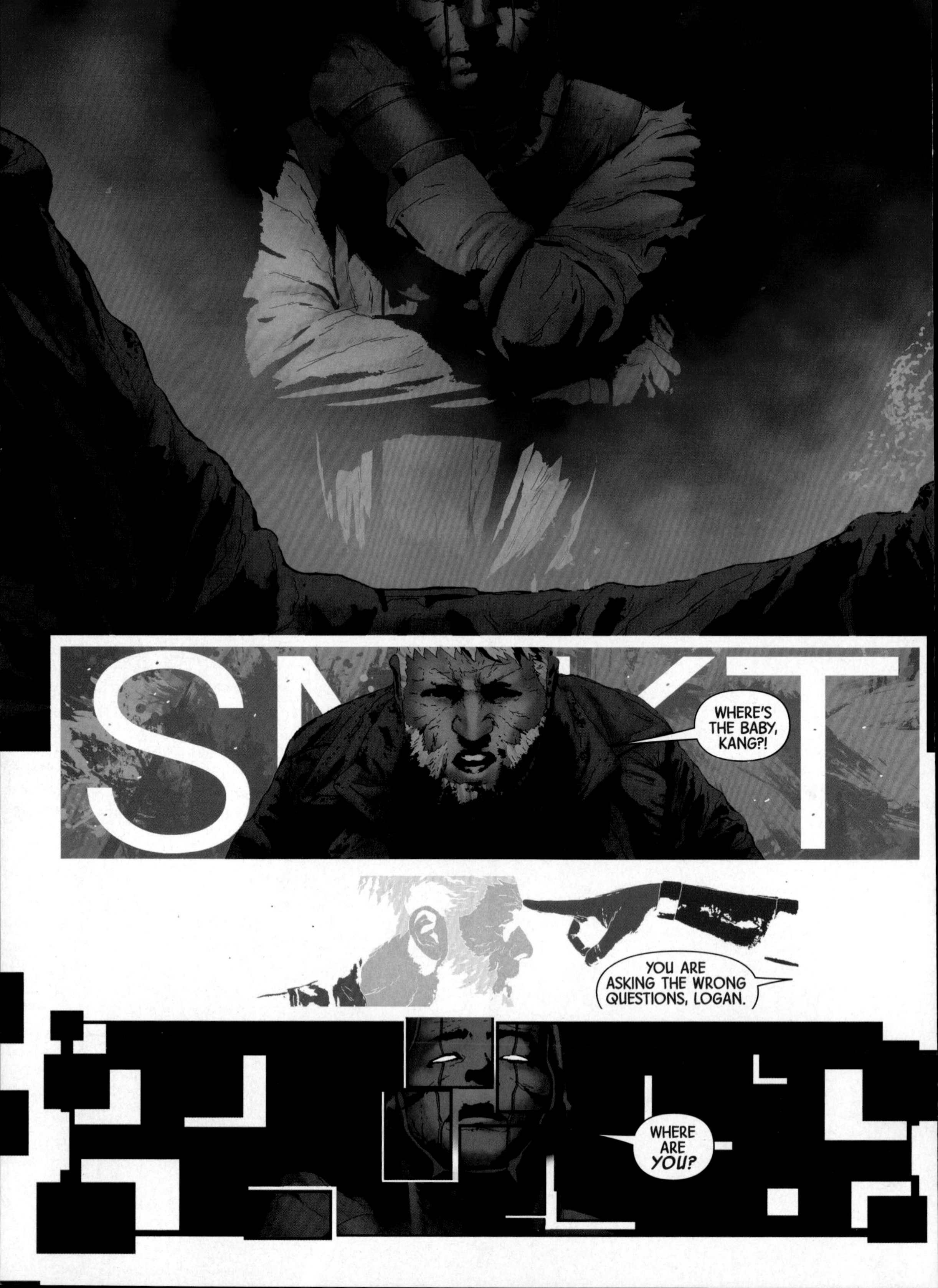
WHERE'S THE BABY, KANG?!
YOU ARE ASKING THE WRONG QUESTIONS, LOGAN.
WHERE ARE *YOU*?

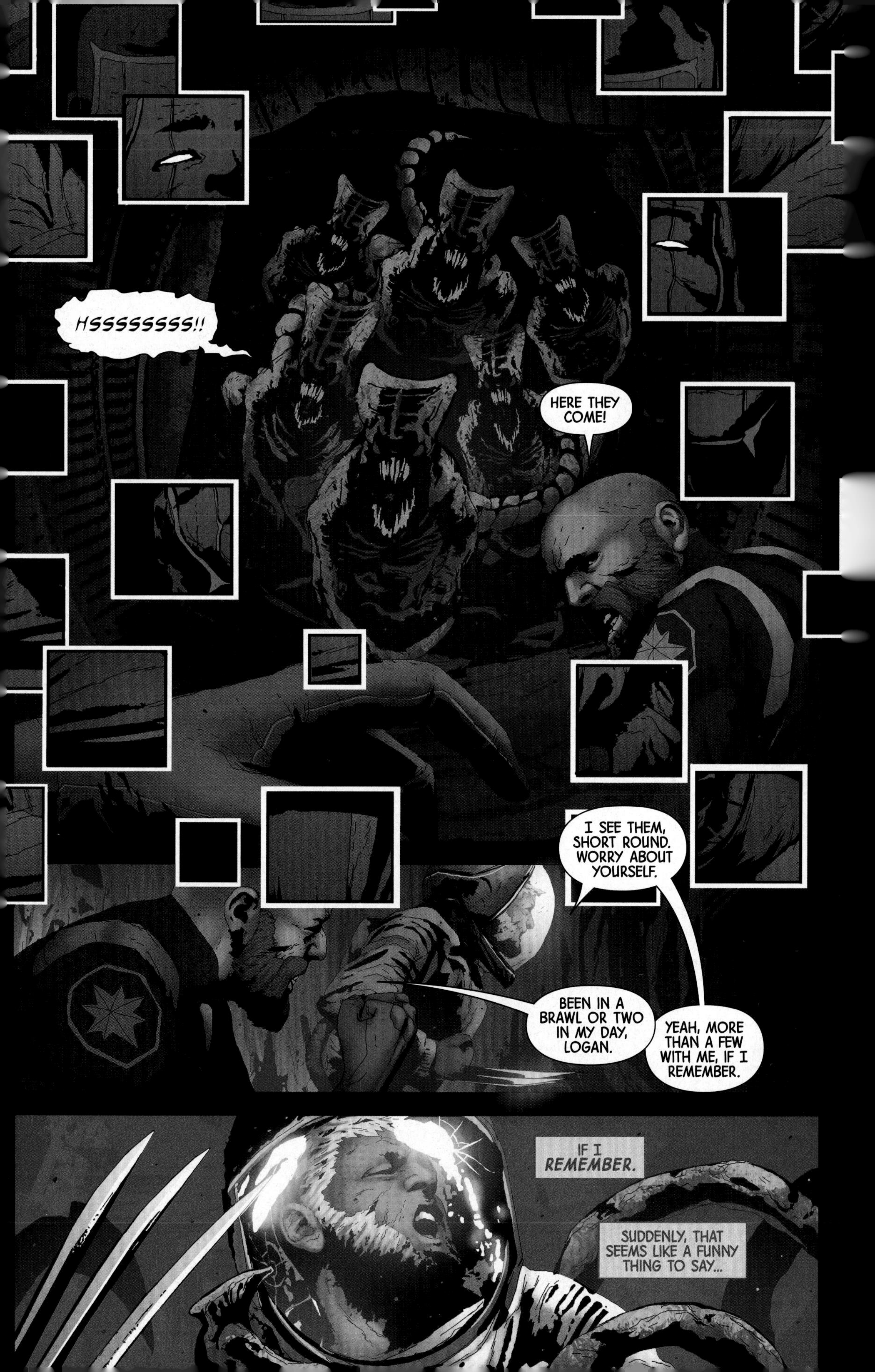
HSSSSSSSS!!
HERE THEY COME!
I SEE THEM, SHORT ROUND. WORRY ABOUT YOURSELF.
BEEN IN A BRAWL OR TWO IN MY DAY, LOGAN.
YEAH, MORE THAN A FEW WITH ME, IF I REMEMBER.
IF I *REMEMBER*.
SUDDENLY, THAT SEEMS LIKE A FUNNY THING TO SAY...

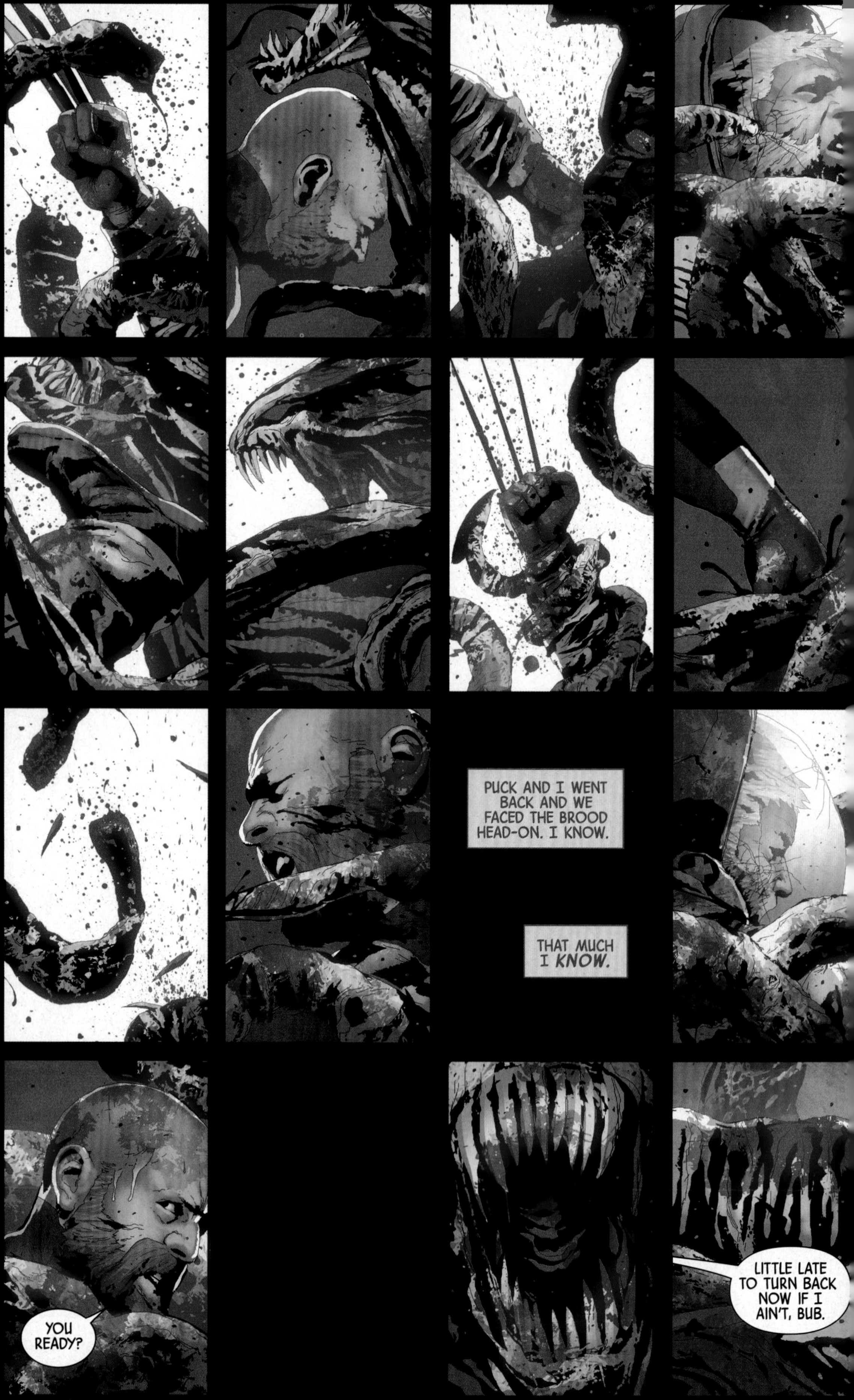
PUCK AND I WENT BACK AND WE FACED THE BROOD HEAD-ON. I KNOW.
THAT MUCH I KNOW.
YOU READY?
LITTLE LATE TO TURN BACK NOW IF I AIN'T, BUB.

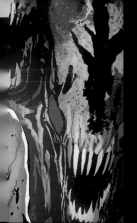

I--I KNOW I'M FORGETTING *SOMETHING* ABOUT HOW ALL THIS WENT DOWN.

KEEP PUSHING FORWARD! BRAND AND SASQUATCH ARE ON THE MAIN DECK!

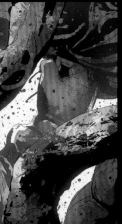

THERE WERE SO MANY OF THEM. JUST KEPT COMING AND WE JUST KEPT SLICING AND DICING. PUSHING FORWARD DOWN THE CORRIDOR.

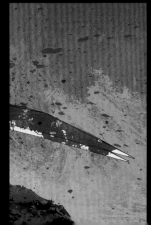

GOOD POINT... BUB.

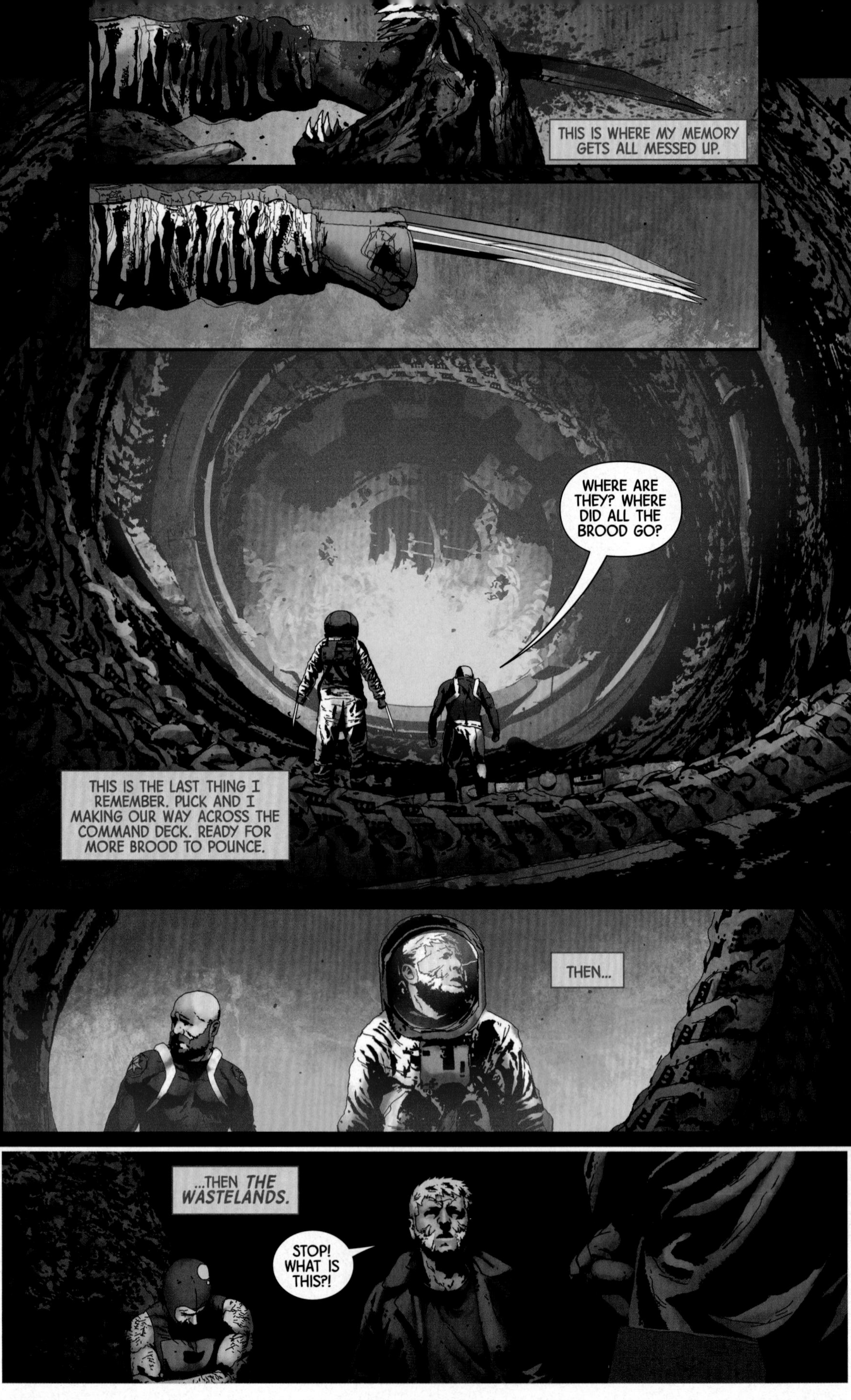

THIS IS WHERE MY MEMORY GETS ALL MESSED UP.
WHERE ARE THEY? WHERE DID ALL THE BROOD GO?
THIS IS THE LAST THING I REMEMBER. PUCK AND I MAKING OUR WAY ACROSS THE COMMAND DECK. READY FOR MORE BROOD TO POUNCE.
THEN...
...THEN THE WASTELANDS.
STOP! WHAT IS THIS?!

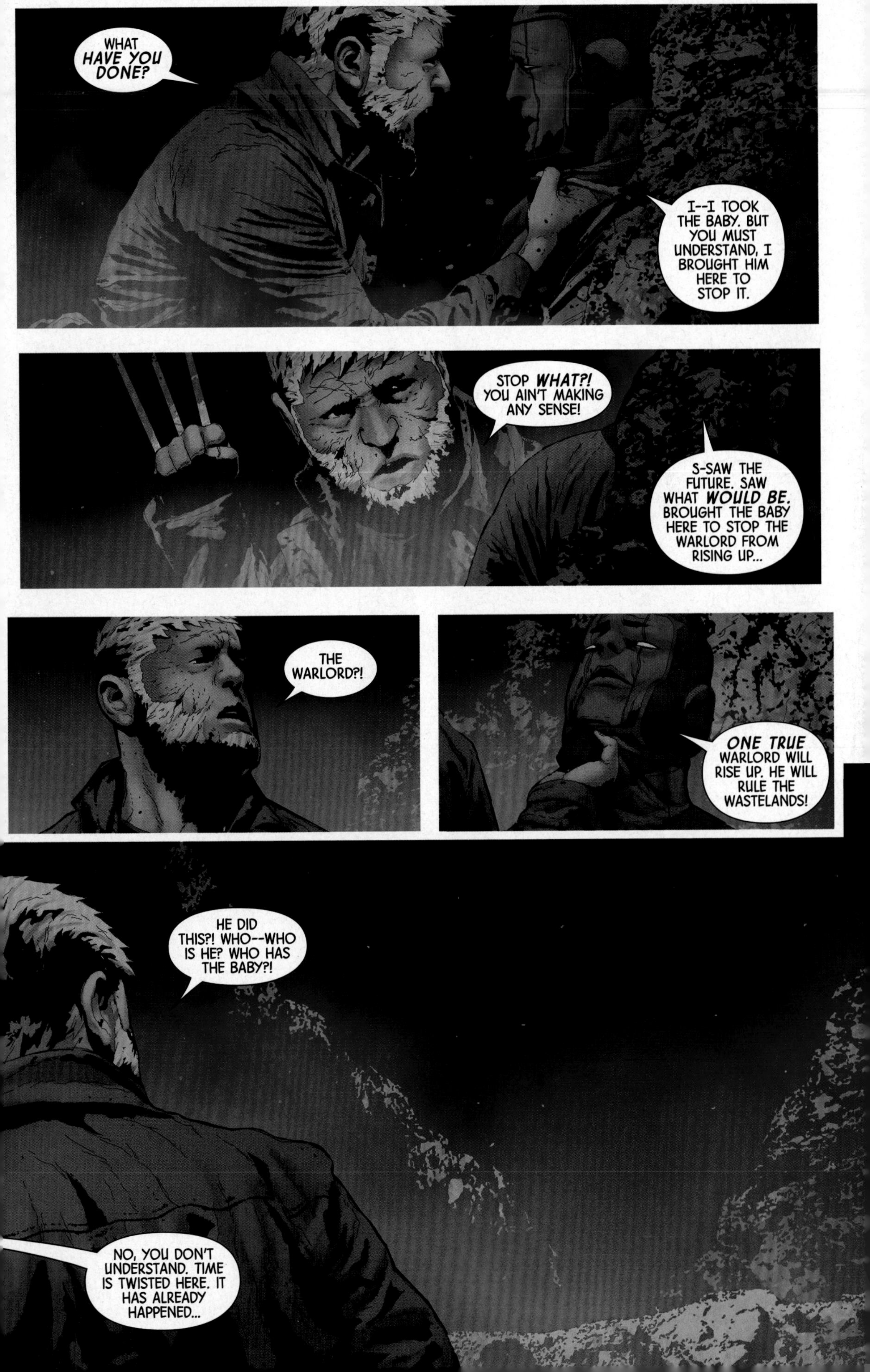
WHAT *HAVE YOU* DONE?
I--I TOOK THE BABY. BUT YOU MUST UNDERSTAND, I BROUGHT HIM HERE TO STOP IT.
STOP *WHAT?!* YOU AIN'T MAKING ANY SENSE!
S-SAW THE FUTURE. SAW WHAT *WOULD BE.* BROUGHT THE BABY HERE TO STOP THE WARLORD FROM RISING UP...
THE WARLORD?!
ONE TRUE WARLORD WILL RISE UP. HE WILL RULE THE WASTELANDS!
HE DID THIS?! WHO--WHO IS HE? WHO HAS THE BABY?!
NO, YOU DON'T UNDERSTAND. TIME IS TWISTED HERE. IT HAS ALREADY HAPPENED...

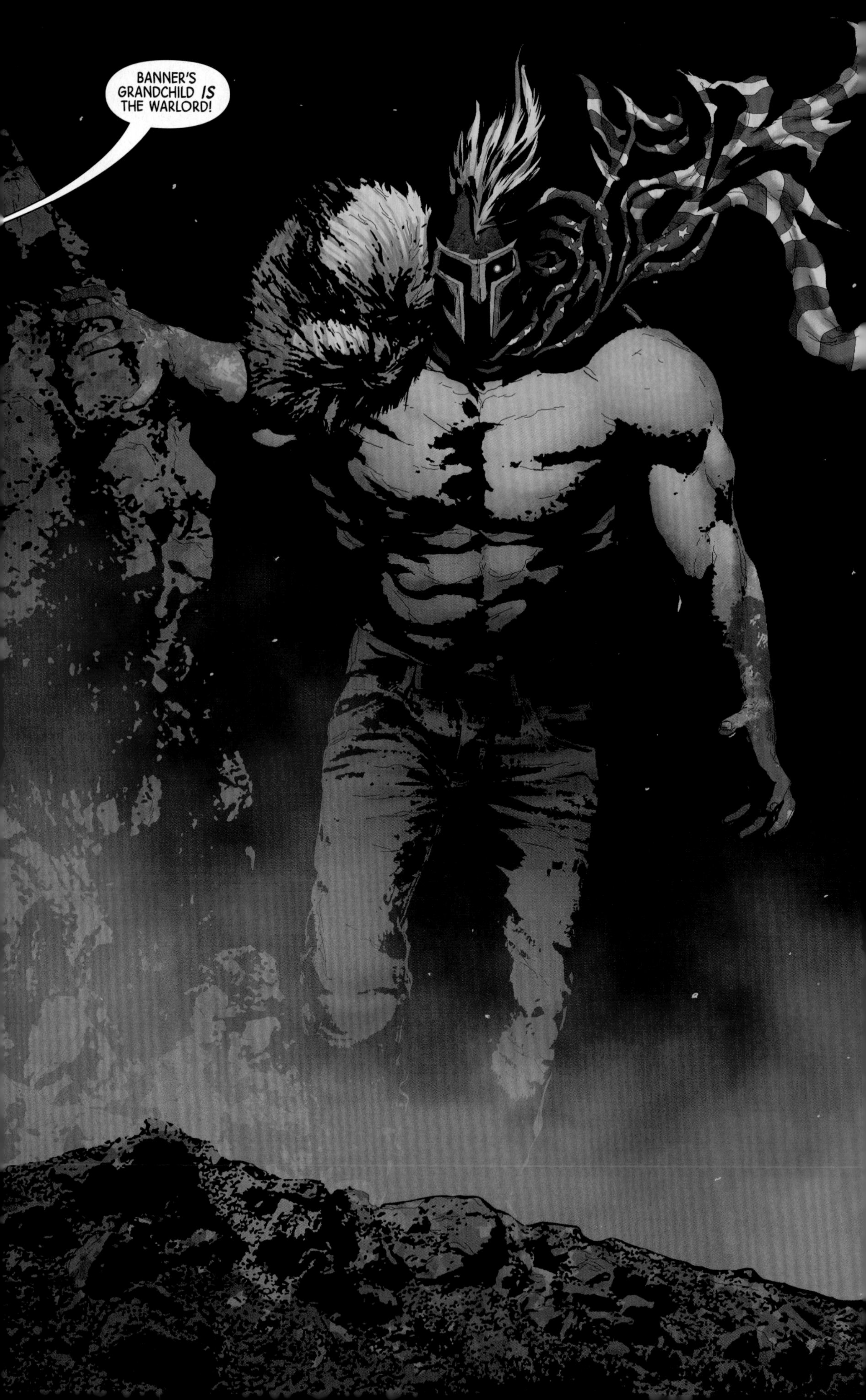
BANNER'S GRANDCHILD *IS* THE WARLORD!

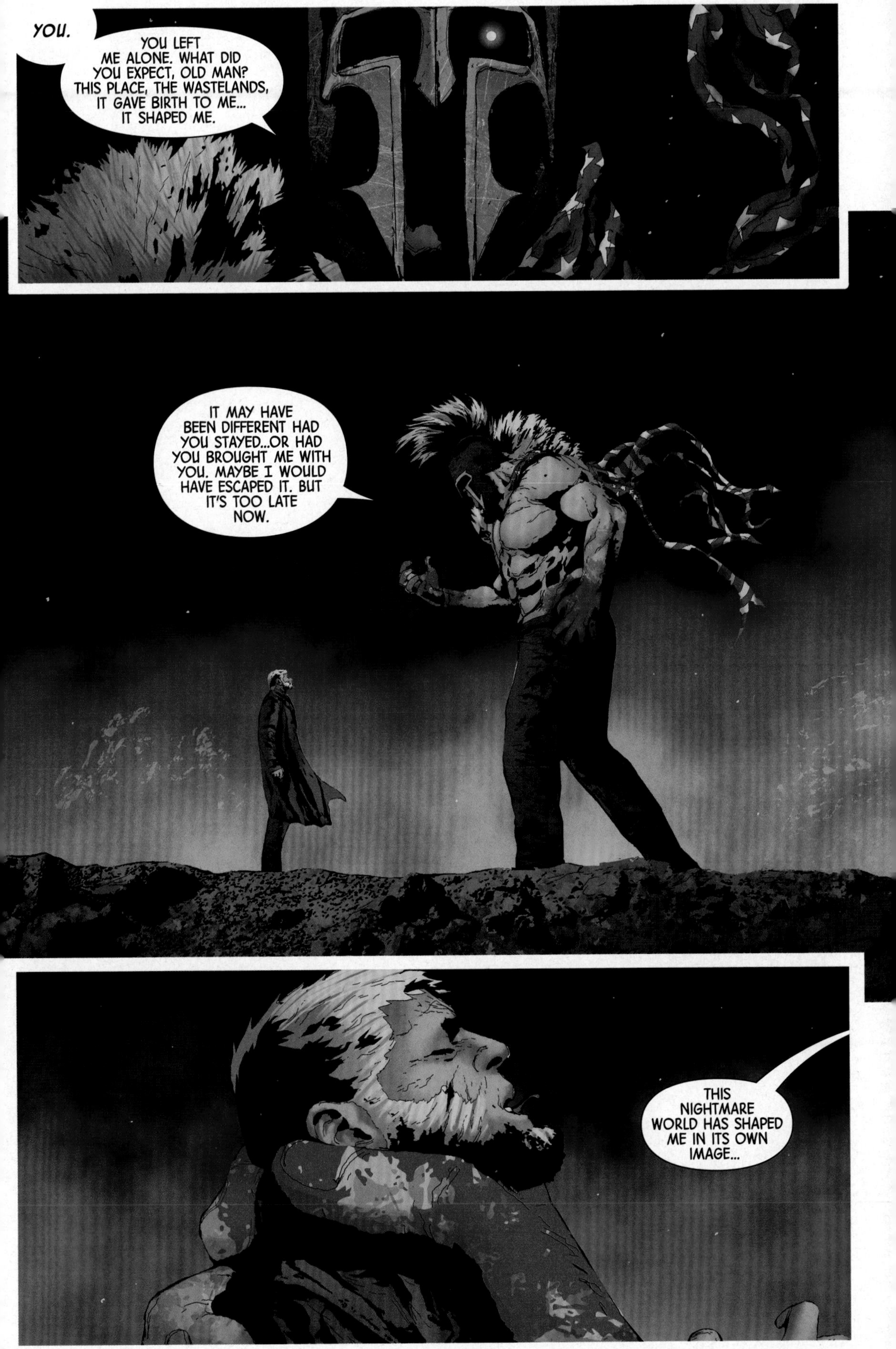
YOU.
YOU LEFT ME ALONE. WHAT DID YOU EXPECT, OLD MAN? THIS PLACE, THE WASTELANDS, IT GAVE BIRTH TO ME... IT SHAPED ME.
IT MAY HAVE BEEN DIFFERENT HAD YOU STAYED...OR HAD YOU BROUGHT ME WITH YOU. MAYBE I WOULD HAVE ESCAPED IT. BUT IT'S TOO LATE NOW.
THIS NIGHTMARE WORLD HAS SHAPED ME IN ITS OWN IMAGE...

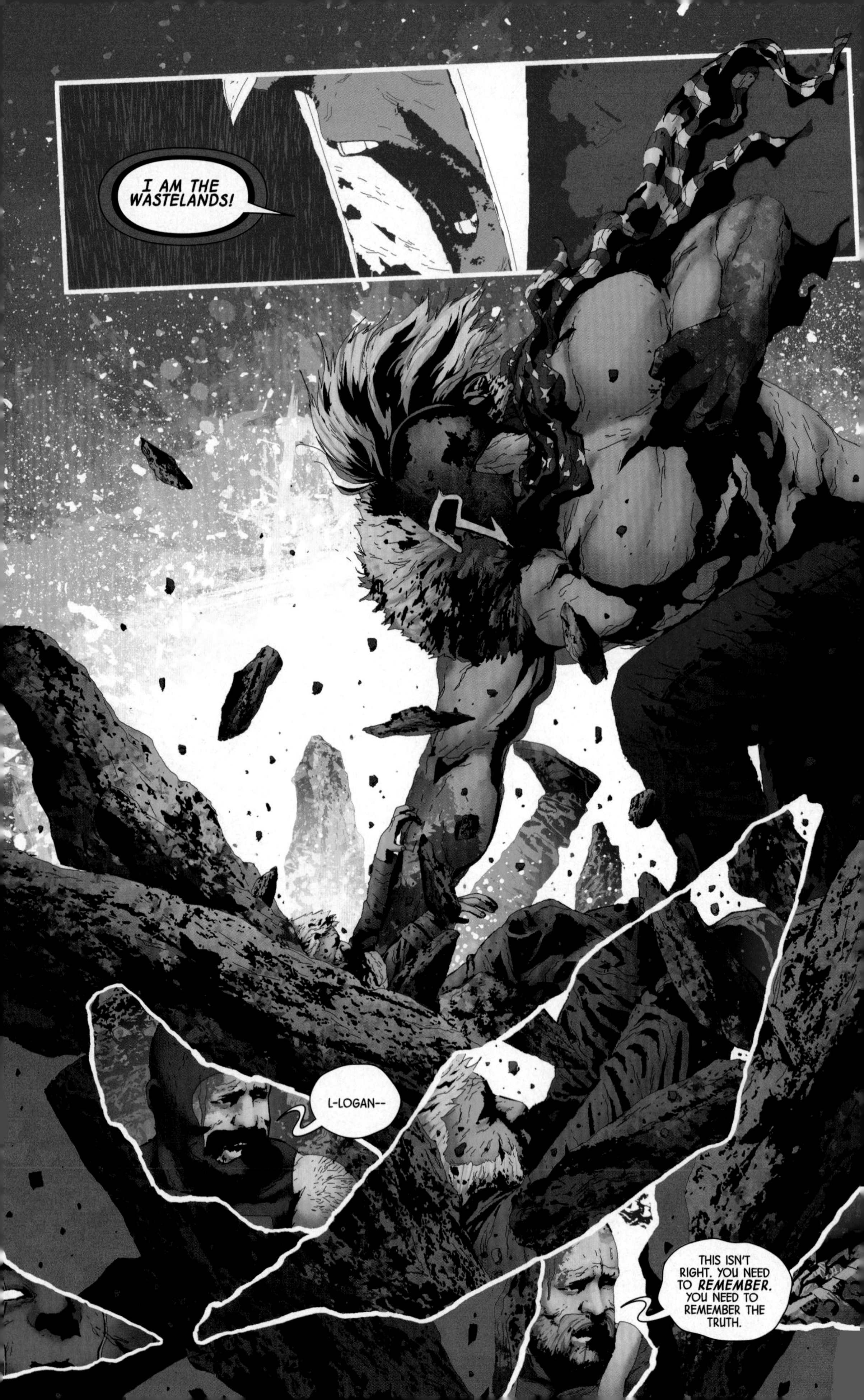
I AM THE WASTELANDS!
L-LOGAN--
THIS ISN'T RIGHT. YOU NEED TO REMEMBER. YOU NEED TO REMEMBER THE TRUTH.

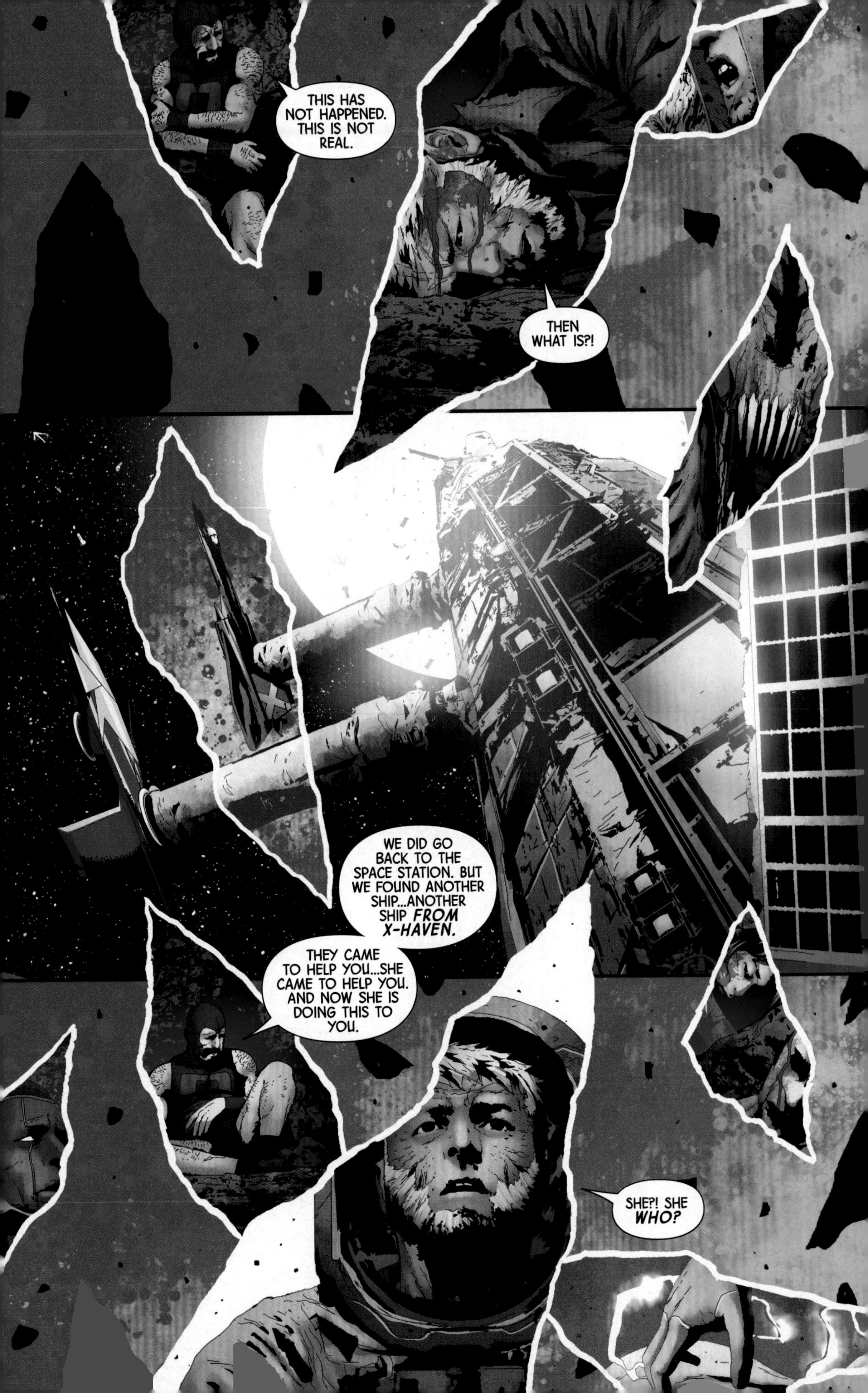
THIS HAS NOT HAPPENED. THIS IS NOT REAL.
THEN WHAT IS?!
WE DID GO BACK TO THE SPACE STATION. BUT WE FOUND ANOTHER SHIP...ANOTHER SHIP FROM X-HAVEN.
THEY CAME TO HELP YOU...SHE CAME TO HELP YOU. AND NOW SHE IS DOING THIS TO YOU.
SHE?! SHE WHO?

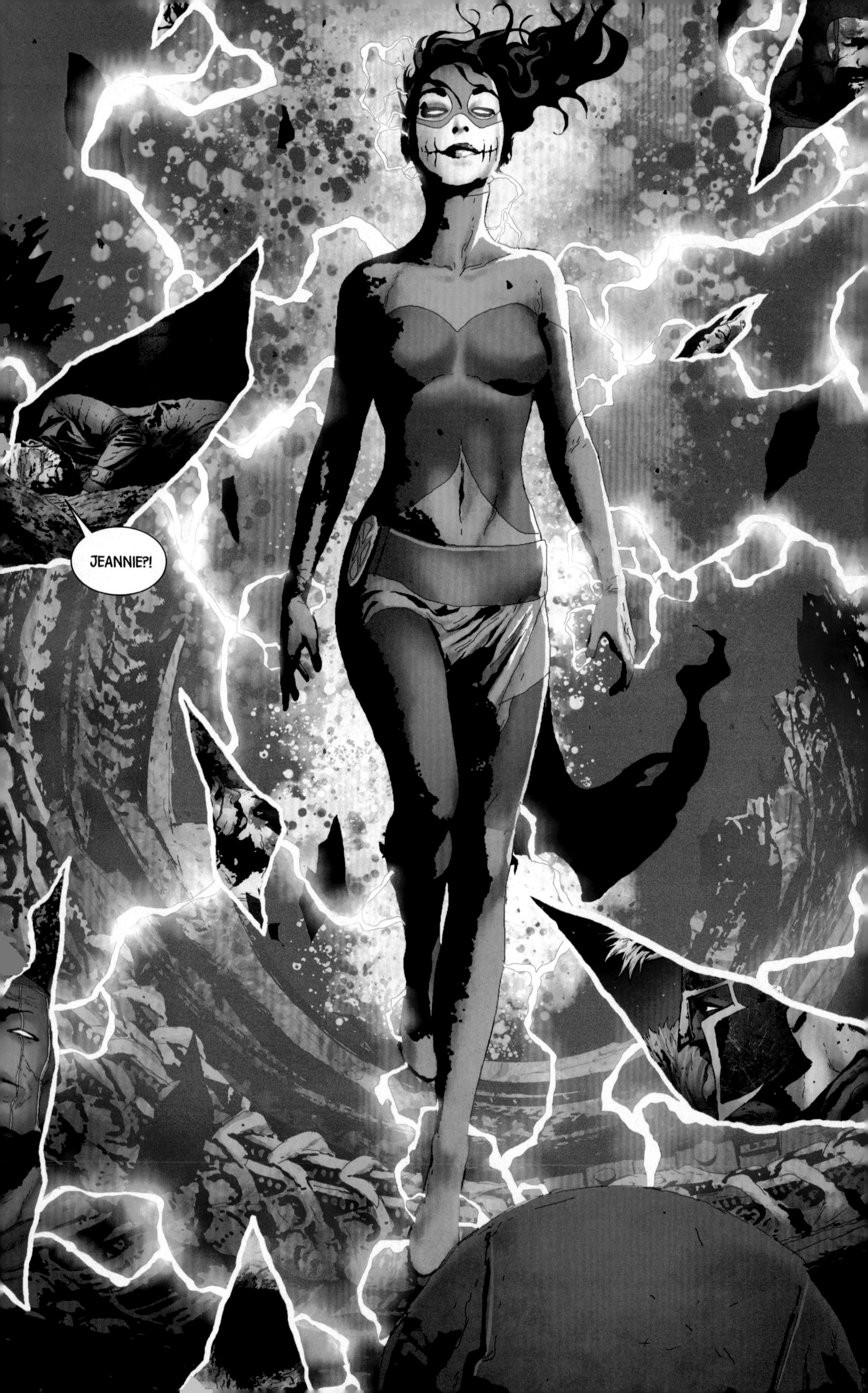
JEANNIE?!

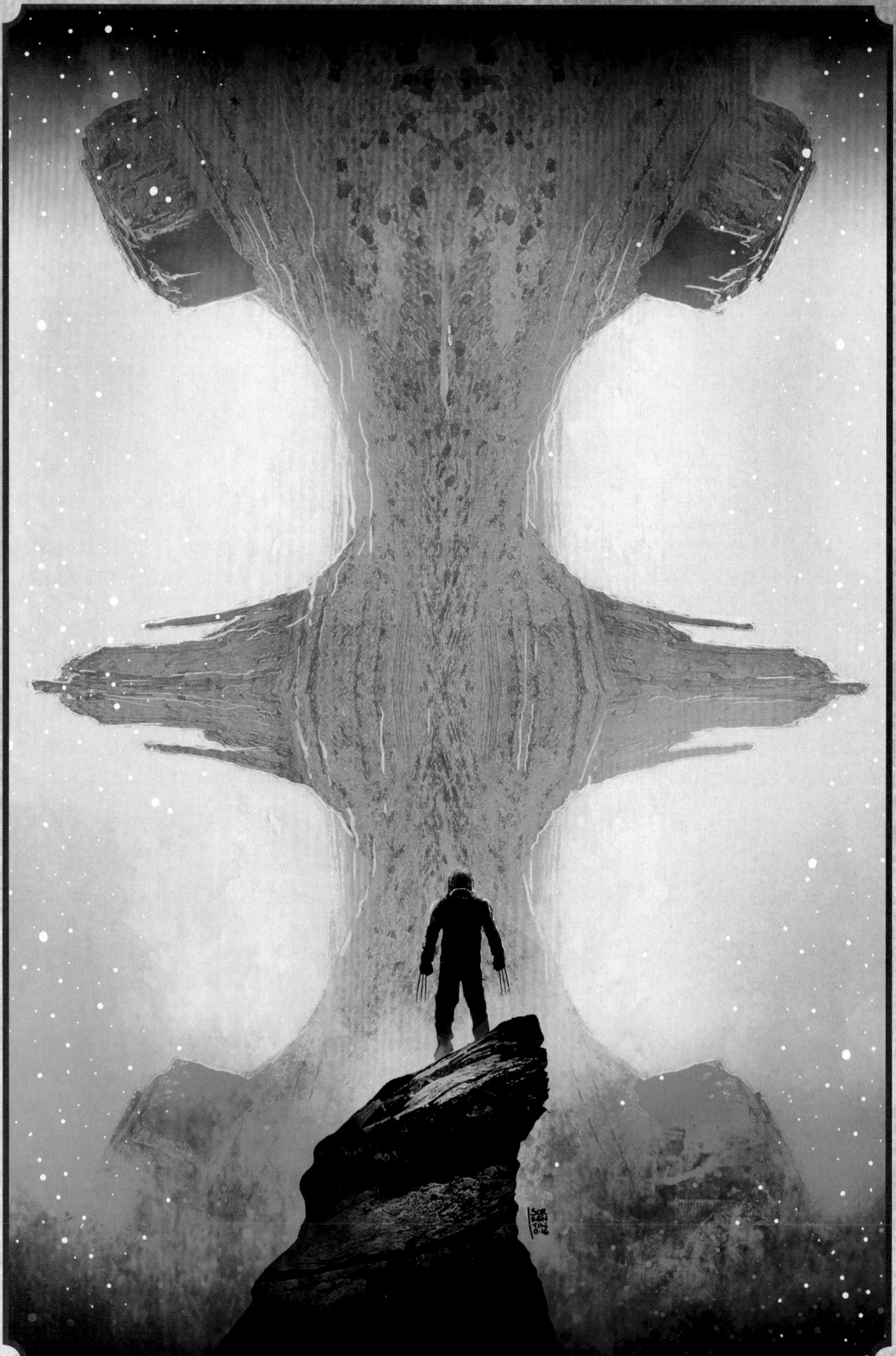

18

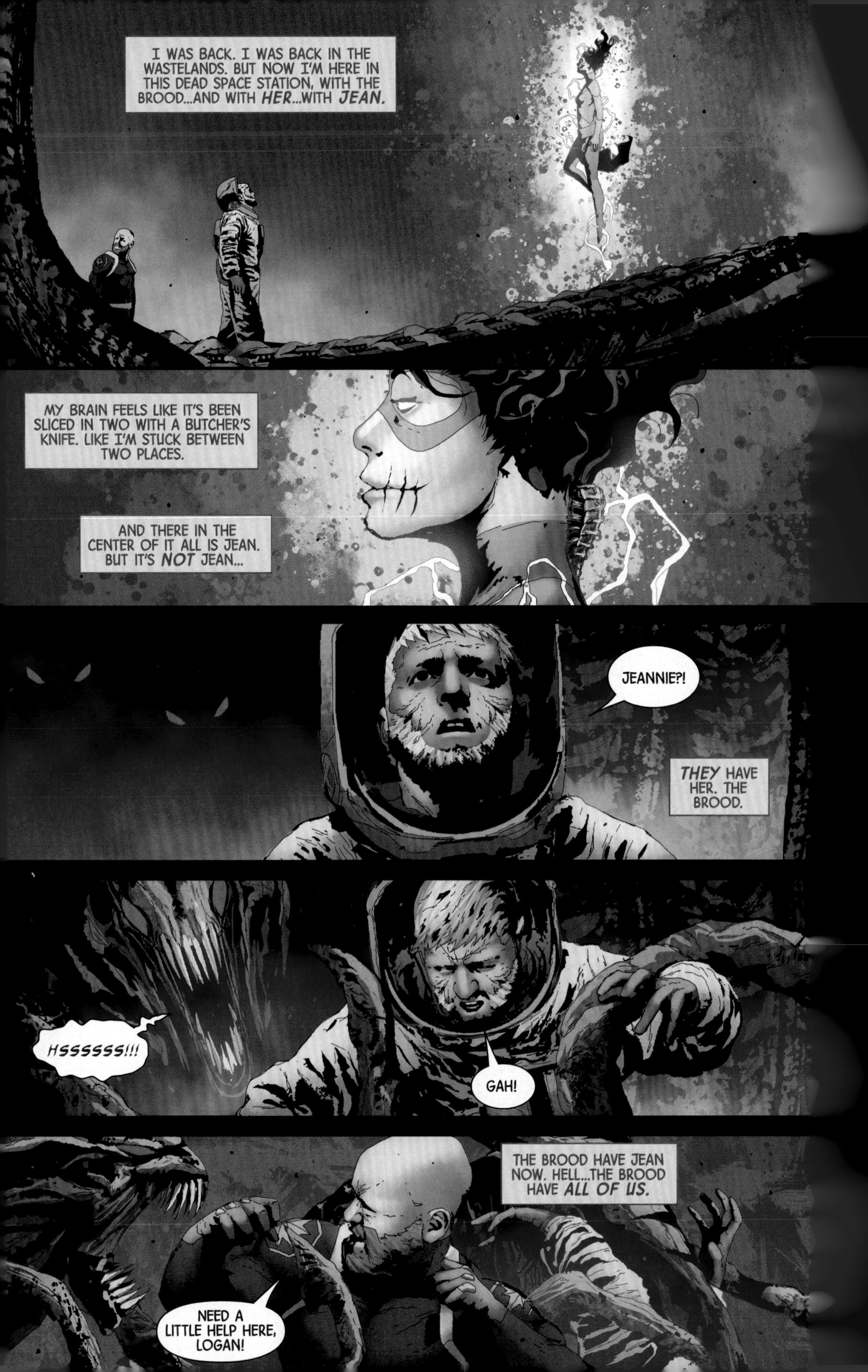
I WAS BACK. I WAS BACK IN THE WASTELANDS. BUT NOW I'M HERE IN THIS DEAD SPACE STATION, WITH THE BROOD...AND WITH *HER*...WITH *JEAN.*
MY BRAIN FEELS LIKE IT'S BEEN SLICED IN TWO WITH A BUTCHER'S KNIFE. LIKE I'M STUCK BETWEEN TWO PLACES.
AND THERE IN THE CENTER OF IT ALL IS JEAN. BUT IT'S *NOT* JEAN...
JEANNIE?!
THEY HAVE HER. THE BROOD.
HSSSSSS!!!
GAH!
THE BROOD HAVE JEAN NOW. HELL...THE BROOD HAVE *ALL OF US.*
NEED A LITTLE HELP HERE, LOGAN!

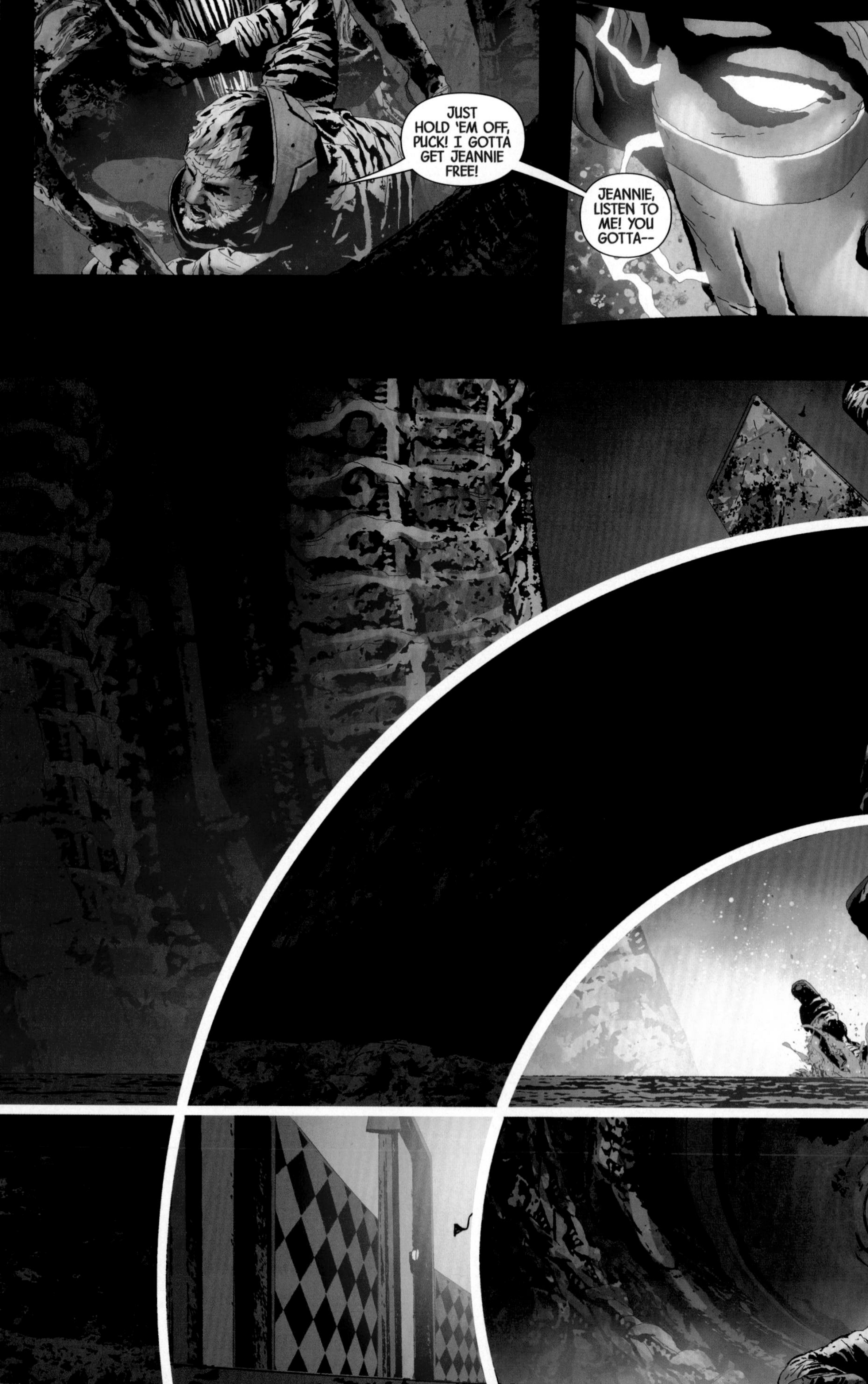
JUST HOLD 'EM OFF, PUCK! I GOTTA GET JEANNIE FREE!
JEANNIE, LISTEN TO ME! YOU GOTTA--

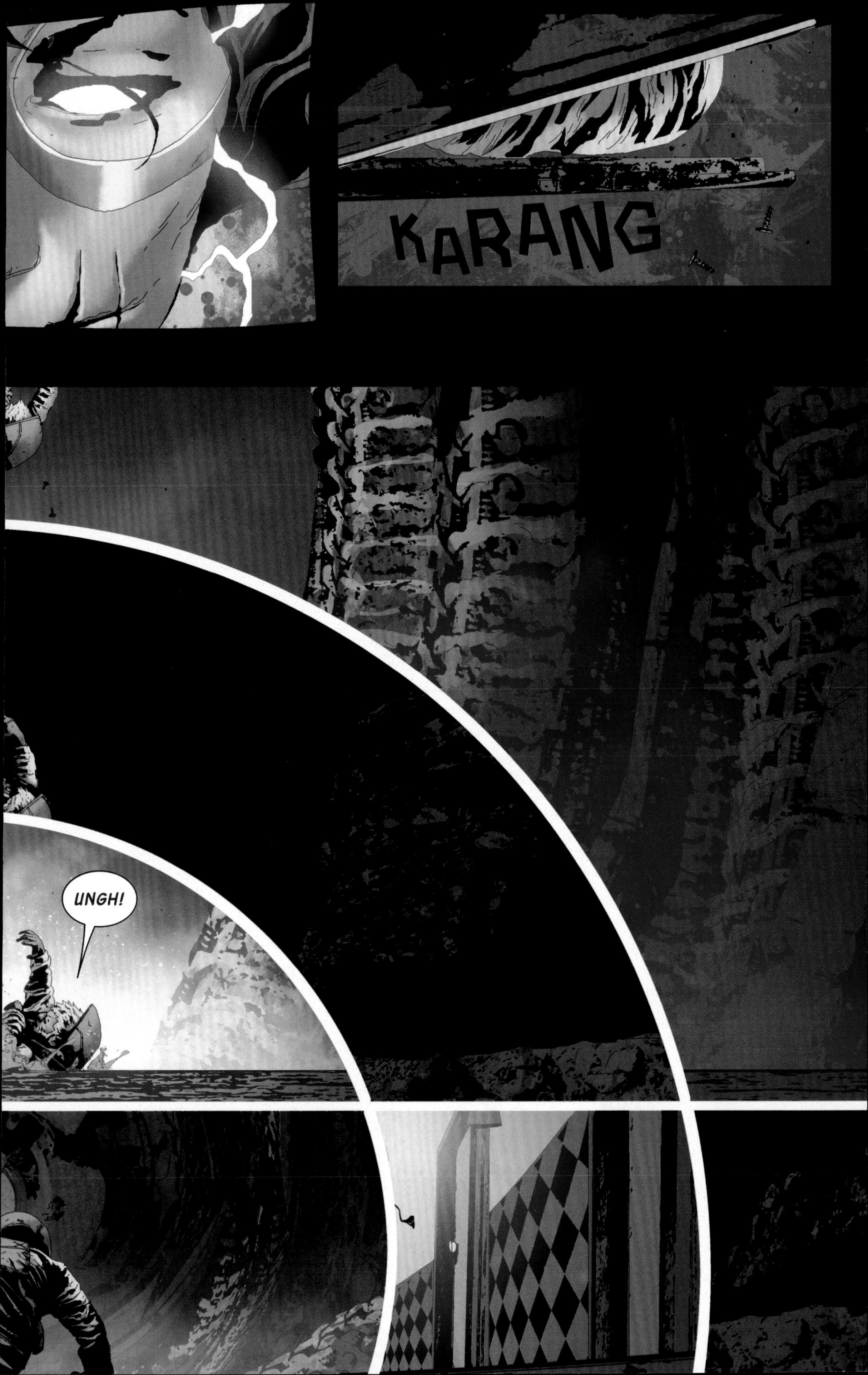
KARANG
UNGH!

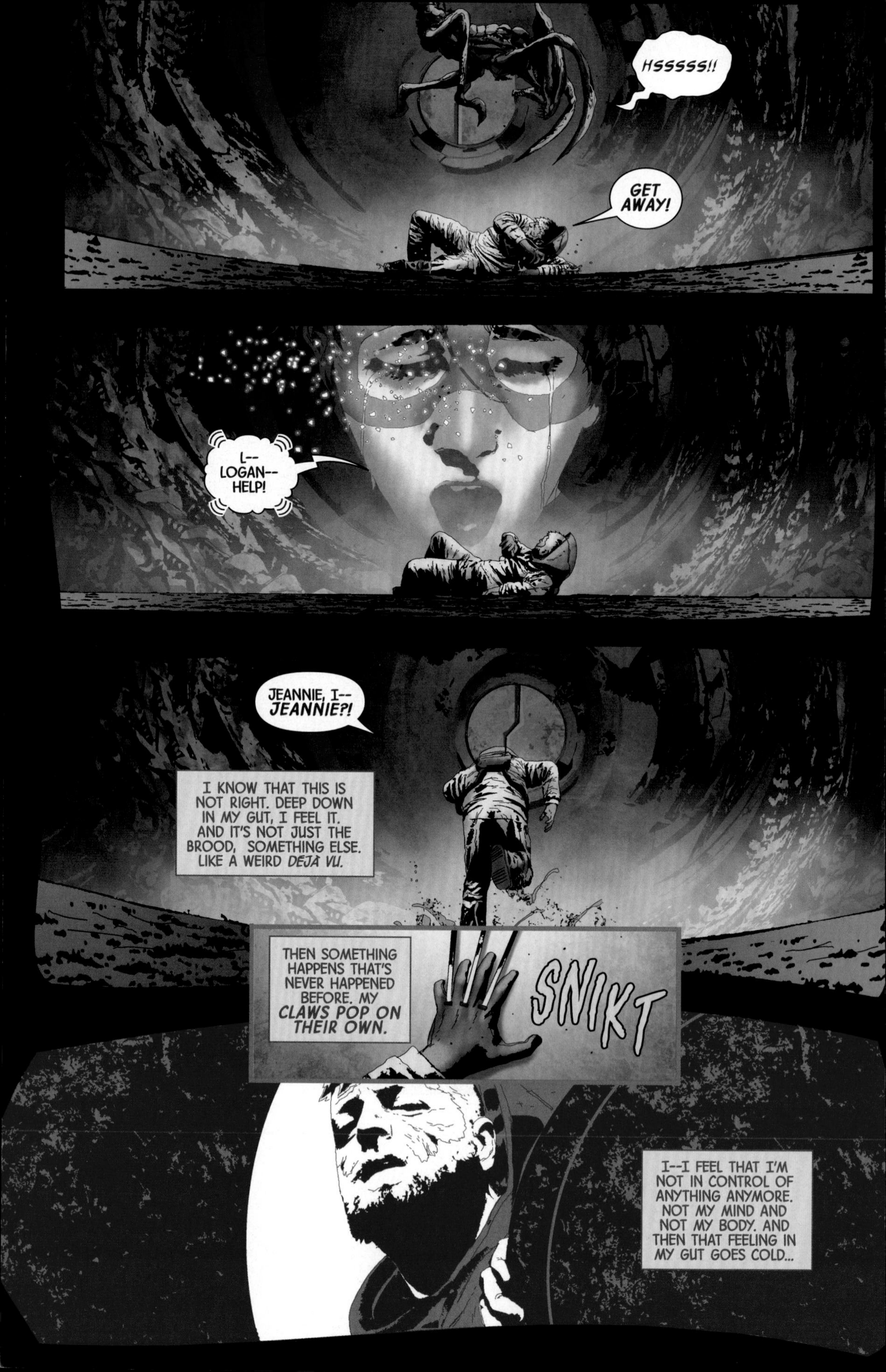
HSSSSS!!
GET AWAY!
L-- LOGAN-- HELP!
JEANNIE, I-- JEANNIE?!
I KNOW THAT THIS IS NOT RIGHT. DEEP DOWN IN MY GUT, I FEEL IT. AND IT'S NOT JUST THE BROOD, SOMETHING ELSE. LIKE A WEIRD DÉJÀ VU.
THEN SOMETHING HAPPENS THAT'S NEVER HAPPENED BEFORE. MY CLAWS POP ON THEIR OWN.
SNIKT
I--I FEEL THAT I'M NOT IN CONTROL OF ANYTHING ANYMORE. NOT MY MIND AND NOT MY BODY. AND THEN THAT FEELING IN MY GUT GOES COLD...

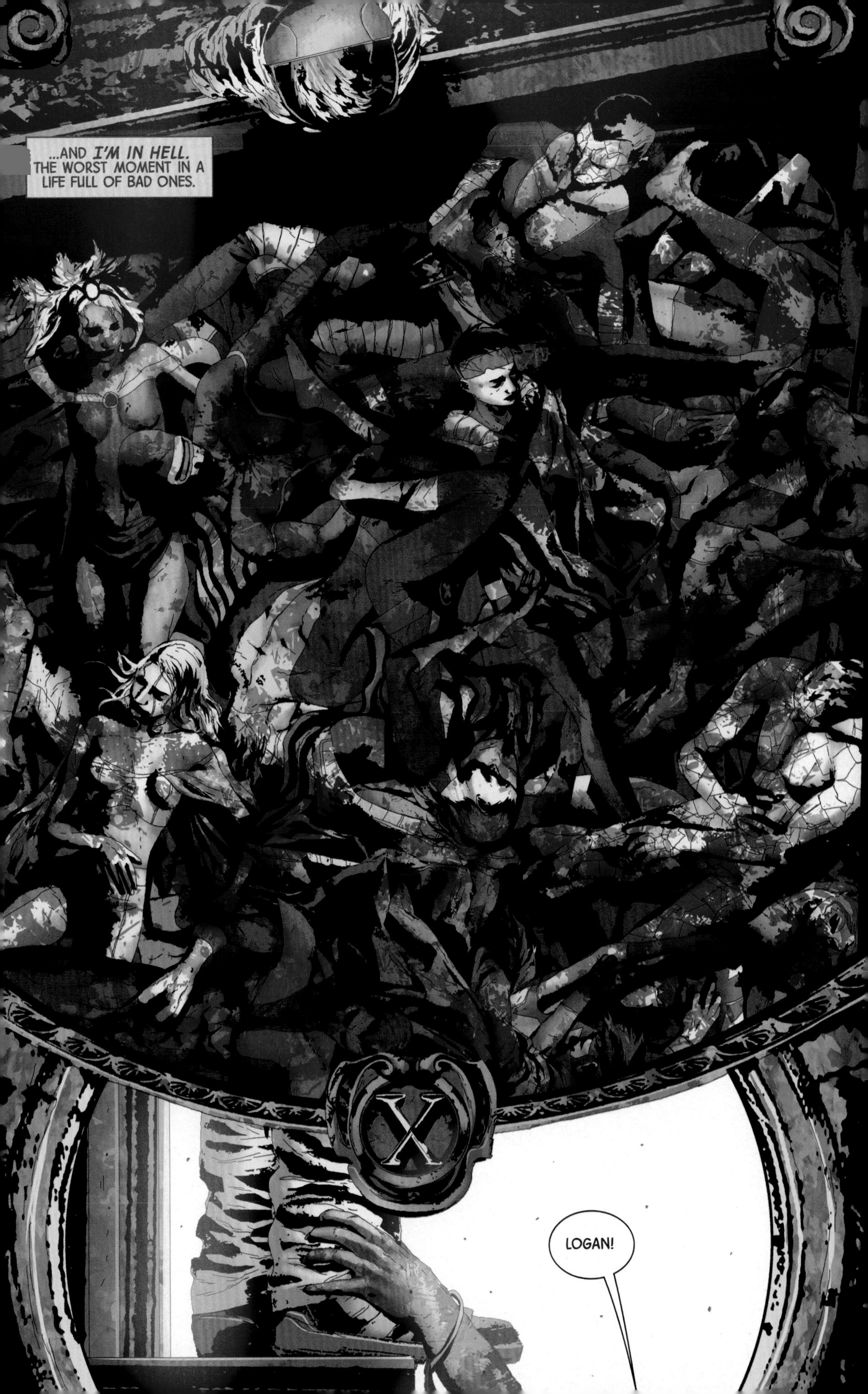
...AND I'M IN HELL. THE WORST MOMENT IN A LIFE FULL OF BAD ONES.
X
LOGAN!

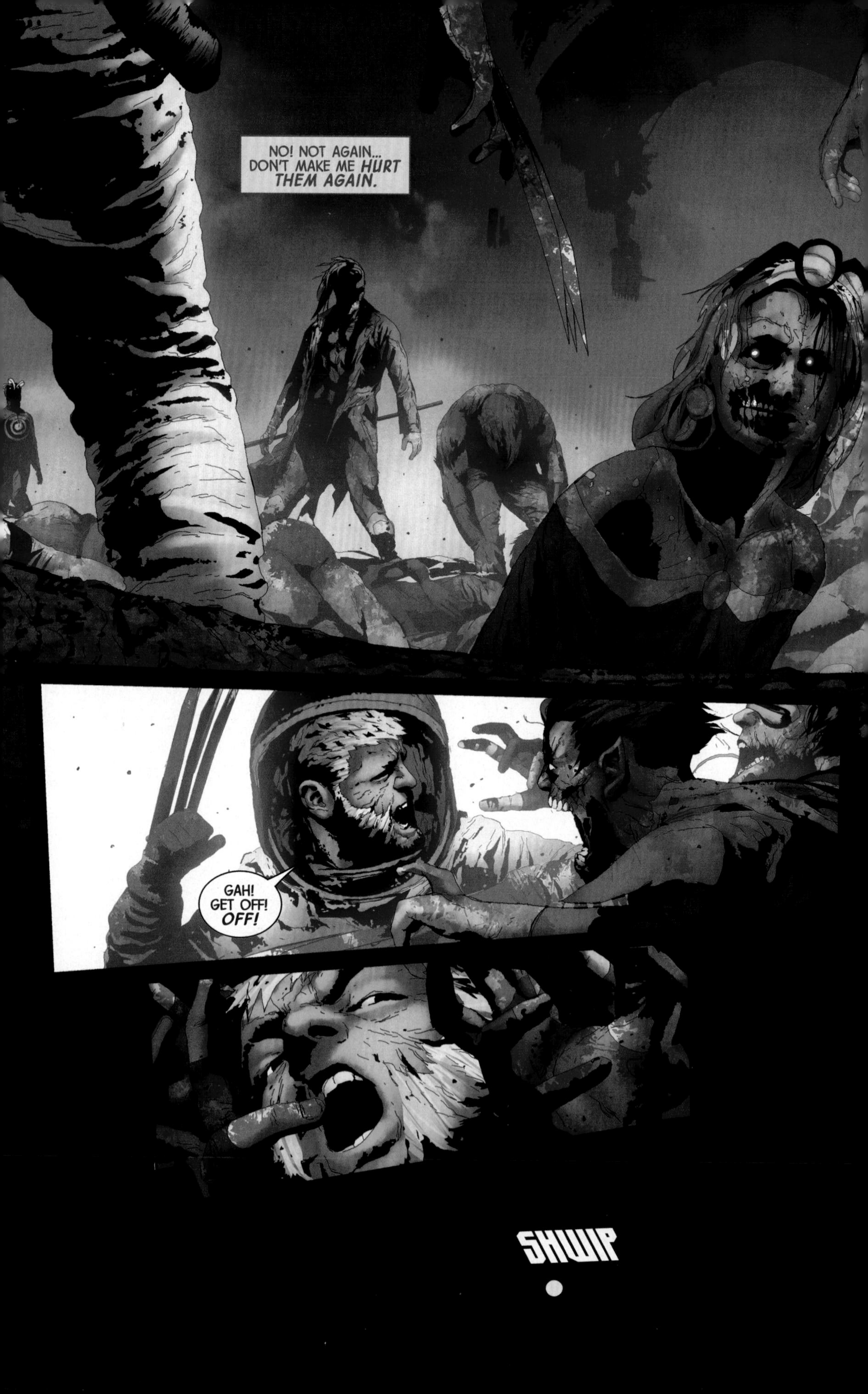
NO! NOT AGAIN... DON'T MAKE ME HURT THEM AGAIN.
GAH! GET OFF! OFF!
SHWIP

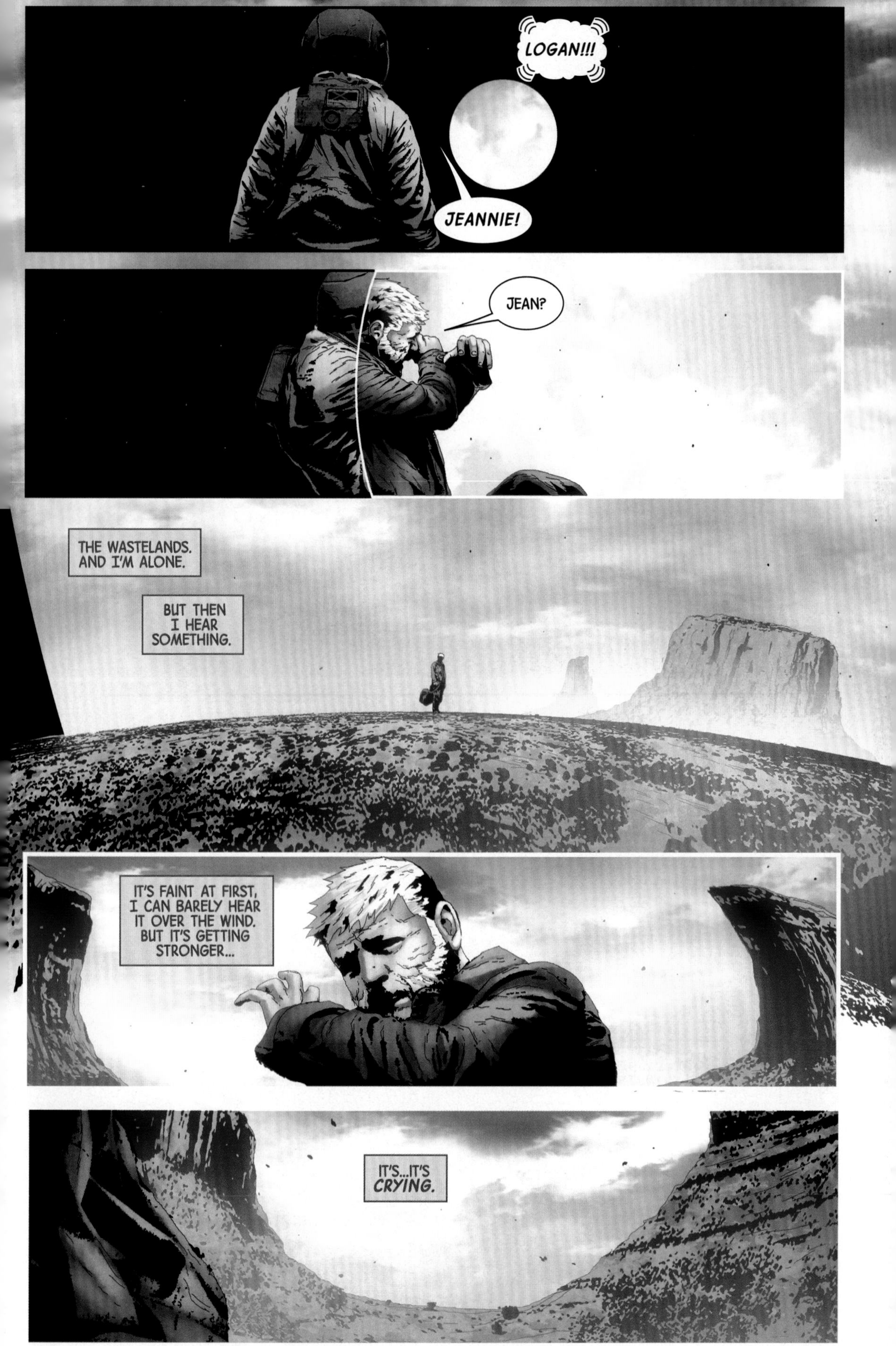
LOGAN!!!
JEANNIE!
JEAN?
THE WASTELANDS. AND I'M ALONE.
BUT THEN I HEAR SOMETHING.
IT'S FAINT AT FIRST, I CAN BARELY HEAR IT OVER THE WIND. BUT IT'S GETTING STRONGER...
IT'S...IT'S *CRYING.*

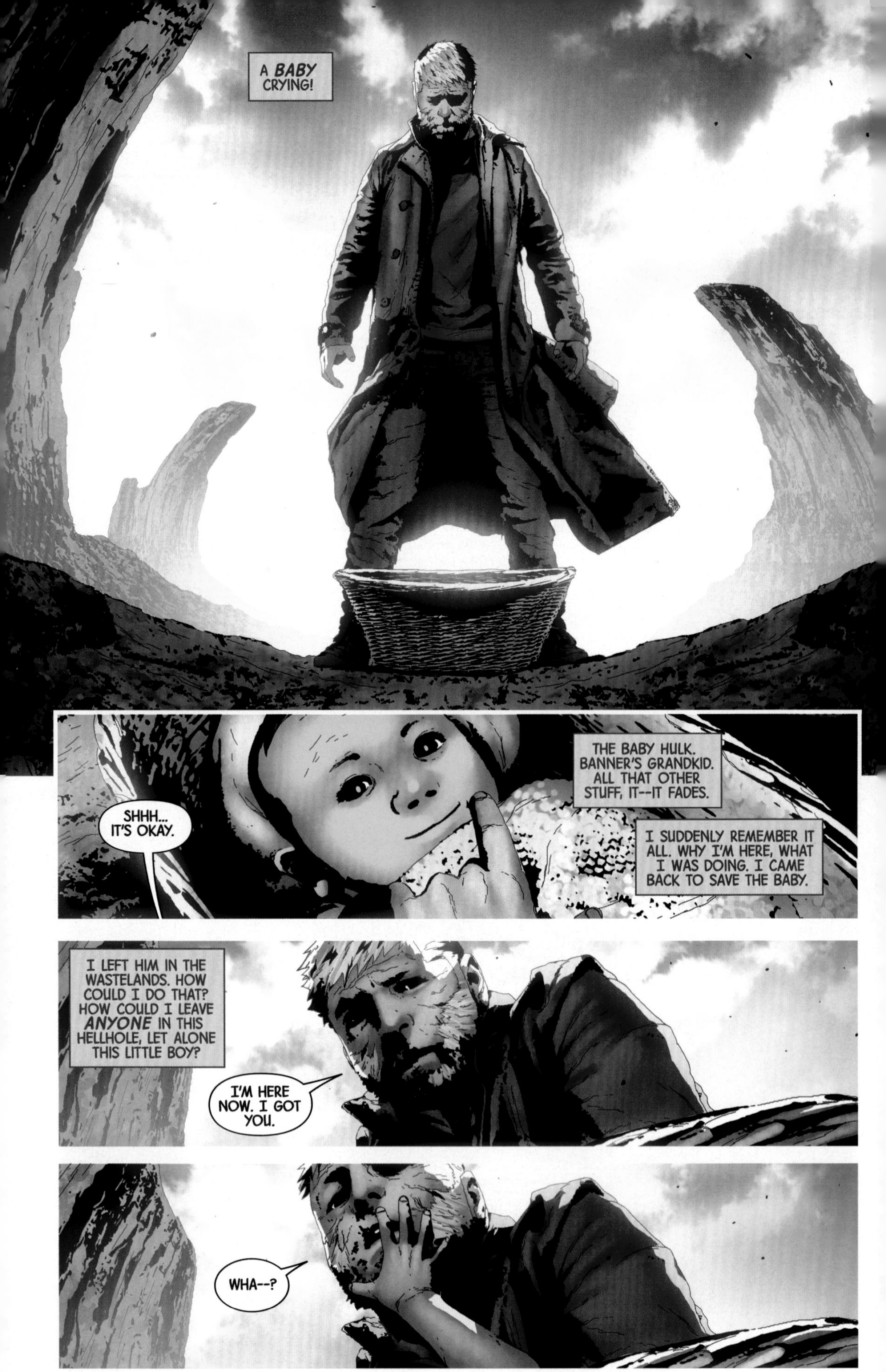
A *BABY* CRYING!
THE BABY HULK. BANNER'S GRANDKID. ALL THAT OTHER STUFF, IT--IT FADES.
SHHH... IT'S OKAY.
I SUDDENLY REMEMBER IT ALL. WHY I'M HERE, WHAT I WAS DOING. I CAME BACK TO SAVE THE BABY.
I LEFT HIM IN THE WASTELANDS. HOW COULD I DO THAT? HOW COULD I LEAVE *ANYONE* IN THIS HELLHOLE, LET ALONE THIS LITTLE BOY?
I'M HERE NOW. I GOT YOU.
WHA--?

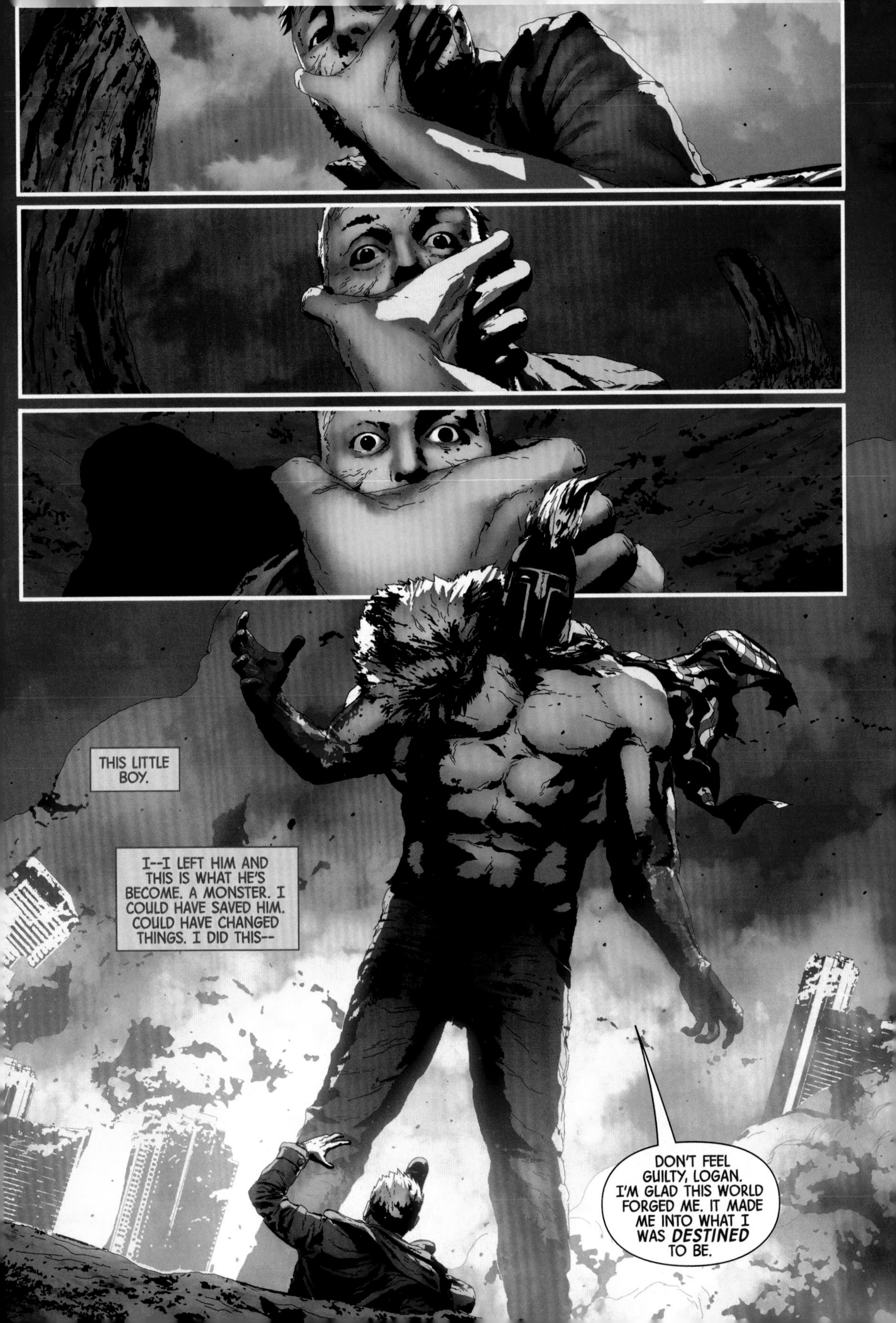
THIS LITTLE BOY.
I--I LEFT HIM AND THIS IS WHAT HE'S BECOME. A MONSTER. I COULD HAVE SAVED HIM. COULD HAVE CHANGED THINGS. I DID THIS--
DON'T FEEL GUILTY, LOGAN. I'M GLAD THIS WORLD FORGED ME. IT MADE ME INTO WHAT I WAS *DESTINED* TO BE.

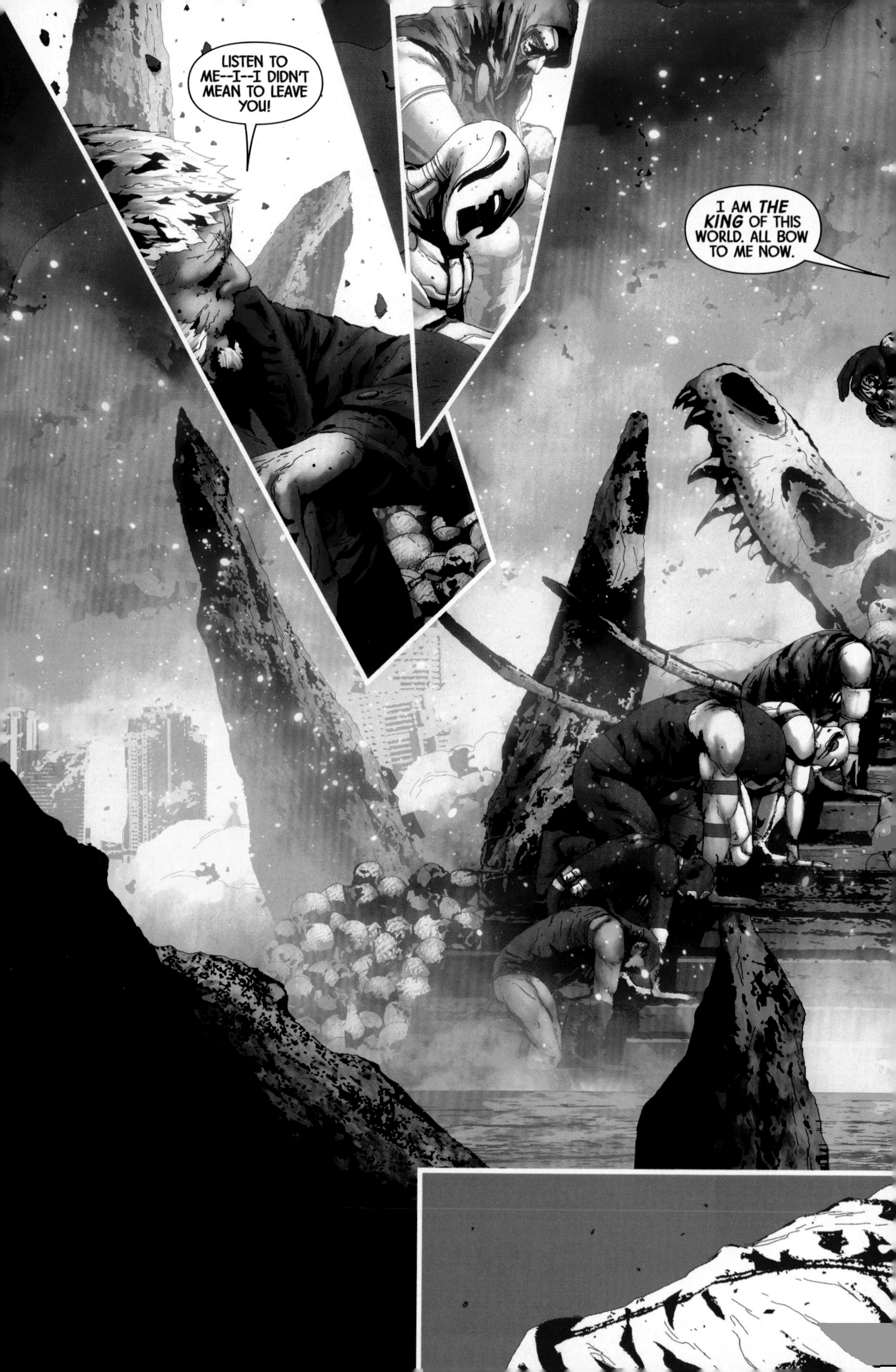
LISTEN TO ME--I--I DIDN'T MEAN TO LEAVE YOU!
I AM *THE KING* OF THIS WORLD. ALL BOW TO ME NOW.

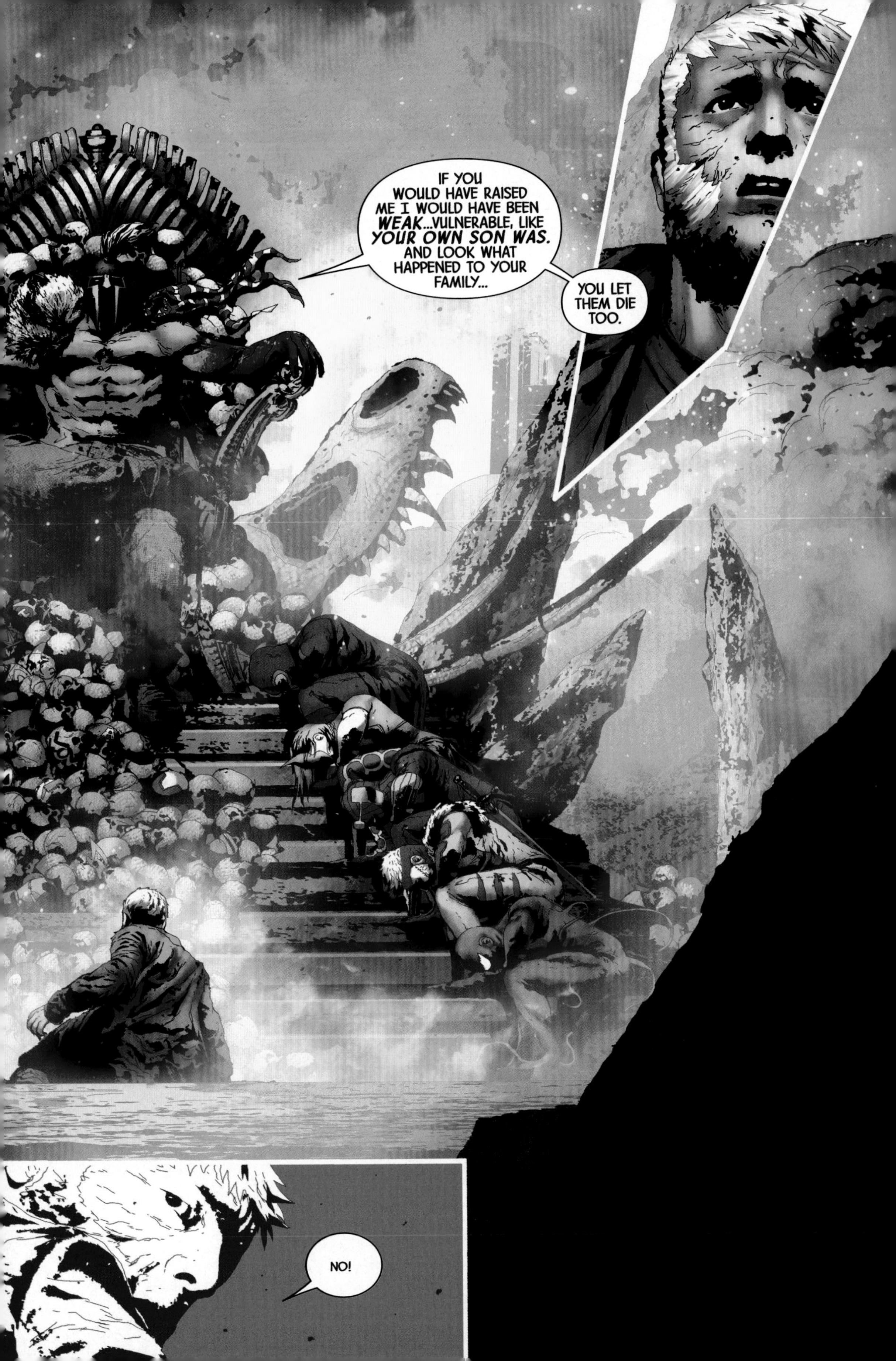
IF YOU WOULD HAVE RAISED ME I WOULD HAVE BEEN WEAK...VULNERABLE, LIKE YOUR OWN SON WAS. AND LOOK WHAT HAPPENED TO YOUR FAMILY...
YOU LET THEM DIE TOO.
NO!

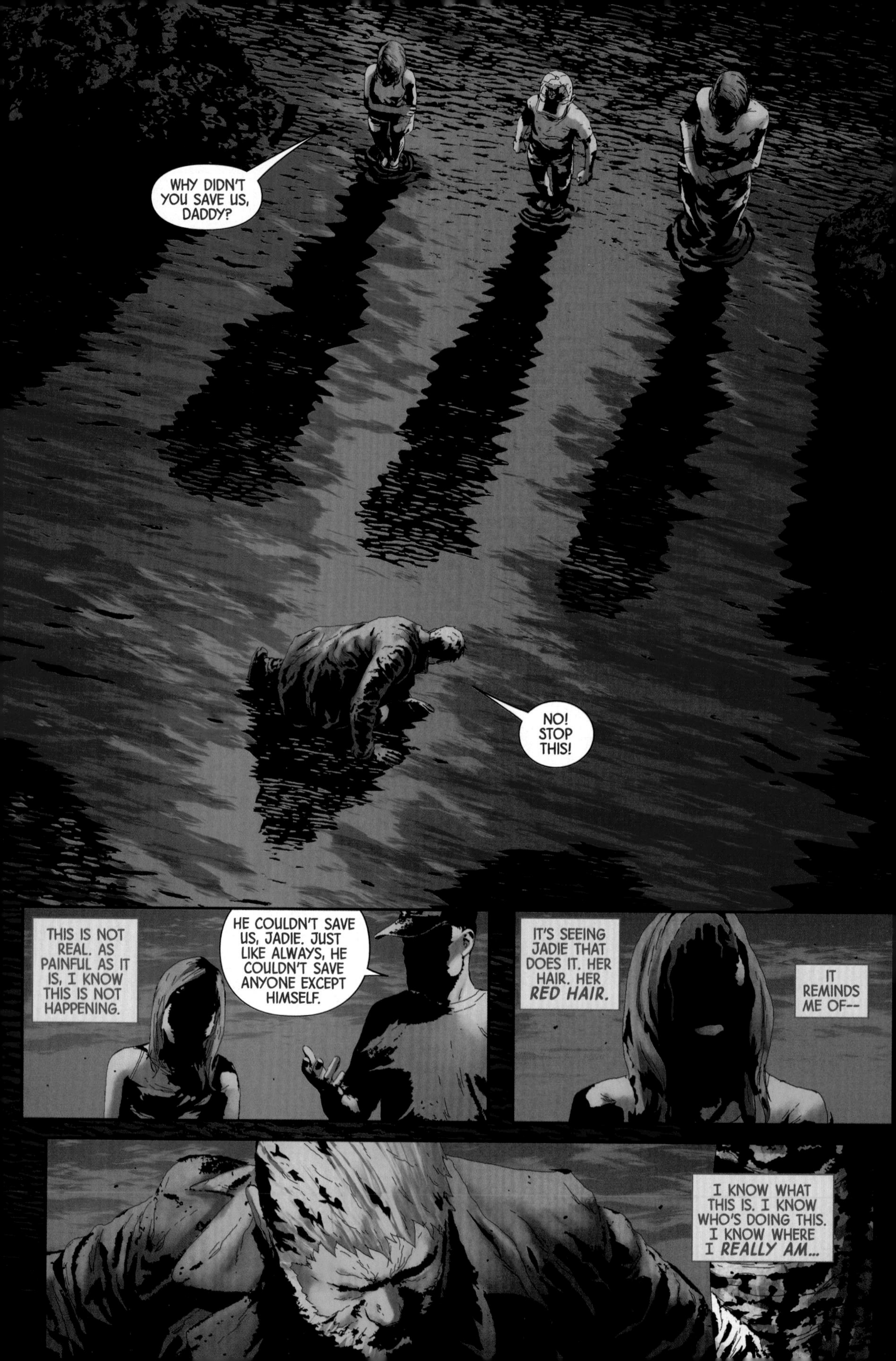

WHY DIDN'T YOU SAVE US, DADDY?
NO! STOP THIS!
THIS IS NOT REAL. AS PAINFUL AS IT IS, I KNOW THIS IS NOT HAPPENING.
HE COULDN'T SAVE US, JADIE. JUST LIKE ALWAYS, HE COULDN'T SAVE ANYONE EXCEPT HIMSELF.
IT'S SEEING JADIE THAT DOES IT. HER HAIR. HER *RED HAIR.*
IT REMINDS ME OF--
I KNOW WHAT THIS IS. I KNOW WHO'S DOING THIS. I KNOW WHERE I *REALLY AM*...

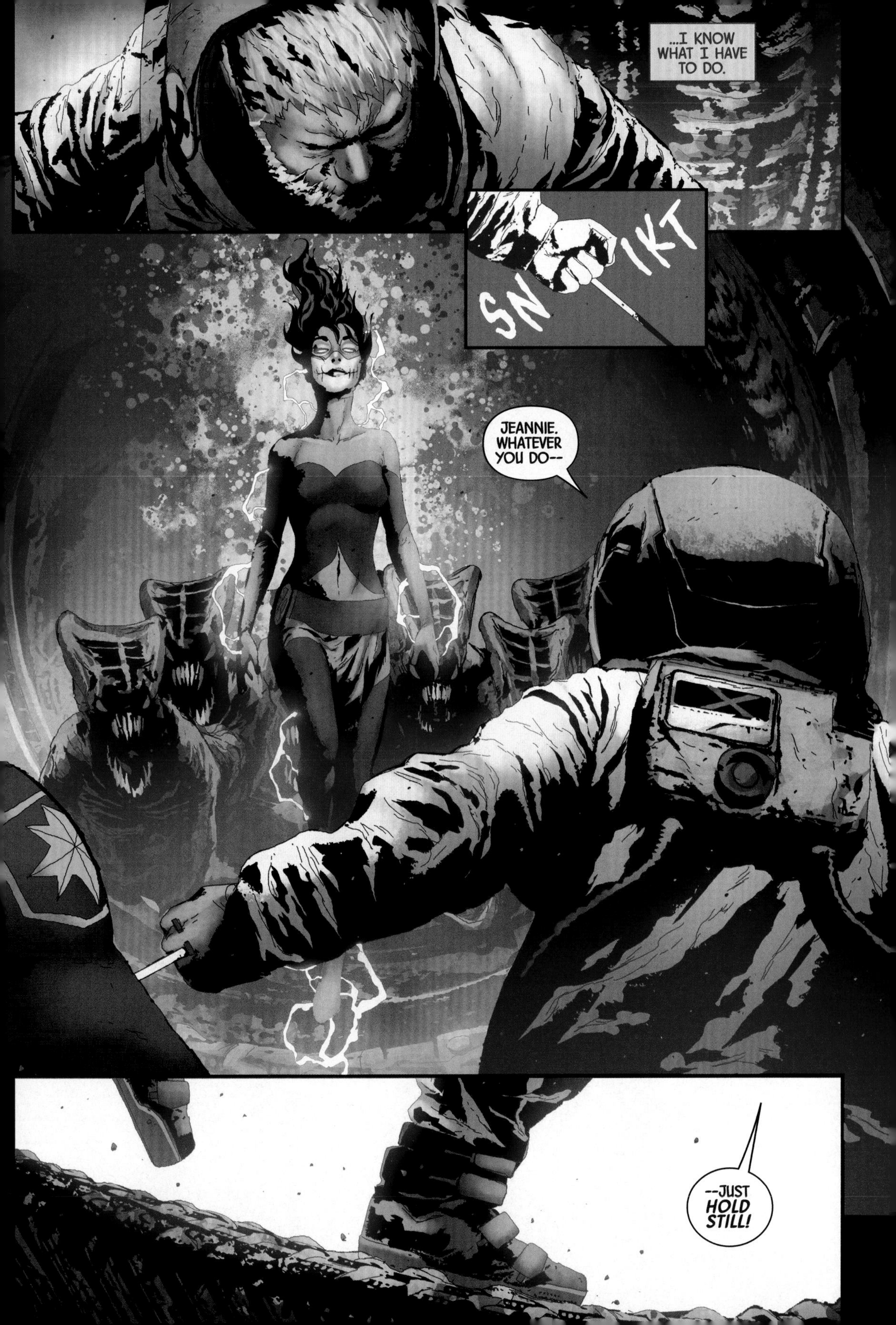
...I KNOW WHAT I HAVE TO DO.
SNIKT
JEANNIE. WHATEVER YOU DO--
--JUST HOLD STILL!

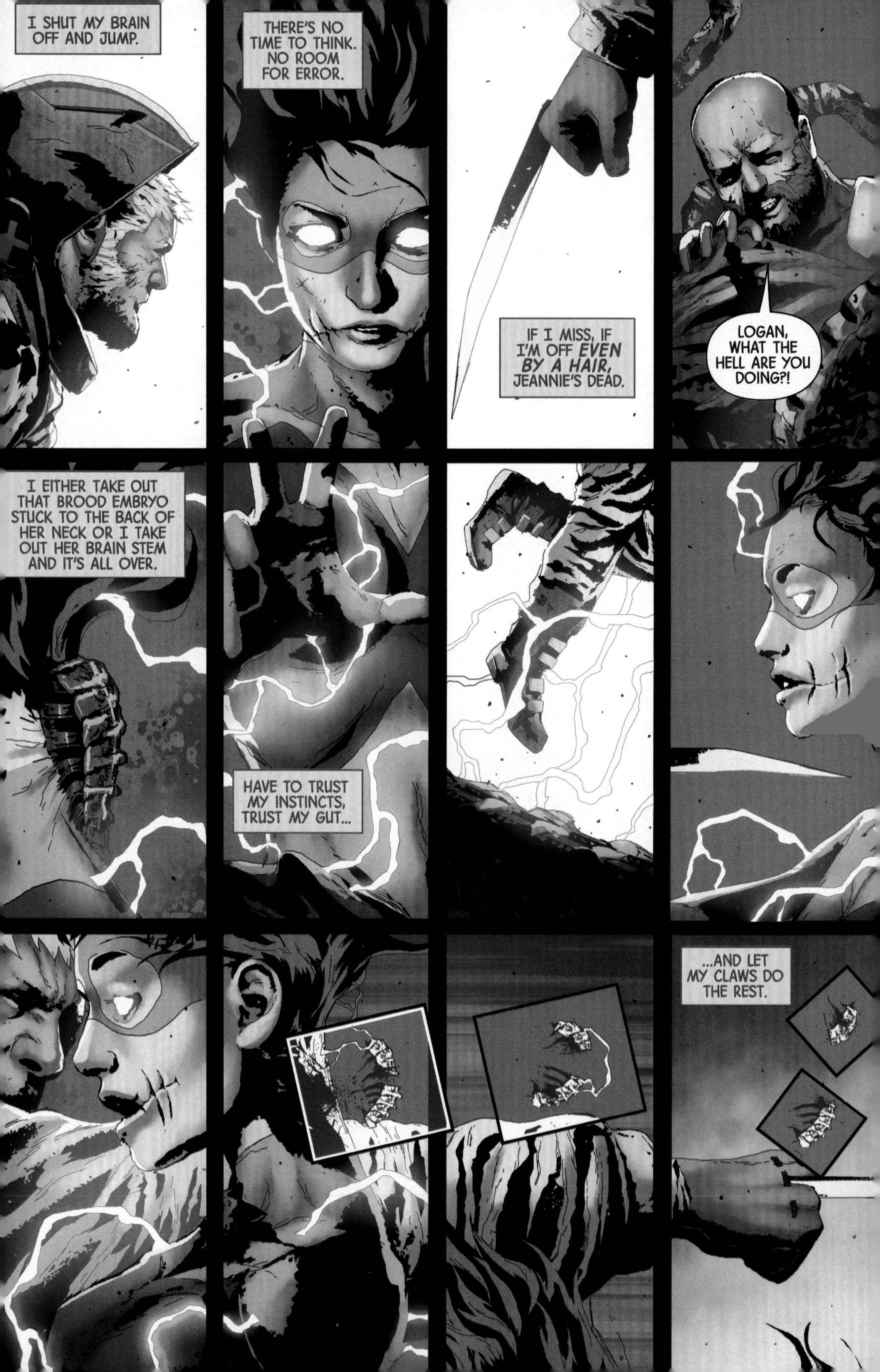

I SHUT MY BRAIN OFF AND JUMP.
THERE'S NO TIME TO THINK. NO ROOM FOR ERROR.
IF I MISS, IF I'M OFF EVEN BY A HAIR, JEANNIE'S DEAD.
LOGAN, WHAT THE HELL ARE YOU DOING?!
I EITHER TAKE OUT THAT BROOD EMBRYO STUCK TO THE BACK OF HER NECK OR I TAKE OUT HER BRAIN STEM AND IT'S ALL OVER.
HAVE TO TRUST MY INSTINCTS, TRUST MY GUT...
...AND LET MY CLAWS DO THE REST.

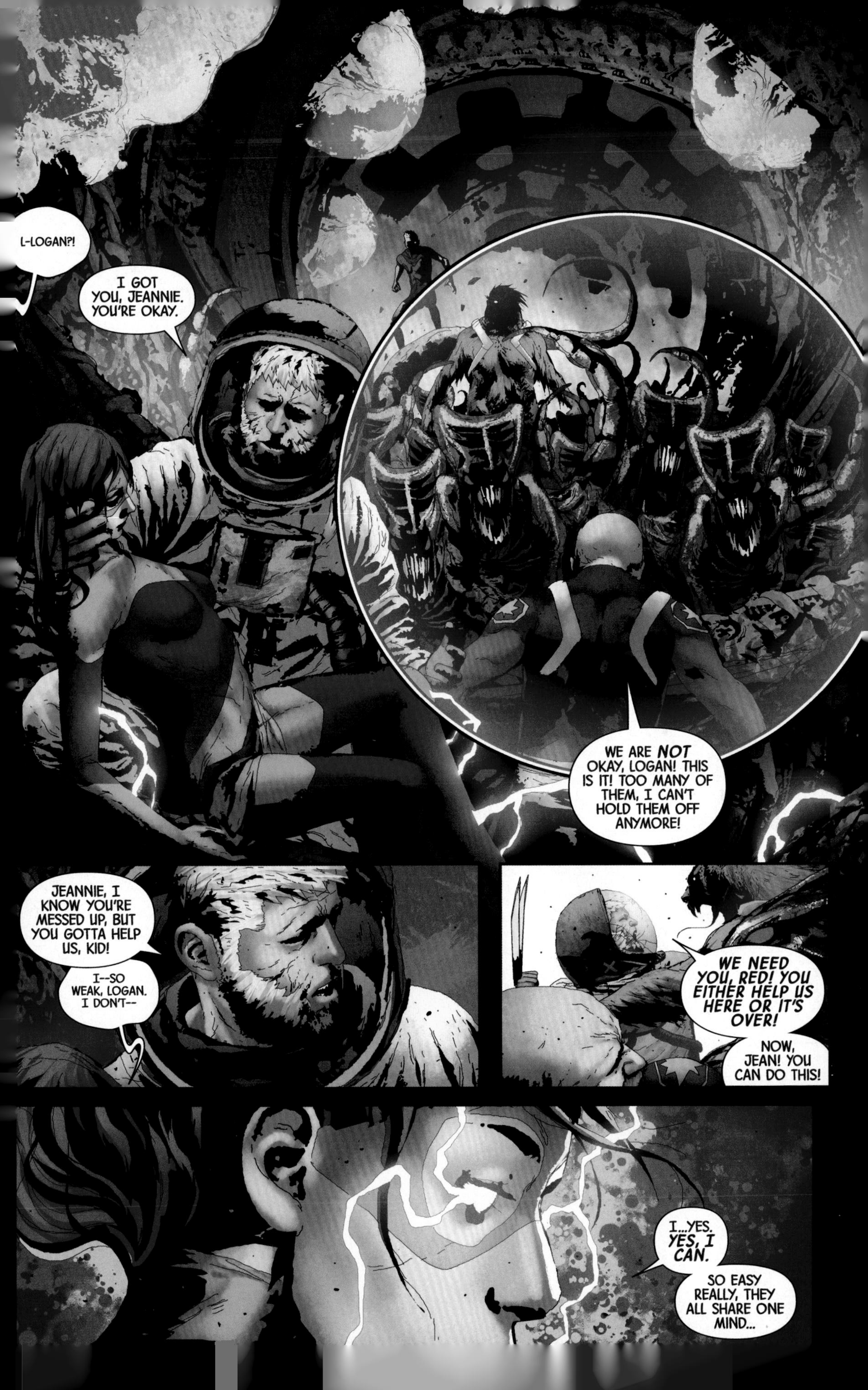
L-LOGAN?!
I GOT YOU, JEANNIE. YOU'RE OKAY.
WE ARE NOT OKAY, LOGAN! THIS IS IT! TOO MANY OF THEM, I CAN'T HOLD THEM OFF ANYMORE!
JEANNIE, I KNOW YOU'RE MESSED UP, BUT YOU GOTTA HELP US, KID!
I--SO WEAK, LOGAN. I DON'T--
WE NEED YOU, RED! YOU EITHER HELP US HERE OR IT'S OVER!
NOW, JEAN! YOU CAN DO THIS!
I...YES. YES, I CAN.
SO EASY REALLY, THEY ALL SHARE ONE MIND...

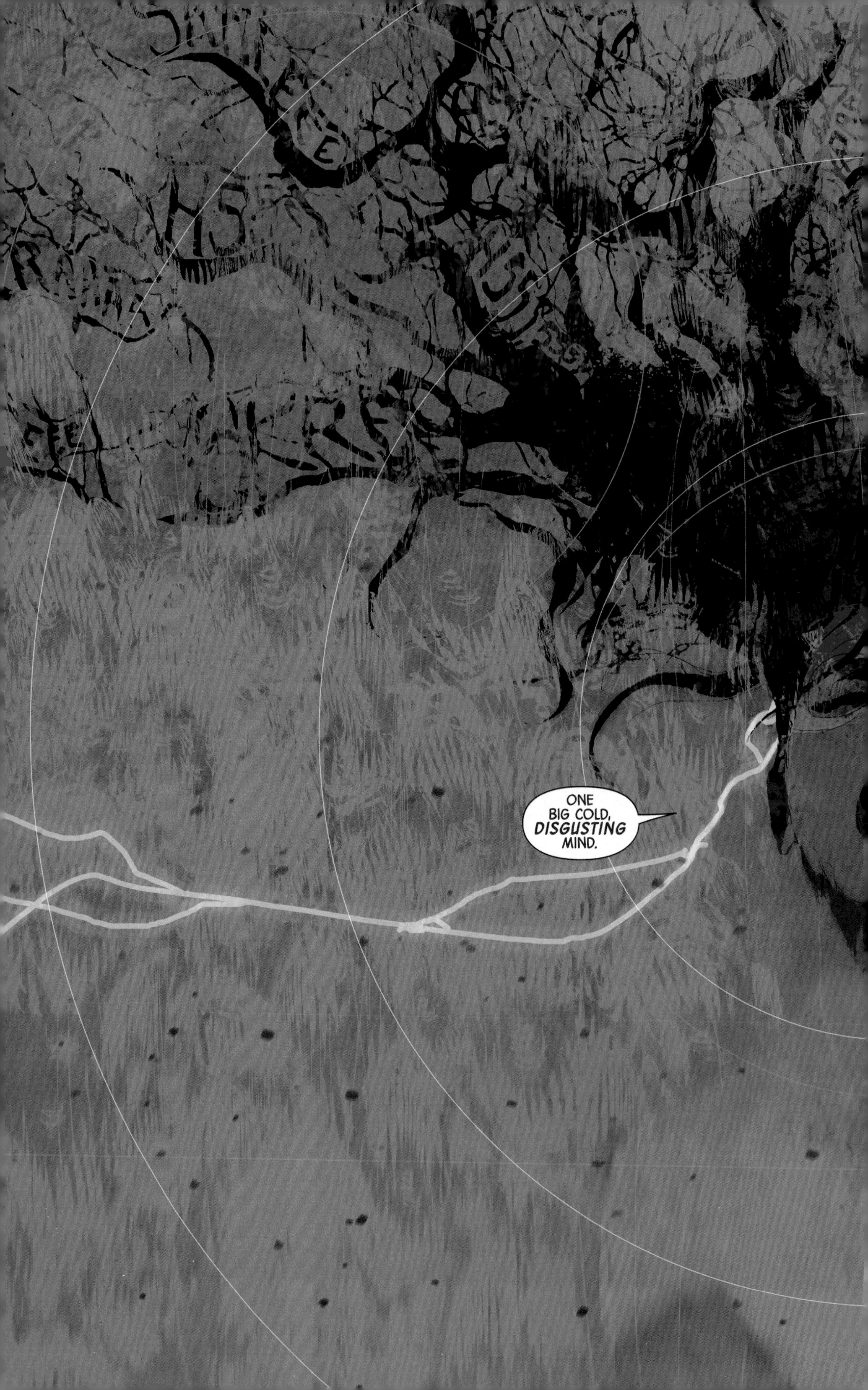
ONE BIG COLD, DISGUSTING MIND.